What experts are saying about this breakthrough book . . .

Jim Friesen's account is not easy to read, but it is becoming all too familiar. This book not only provides encouragement for the lonely and isolated victims of satanic ritual abuse but it is also vitally instructive for counselors who work with dissociative states and multiple personality disorder.

WALTER LINN, Ph.D., Director
Genesis Counseling Services

In this book Dr. Friesen has answered many of the questions asked by professionals and victims of ritual abuse. He gives hope for restoration and he underscores the importance of a balanced approach to recovery. His commitment to those whose lives have been devastated by this horrendous evil is borne out of his understanding that Jesus truly came to "set the captive free."

JAN FRANK
Author of **A Door of Hope**

Jim Friesen's clinical expertise and spiritual maturity put him at the forefront of those therapists working with MPD. This book will educate, amaze and inspire you!

SANDRA D. WILSON, Ph.D.
Author and Family Therapist

It has taken fifty years for society to awaken to the reality of child abuse. Hopefully it will take only a fraction of that time for us to become aware of the reality of satanic ritual abuse. This book will carry us a long way toward that goal.

H. NEWTON MALONY, Ph.D.
Professor of Psychology
Fuller Theological Seminary

This book is deadly serious about the destructive forces of cults. The scenes presented are accurate accounts of many cult activities. **Uncovering the Mystery of MPD** is bound to outrage even those who imagine themselves outraged already. It might even inspire concerned communities to work toward combating cult activities.

SHERI DE GROM
Forensic Criminologist

Dr. Friesen has described one of the least understood yet most destructive sources of emotional terror and anguish that can occur for humans. His presentation of satanic ritual abuse and the resultant psychological defense of multiple personality disorder (MPD) is clear and persuasive without drawing on sensationalism. The interested reader will gain a significant understanding of the diagnosis and treatment of MPD and will more easily recognize the place for spiritual intervention.

GRANT L. MARTIN, Ph.D.
Author and Psychologist
Crista Counseling Service

An excellent but naturally anecdotal, subjective book on a major frontier for both religion and psychiatry, pointing to the desperate need for scientific research on the subject of demonic possession in all of its ramifications. When will we listen? When are we going to get serious about looking at this reality?

M. SCOTT PECK, M.D.
Author, **The Road Less Traveled**

Uncovering the Mystery of

MPD

JAMES G. FRIESEN, PH.D.

Wipf and Stock Publishers
150 West Broadway • Eugene OR 97401

Uncovering the Mystery of MPD
by James G. Friesen, Ph.D.
Copyright© 1991 James G. Friesen, Ph.D.

ISBN: 1-57910-062-7

Printed by *Wipf and Stock Publishers*
150 West Broadway • Eugene OR 97401

This book is dedicated to
my wife, Maureen.

She has devoted countless hours
to household duties and family activities,
filling in for her absent husband
while he was devoted to the writing of this book.

It was a team project,
and she has been a wonderful team player.

Other team members
who have made key contributions are:
Jim Wilder,
Jane Willard,
Sandra Sanders,
Robin Brooks,
Charlotte Smith,
Pat Hayes,
Juanita Stephenson
Many thanks to each of them.

CONTENTS

PART ONE: UNDERSTANDING

   - My First Battle
   - Incubus
   - A War With No Casualty List
   - Profile of Occult Victims
   - Stretching Horizons

   - How I Discovered It
   - Alter Personalities Taking Control of Behavior
   - Internal Voices
   - Amnesia—The Clinching Clue
   - Switching—A Subtle Sign
   - Hiding Traumatic Memories
   - The Uncontaminated Person

   - Facts and Feelings
   - What Is Satanism?
   - SRA and MPD
   - A Journalist's Account
   - A First-Hand Account
   - A Parent's Account
   - How Widespread Is the Damage?
   - What Can I Do?

PART TWO: PSYCHOLOGICAL RESTORATION

   - Guidelines for the Multiple
   - When the Diagnosis Is Wrong
   - Roles and Systems
   - Components of Dissociation

PART THREE: SPIRITUAL RESTORATION

ILLUSTRATIONS

The more a person is at one with himself
and inwardly undivided,
the more varied and profound things
does he understand without effort,
for he receives the light of understanding from above.

Thomas à. Kempis,
The Imitation of Christ (1441 A.D.)

There is nothing concealed that will not be disclosed,
or hidden that will not be made known.
What you have said in the dark
will be heard in the daylight,
and what you have whispered in the ear in the inner
rooms will be proclaimed from the roofs.

Jesus
speaking to His disciples
in Luke 12:2,3

You will know the truth,
and the truth will set you free.

Jesus
from John 8:32

FOREWORD

Let me, along with Jim Friesen, stick my neck out.

His book is important for at least two reasons. First, he says things many of us would be reluctant to say because we cling so desperately to the good opinion of our colleagues. One must be careful not to express oneself too freely. It is risky to depart any distance from what current intellectual and religious fashion dictate to be prudent. We fear for our reputations. This book could win incredulity and scorn for Jim. To many it will sound wild, far out. For those who have had no experience of the things he writes about, and who perhaps have doubted occasional newspaper reports, it is understandable that this should be so. Nevertheless, Jim has had the courage to put duty before personal ambition. I am therefore glad to stick my neck out and join him, for I, too, have encountered a little (but enough) of the horror he writes about.

Second, it is the first book to discuss ritual torture, murder and sexual abuse, while at the same time offering spiritual (and not only psychological) solutions. With good reason Jim places multiple personality disorder in its correct context—warfare with dark powers. Other books have dealt with the problem, some sensationally, others with restraint. So far as I know, this will be the first to point to the real source of help for the victims.

Quite correctly, Jim has shared with us his personal journey as he stumbles onto the activity of the powers of darkness and of the treatment for multiple personality disorder. The history of his inner struggle becomes an open book for us to read. It is better this way. Writers are of two sorts, those who dig up facts and theories and describe them, and others who, from the depths of their personal struggle with truth, speak from their living experience. Jim Friesen is the latter. He knows whereof he speaks.

It is difficult to discuss satanic abuse without opening oneself to the accusation of sensationalism. Some news is by its very nature appalling and sickening. Yet how can one convince the public of the horror without describing it—at least to some extent? Description of satanic ritual abuse is nauseating, horrendous. However, unless we grasp the horror we will never understand, much less be able to heal, the pitifully damaged victims.

When I read the account of the first court proceedings in Canada,[1] I was strapped into the window seat of a large aircraft. I have a strong stomach. I have seen mangled and bloody messes in emergency departments of city hospitals, know the smells and sights of post mortem examinations, carried out major surgical procedures, been involved in war. Nevertheless, as I read what happened to two little girls aged 3 and 5, I tugged frantically at my seat belt so I could head for the toilet and vomit. My nausea had nothing to do with flying—the flight was smooth as glass.

There are many reasons Jim's descriptions will sound incredible. There have, of course, been false reports, so we are skeptical of all reports. Another reason for skepticism is, we have no idea how dark the darkness of evil really is. In fact, we do not want to know. Faced with it we shake our heads. In particular, police personnel and judges until recently wanted not to know. Now, little by little, the evidence mounts, and official incredulity gives place to horrified recognition of reality. Sadly, even police officials, lawyers, judges, doctors and psychiatrists are found among the perpetrators of unmentionable ritual evils. Community leaders can be active agents of the spreading darkness.

Jim faces not only the incredulity of the public, but also the dismissal of his views by some of his psychology colleagues. For too long, the human sciences have buried their heads in the sand regarding the supernatural. Even with the trend changing, the fashion is to welcome what comes from the Orient as enlightened and sophisticated but to despise traditional Christian concepts. Scriptures are "regressive, outmoded."

I have great respect for the truths Jim has discovered. He and his colleagues have contributed immensely to our understanding of the multiple personality syndrome. Clearly we have more to learn, and now understanding about things once considered the exclusive prerogative of professionals is being given to the people of God *as* the people of God.

I am delighted, therefore, that this book will be available to the public. It goes with my own prayers that Christ will triumph as the powers of evil are exposed and put to flight.

JOHN WHITE, M.D.
Former Associate Professor of Psychiatry
University of Manitoba

PREFACE

Just a few years ago I knew nothing about multiple personality disorder (MPD) and had not even heard of satanic ritual abuse (SRA). I knew about spiritual warfare, but I had had no first-hand experience with exorcisms in a therapy setting.

My preconceptions about therapy and about people began to change when I read *People of the Lie: The Hope for Healing Human Evil*.[1] That book led me to be more open to the clinical benefits of exorcisms, and it prepared me for contact with evil.

If you would have told me then that I would be writing this book, I would not have believed it. I would have told you that MPD is virtually non-existent, that practically no people on earth would be ruthless enough to participate in SRA, and that exorcisms are extremely rare.

People who talk about these things are considered eccentric and peculiar, and the accounts are seen as unverifiable and/or non-scientific. This book describes my eye-opening experiences in all three areas. Many people support my observations, but they are reluctant to talk openly about the subject because the accounts *are* so unverifiable and because therapists have not been properly trained in those areas.

I have been featured at seminars in California, Pennsylvania, Colorado, Georgia, Michigan and Vancouver, and the response at each has been surprisingly positive. Therapists all around the country are observing the same things I have found and are eager to participate in open forums on MPD, SRA and psychological and spiritual restoration.

It is time to put the content of those seminars into book form so that more people can learn more about how to help the troubled survivors of human evil.

This book is intended to assist therapists and friends of victims who are seeking restoration. It will give victims permission to believe the memories which emerge during therapy. They will not make progress, and many will even drop out of therapy, unless their therapists and friends believe what they tell them.

The magnitude of their suffering is tremendous.

They have not been able to open up before because the accounts of the things they have seen and heard are repulsive to the listener. The time has now come when they can tell everything, unreservedly. Now they can be believed. That is the first step in their restoration.

PREFACE: PART II

Why did I write this book? Because I don't like to see people suffer.

Too many clients have told me they cannot tell their story without it and their feelings getting minimized or even completely disregarded. Too many clients have received psychological and spiritual healing in my presence and have lamented that they have not found both kinds of help in any other single place.

Please, clinicians, offer help in both dimensions.

The more I help people from both frameworks, the more I see them intertwined. Psychological and spiritual healing can promote each other—or they can create blockages for each other. Be bold. Go ahead and find out if they really can work together.

Clients need to seek help in both areas if they are to recover fully. Therapists need to seek what is best for every client. If spiritual healing is necessary for any client and the therapist ignores that, the integrity of the therapist could be called into question. Survivors of abuse have endured enough. Provide healing in ways that hold the promise of optimal relief from suffering.

This book will offer suggestions about how to use both the spiritual and the psychological approaches to restoration. If a therapist is familiar with only one of these, suffering may go unrelieved.

THE AUTHOR

GLOSSARY

Alter personality, alternate personality or alter: A personality state which is amnesic to one or more of the other personality states within the same person (see page 62).

Amnesia: a period of time which is disremembered. For dissociators, the segment of memory which is lost by particular alter(s) is retained by other(s) but is blocked from the former by the dissociative process. **Partial amnesia** occurs when one or more dissociative components are disremembered but another is retained (see chapter 2).

Borderline personality (BP): A particular kind of personality disorder which has been resistant to progress during treatment. I believe that when borderline personality clients are treated using the dissociative framework, progress may be better (see page 195).

Components of dissociation: This book uses four components, or layers, of dissociation to explain the phenomena which dissociators encounter—the mind, the emotions, the body's experience and the will. One or more of these may be dissociated during a partial dissociation. When all four are dissociated, the amnesia will be total and an amnesic episode will occur (see page 113).

Core personality: The unified (or unifying) amalgam of alter personalities which are (or are being) united to define the (emerging) personality. This term refers to the developing unity of personalities within a system, during the integrating process in therapy (see page 182).

Dissociate or dissociation: When used as a verb, this term describes what happens when a particular alter gives up or loses executive control. "Switch" is a good synonym. When used as a noun, it is a defense mechanism, which is highly successful in forgetting a traumatic event (see page 62).

17

Ego state: Part of a person which responds in a distinctive manner. There may be a large number of ego states within a person with no amnesia between them (see page 190).

Executive control: This refers to when a particular personality is literally in control of the body. If a switch occurs, a different personality gains executive control. This usually happens automatically with cues and signals from the environment, but it can sometimes involve a struggle to gain or retain executive control (see pages 111-13).

Fusion: The point at which two or more alters become one. It is somewhat like when two X rays are placed on top of each other. The integration process continues to finish up after fusion takes place. "Joining" is a good synonym for "fusing" (see page 178).

Host personality: The personality who is "out" more than any of the others. Note: When a "host" vanishes for days or weeks, or even longer, during therapy, it really is not a useful designation to apply to any personality. When a system is in flux it is not important to figure out which is the host. It is just important to try to get stability (see chapter 2).

Integration: The process which takes place while the amnesia is being eroded. Alters are learning to know each other more fully while integration is taking place. "Merging" is a useful synonym (see page 178).

Non-Amnesic Dissociator: This term describes a person who uses partial dissociation as a defense mechanism. These people have ego states which have partial knowledge about each other, and no "alter" is fully isolated by complete amnesia (see page 188).

Personality system: The total of all alter personalities within an individual (see chapter 2).

Switch: A change in executive control of the body. "Dissociate," when used as a verb, is a good synonym.

PART ONE:
UNDERSTANDING

1

SPIRITUAL WARFARE:
Three Levels

> **WARNING**
> This is an intriguing and powerful story, and I don't tell it often. Whenever I do, I make a strong point at the beginning and end, and here it is: **Don't try this stuff.** Don't get interested in it; don't set yourself up for any kind of experimental dabbling. It can only lead to trouble.

I DID NOT ASPIRE to become a spiritual warrior—there was no quest to gain recognition by casting out spirits. I did not hear about spiritual warfare first, and then join up for the battle—I literally walked right into the middle of one. During my sophomore year in college I walked over to a friend's room in the dormitory one afternoon. I cannot remember just why I went there, but it was a fateful destination—it brought me to the first lesson in my as yet unrecognized training in spiritual warfare.

MY FIRST BATTLE

The door was closed. That was not particularly unusual, but as I knocked on the door and was invited in, a strange feeling came over me. A few students sat around a small metal typing table. Their hands rested lightly on its top, and their little fingers overlapped to form an unbroken ring of human contact. "What's going on?" I asked.

The reply: "A seance."

I did not know how seances were carried out, so I just went over to the other side of the room and quietly watched as the students continued. In subdued voices they were asking questions of a spirit. The table would tip to one side for yes, to the other for no.

To spell out a word, it would tip once for *A*, twice for *B*, and so on to twenty-six times for *Z*. The table was spelling out a sentence when I came in. The participants, fascinated and totally involved, hardly noticed my entry. I was not surprised at what I saw. Without any direct human help, the table tipped from side to side—and the students were in contact with the spirit world. It was right there. I could not help but believe what I was seeing.

After about twenty minutes I realized this was more to these students than just a novel way to spend the afternoon. They excitedly sensed a mixture of belief and disbelief at what they were discovering. They were in contact with a spirit who had spelled out its name as "Hoz," and who claimed to have been a court magician from the Middle Ages. Spinning out its story in answer to the students' questions, the spirit drew them deeper and deeper into the mysteries of Hoz's life and death. The seance had begun about a half hour before I came into the room, and I began to marvel at the whole experience. "Hoz" had told how he died and who the king was that he worked for, and he had given a lot of incidental information about life during the Middle Ages. Those sitting at the table would *never* forget that day.

I had been taught the Bible throughout my childhood. My mother would read to me for hours from a Bible story book, and I had been a Christian for several years. I knew the accounts of Jesus casting out evil spirits in the New Testament[1] and had heard missionaries from third world countries tell how they, in the name of Jesus, had cast out evil spirits. It occurred to me that I had such an entity in front of me. I found myself with a chance to discover if using the name of Jesus really would expel an evil spirit.

Thinking things through, however, I ran into a dilemma. If I spoke the words out loud, "In the name of Jesus I command you to leave," the students could take their hands away from the table, or somebody could hold the table down to prevent any tipping. I might not know if the name of Jesus could be used effectively. So I decided to just think the command.

I directed my gaze toward the table and thought the instruction: *Hoz, in the name of Jesus I command you to leave!* The students had no idea that I had just cast Hoz out. The table was in the middle of spelling out a word, and at the very second I finished my thought-command, it stopped. The students kept their hands as they were and tried to figure out why the contact had been broken, but they could come up with nothing. The table would not move, *period.* They backed off from it and glanced back and forth at each other, shocked and puzzled.

I told them what I had done. They expressed irritation with me and tried to start the seance again, but they could not conjure up Hoz or any other spirit. That was the end of the seance—and the power of Jesus' name had been demonstrated to me.

Growing Intrigue

The nature of spiritual warfare had not yet become apparent, but within a few days I realized that the "innocuous" table-tipping was leading to great peril for those involved.

The story about the seance spread across the small campus within just a few hours. By that evening at least three groups of students were trying to contact the spirit world through seances, and all the college dormitories had been drawn into the intrigue. There were doubters and proponents; there were those who acted as though they knew everything there is to know about the spirit world; there were missionary kids who had seen similar things happen. Practically the whole campus got into discussions about what was going on. Two nights later the situation had gotten so intense that at one o'clock in the morning a collection of doubters and "experienced mediums" decided to stage a seance right in the middle of the student hall! Somewhere between thirty and fifty students came into the auditorium and watched intently. A friend came and got me out of bed because he knew I'd be interested. When I came in, the table was tipping out an answer and one doubting student was on his knees, trying to figure out just how those charlatans were tricking everyone into believing that a spirit really was moving the table! He found no evidence. This was no human trick. The table was being moved by an unseen force, and there was every reason to believe it was indeed a spirit. The student finally quit trying to figure out the "illusion," and he watched with the rest of us, but he declared that there probably were magnets in the ceiling (some twelve feet overhead) which were responsible for the illusion.

Various students would ask questions from where they were, and the table would answer. It became a forum for asking all kinds of questions about religion, philosophy and science. One very intelligent student asked the table this question: "Is Jesus Christ the only way to overcome Satan's power?"

He had asked *the* question for us all. We were all young people taking our first shot at establishing independent living, and we wanted a definitive answer to that question. Did we really need to rely on Jesus?

Everyone's attention was riveted to the table. Those sitting at the table kept their hands lightly poised, waiting for the answer, which was slow in coming. Then the table started to tip, very slowly, toward the yes side. It continued to tip more and more—until it fell to the floor!

We were all stunned!

No one had heard of a table tipping so far it would fall over in answer to a question! I'm sure no one in that room could ever be convinced that there was any other way to overcome Satan's power. People broke into small groups, and they talked quietly and earnestly.

That night I stayed up until daybreak, talking with a few guys who needed to express deep, pent-up emotions. One fellow whom I had known for years started crying as he got in touch with feelings of neglect by his father. Things began to come to a head. People were getting out of their customary routines. Their emotions were volatile, especially those who had been sitting at the seance tables. They missed classes and let their school work slip, and a cloud of discontent hung over the whole campus. One girl even collapsed on her way to breakfast the morning after she had been involved in a seance. Her pastor was called to the campus and she took a leave of absence from school. I don't know if she ever came back.

The "Spirit Zapper"

In the meantime, I was getting a reputation as a "spirit zapper." On the evening of that first afternoon seance, I had stumbled onto a second one, in the room next to mine. Four students sat around a small table, attempting to duplicate the earlier seance. I quietly stood by and watched them ask the table to answer questions about themselves, as well as about the life and times of the spirit. This was not Hoz, but one of the other spirits contacted at the campus during that week. I wondered if the name of Jesus would have the same effect, and once again I issued the thought command. The seance ended immediately, just as it had the first time. These students were almost thankful I had stopped the process.

After we discussed why I cast the evil spirit out, they agreed there was something unsettling about it anyway. Not only was it scary to get things from an unknown source, but it also was upsetting to think the spirit world could actually give accurate answers about our inner life. It was spooky to think we could be "tracked" by the evil side. Those students decided to stay away from further involvement with seances. I took that lesson to heart, silently zapped spirits at two other seances, and began to spread the word—this stuff is dangerous!

As the school week ended, a divergence of opinion arose about the seances. The school was splitting along two lines: Some people were getting pulled more deeply into the experience; others were expressing caution at what they saw. By Friday night, a ban on seances had been issued by the school administration. Yet Saturday night, despite the official ban, some of the students conjured up another spirit. The news spread again, the room filled, and somebody came and got me. Those at the table didn't want me to enter the room—they didn't want me to silently cast out the spirit. They were relishing the moment.

I bargained with them. "I won't cast out the spirit if you will let me come in."

They agreed.

I took my place in the crowd, and I watched them ask questions that fanned flames of upset, like which person present would have certain things happen to him. These students were being seduced into progressively more upsetting areas of questioning.

I could not see any benefit from letting the seance continue, but had promised not to perform any expulsion, so when I got a chance, I asked, "Is it okay if I ask the table a question?"

The table tipped to the yes side, ever so slightly.

"Is everyone on the table opening themselves up to Satan's power?"

In a split second one of the students yanked her hands off the table. She didn't want to see the table tip—everybody *knew* the answer to *that* question!

That was the whole point of the warfare. People were opening themselves up to Satan. They were asking spirits to work through their hands—they were inviting and allowing entities from "the other side" to enter them, and it was no minor risk. Through the innocent curiosity of a few students, the whole campus had been drawn into a spiritual crisis.

In general, the good side won over the bad side. The battle had begun insidiously, but the enemy was subdued because there were enough of us around who recognized it as warfare.

The meeting broke up, and that was the end of the seance caper at that campus. Most students were convinced those activities were not worth the danger involved. I have kept in contact with a few of the students, and none has been involved with any more seances. Once was enough.

Level 1 Warfare

Years went by and I had told the story to only a few people. The experience had strongly shaped my world view, but it just sat in my memory bank with no particular purpose. I did not run into any more people who were doing seances or conjuring up spirits. I just went about my life—getting married, having children, and getting through graduate school. I obtained my license as a psychologist but had to keep my story about the spirit world separate from my scientific training.

I finished my course of study at a school where I was granted a master's degree in theology and a doctorate in psychology, but even there I did not tell people about the seances. Well, I did mention it once in a classroom discussion, but it raised so much resistance that I dropped it flat—and nobody ever talked with me about it afterward. Most people apparently discount stories like that, or at least they try to dismiss the implications of how their way of thinking would have to change if those things really happened.

The seances can be understood as an example of "level 1" warfare, the "dabbling" level. The degree of upset at this level was not nearly as serious as what I was to find at the next level. Although it was still years away, my next lesson would involve "level 2." People who have been subjected to that level of spiritual oppression suffer more. "Level 3" oppression is worse yet, but I would not learn about that until well after my encounter at the second level.

INCUBUS

Four years into my career as a psychologist, I moved from a public clinic to a Christian counseling center. Even in this Christian setting, I did not talk with my co-workers about the seances which had taken place in college thirteen years earlier. About two years after I came to the center, I was introduced to level 2 spiritual warfare. A call from the boyfriend of a client awakened me in the middle of the night. My 19-year-old client was in some kind of a trance, and her boyfriend could not wake her. He said, "She is on the bed, and I've been trying to wake her up for twenty minutes, but she won't talk to me. Now she is rigid, and I can't move her from her position."

Level 2 Battle

I certainly did not know what to make of it. I had learned nothing in psychology to help me know what to do in this situation. I said to him, "It seems to me there might be something spiritual going on." I don't know how I came to that understanding right then—maybe the process of elimination. I knew of nothing medical or psychological that would account for what I was hearing.

The boyfriend said, "Yeah, I agree something spiritual must be going on, but I'm not a religious person, so I don't know." Then he added, "At first I wasn't going to tell you this, but now that you've brought up 'spiritual,' I will. When this started, I saw her being picked up off the floor and moved over to the bed in some kind of levitation."

He said he could hardly believe it himself, and maybe it didn't really happen, but he insisted that he really did see her carried to the bed by some unseen force. He was trying hard to remain factual, but began to get a little hysterical. I prayed with him over the phone, and while we were praying he said, "She's starting to wake up."

In a minute or two she got on the phone, in a very disoriented state. Without telling me anything specific about what had just happened, she said she wanted to see me right away. She came in first thing the next morning, and when she described what had happened to her, I believed her. There was no reason for her to make up any story—I knew her well, and she was not a liar, nor was she psychotic.

She said she had been raped by a spirit. It was practically impossible for her to describe it to me—she did not believe in that sort of thing. Her body had been "captured" by the evil spirit, who put her into a motionless, muted state while he violated her sexually. She said that although her eyes were closed she was not asleep. She could hear her boyfriend and feel him shaking her, but the spirit was continuing with the rape. She experienced all the bodily sensations of the sexual experience, and she was simultaneously full of repulsion and great sexual pleasure, but until it was over she could not make a sound.

To find out if people really could be raped by a spirit, I called a retired missionary I knew about from Haiti, named Martin. He had thirty years experience working with various forms of spirit possession and he had a good reputation among some of the therapists I worked with.

Our discussion that morning was an important lesson for me. He told me of many incidents in the culture in which he had worked, a culture permeated with spiritism. He said, "When people open themselves up to Satan, they are controlled by him. It is very much like some horror movies where people want to gain something from Satan, like money or the knowledge of future events, or maybe they want to contact a dead friend. When they open themselves up to Satan, they always pay a price, and that price is often their sanity. Sometimes a person even forfeits his life, after spending years in agony."

Martin added that my young client had probably opened herself up in some way for the attack, and that could result in demonic rape. He said that would be consistent with what he had seen in Haiti.

After I spent a few "crisis" hours with her that week, my client accepted what had happened to her and began to protect herself from future attacks by deepening her spiritual life. We talked about how she may have been opened up to an evil spirit, and we pinpointed the opening as a time with a friend of hers who was a self-proclaimed "white witch." With my client's spiritual growth and the distance she kept from this particular friend, she experienced no further demonic episodes.

I found some Christian counselors to consult with about the demonic rape, but although they seemed to accept that it could happen, they had never heard of it. Eventually, I talked with someone who knew what it was called—"incubus." We went to the dictionary, and there it was: "A spirit or demon thought in medieval times to lie on sleeping persons, especially women, with whom it sought sexual intercourse."

It did not take me long to uncover more information about incubus. I found references to incubus accounts in *A Treasury of Witchcraft*. That book cites St. Augustine with the earliest record, at about 400 A.D.: "It is a widespread belief that . . . incubi [plural] have frequently molested women, sought and obtained coitus from them."[2]

Another reference dating from the 13th century, comes from a man named Albertus Magnus: "It is truly recorded of incubi . . . demons and we ourselves have seen persons known by them."[3]

In the 15th century, Walter Mapes wrote: "We have heard of demons as incubi . . . and that their intercourse is fraught with danger."[4] (The interview with Fran in chapter 3 strongly supports this. She described the painful demonic rape as "searing.")

It was affirming to my 19-year-old client to learn that she was not crazy—these things have been recorded for centuries. As time went by, four other women gave similar reports to me, and they were also happy to find somebody who believed them.

The incubus experience is a level 2 battle, where there is a deeper struggle for the victim's soul. The invasion by the spirit is more threatening and debilitating than in level 1 battles. There is more suffering, and the recovery is more arduous.

Level 3 Battle

Nobody is truly ready for the agony that awaits a person when he enters level 3—union with Satan. People who knowingly sell their souls to the devil and follow their leader's orders often give up their physical lives as well as their souls. They are casualties of spiritual warfare.

A WAR WITH NO CASUALTY LIST

The free press keeps us informed about developments in on-going wars around the world. Casualty lists are made, recording the names of those who have been wounded or who have died, and we get a general sense of concern from reporters about sinister developments wherever they occur. It is usually easy to tell which side is winning. The press tells us about the shocking number of innocent victims who have succumbed in unnecessary raids on villages, and we are deeply moved. Outrage wells up within us as we hear about senseless deaths in places like Beirut, Afghanistan, China and Iraq. Editorials appear, and sometimes official action is taken to protect civilians. The citizens in our country are informed about these wars, and we are prepared to intervene whenever it is considered prudent.

There is another war being waged, this one with no casualty lists, and there is no way for many people to determine which side is winning. The public has no inkling about what is really going on in this war and is getting just a hint as to its magnitude.

The few journalists who glimpse its sinister nature seem reluctant to report it thoroughly or to estimate the number of casualties. Thanks to them, though, we do have at least some of the facts, and in due time, we may be able to estimate the extent of casualties. This may eventually lead our country to intervene and protect its citizens.

I believe people will be ready to take protective action only after the war has been openly exposed. In most cases the victims are suffering quietly, because their experiences are beyond belief. Let me lay out just two published cases which illustrate the kind of war it is. It can be lethal to innocent people like you and me. Further battles need to be prevented, and aid must be given to the wounded. This is level 3.

Case No. 1 — A Double Suicide

> **NOTE:** The following cases are citations of published material, but the names and circumstances have been changed here to protect the people involved. Cited published accounts may be consulted by those who wish to compare these versions with the originals.

A tragic account was given in the *Los Angeles Times* (April 1, 1989), with the headline, "A Choice to Share Death: Final Act of Couple's Mystical Beliefs Confirmed 6 Years Later." In this case the facts which point to the true nature of the battle are imbedded in the article, but here is the picture that emerges when those facts are interpreted in a spiritual warfare framework.

The headline calls the deaths "mystical." The two subjects of the article had killed themselves in Griffith Park, which lies in the center of the Los Angeles area, and their bodies were not discovered until six years later. The reporter visited the couple's relatives and friends and assembled quotes which made the story seem like a case of Romeo and Juliet. The truth is, though, that these two were casualties of spiritual warfare, and the clues that lead to this conclusion are readily seen.

The article starts with an important consideration: These two young people were married in an occult shop, and their appearance showed who they followed:

The wedding was unusual, even for Hollywood. The setting was a storefront occult shop near Hollywood Boulevard. The young bride and groom wore matching black sweat shirts with metal studs. In the glow of candles, they vowed to merge together into "the light." A ceremonial priestess then conferred upon them a marriage of the spirits. They very much looked a couple. Both their heads, even their eyebrows, had been shaved.

The young man, Robert Warman, was "a one-time professional dancer who claimed to have the power to contact spirits," recalled . . . one former housemate.

The article described Warman further:

His head was shaved, he was sallow and extremely thin, and wore a dark goatee. His most striking feature, acquaintances recalled, were his eyes: a piercing, clear blue. He had had a tough childhood, mostly in California. He had once been married. He had rings and a belt buckle embellished with the designs of human skulls. "He was withdrawn unless he knew you," one former acquaintance said. "But he could be witty, sociable. He was not a threatening monster. There was a definite fascination, a strange fascination, about him."

Referring to the people who were living together in the same house as the deceased couple, the story continues:

They dabbled in mysticism and meditation. Occasionally they walked to the Goathead Center, a storefront occult shop, to buy candles, herbs and incense. They told their own fates with tarot cards.

One of the housemates said she . . .

met [Warman] through a friend. Warman seemed to have an instant telepathic understanding of her. "He had almost a shine in his eyes." . . . Before long, all of the housemates came to believe that Warman could contact spirits in a calm, candle-lighted room.

Warman's former wife . . . who now lives in Oregon, said Warman had many psychic talents ranging from telekinesis to astral travel. According to [her], Warman once locked his keys in a truck. "We really wanted to get home," she said. "He stroked the glass and popped the plunger up," which unlocked the door. "I witnessed that" . . . [She] said Warman read extensively on death and the occult, [including] Anton LaVey's *The Satanic Bible*. Whether by design or coincidence, Warman's shaved head and the goatee were trademarks of LaVey, who founded his Church of Satan in 1966.

[My comment: If these were the trademarks of LaVey, it is significant that both partners had shaved heads at their wedding. It must have been a satanic wedding.]

[Lilly May] became infatuated with Warman almost as soon as they met . . . Before long, Warman moved in and shared May's bedroom. [One of the housemates] resented the attention she gave to him. At the same time, interest in the occult within the house flared. "Things got very intense," the housemate recalled. "It was kind of like a freak show. . . . He would call spirits from beyond and pull them down for knowledge. He'd light a candle; he'd say the spirit has come down. . . . You would experience feelings, sensations. A presence was very apparent. It was pretty amazing. He wasn't real."

[This housemate] was open-minded to Warman's professed powers. Twice, she said, Warman helped her to concentrate on an ordinary egg-timer and the sand stopped flowing. [The deceased] May shocked the roommates when she shaved her head. Then came the spiritual wedding—not a legally recognized marriage—at the Goathead Center. The shop had a small chapel in the back and, hidden away, a rich inventory of ghoulish objects— bottled fetuses, skeletons, even a shrunken head.

Just a day or two before the double suicide, the girl's father

talked with his daughter by phone for what would be the last time. The conversation was like any other. . . . She gave no indication of anything being wrong.

Warman's former wife, who also knew May, said both were ill and looking for a way out. "They jumped into the abyss holding hands," she said. "I think it was a love story, in a way." But May's father insists that she was brainwashed or drugged. Her former housemates say she may have simply taken a wrong turn. "Lilly was not sick," the father said. "I never saw an emotional drama inside her. I never saw her angry. I never saw depression. I've tried to figure this out a thousand times, and I guess I'll never know."

There are remarkable similarities between the above story, and the one which follows, although they **were** written by different authors. They both describe dabbling in the occult, increased fascination with spiritual power, deterioration, and the destruction of peoples' lives—casualties, dead and wounded.

That is a frequent result of spiritual warfare at the third level.

Case No. 2 — Satanic Worship in the Rockies

The *Los Angeles Times* (October 19, 1988) carried this report: (Headline) "Satanists' Trail: Dead Pets to a Human Sacrifice." The story begins:

> The moon, just out, hung over the Rockies like a pale opal. Soon families would be saying grace over Sunday dinner; children would be clamoring to turn on the Christmas lights. It was time to go home.
>
> But in the darkening woods, four teenagers lingered, enjoying the rush they always felt when they killed something. A kitten lay crumpled nearby. Sharing some unspoken secret, the boys exchanged furtive glances in the fading light. They were growing edgy. Suddenly, John Hadley heard a voice give the command: "Do it now!"
>
> John felt his baseball bat smash into Sean Newport's face and saw Sean's eyes widen in terror as he cried out, staggered, then turned to run. The others gave chase, sneakers scrambling madly through the loose gravel and dead leaves. Sean was big and slow. He wheeled around to face his friends as they closed in. "Why me, you guys?" he begged. "Why me?"

After the murder, the other three boys were implicated in the crime. All were well known in the community and attended a local high school.

> It took the police . . . less than a day to follow the whispers and warnings that led to John Hadley, Porter Roman and Roy Calby, who admitted almost matter-of-factly that they had clubbed Sean to death with baseball bats, tied a 200-pound boulder to his body and dumped him into a well.
>
> They did it, they said, partly out of curiosity: They simply wondered what it would feel like to kill someone. But they also did it out of devotion, for Sean Newport was dying proof, that winter's eve, of his young friends' faith in Satan. He was a human sacrifice. . . .
>
> Despite their disparate backgrounds, Roy Calby and John Hadley forged a blood-brother friendship. Heavy metal music, drug use—and eventually Satan—became their common bonds.
>
> Each blames the other for instigating what became an obsession with the occult. It was all talk at first. Then they began poring over library books on witchcraft and Satanism. They repeated chants in vain attempts to summon a demon. They drew pentagrams and other symbols, first on notebook paper, later on buildings. They mimicked the horned-hand greeting their

favorite metal stars flashed at concerts, with the pinky and index finger extended and the thumb over the other two fingers. . . . .

"Satan is my lord," John would proclaim.

In truth, Roy was starting to get scared.

Late that autumn of his 15th year, Roy came to believe that demons were trying to possess him. He was drifting off to sleep one night when his head began to throb, the pain pounding against his eyes like a jackhammer.

"I felt like there was someone else inside my head . . . but I couldn't understand what they were saying," he told close friends and, later, psychiatrists.

He was dropping out of the Satanism thing. John was sympathetic. He thought he had been possessed himself half a dozen times.

But Roy's declaration had little effect on his life style. He still liked to party and thrash his head to the music. In detention hall, he filled a school work sheet with satanic pentagrams—five-pointed stars that stand on one point instead of two.

[Later,] Roy claimed he could make out the words of the strange voice in his head. "Watch out," it urged. "Kill someone."

The summer before their senior year, while Roy was away in Arizona, John and Porter grew closer. Joined occasionally by other boys in the party crowd—among them Sean Newport—they tortured animals to death so many times they lost count. Sometimes there were three or four in a day. Occasionally, people might come across the pathetic carcasses, but they never reported it until the murder stirred up all that talk about Satanism in Jansen County. . . .

Porter reported that he, too, had heard voices inside his head instructing him to do evil, and that he would return to the woods and old mines where he and John butchered the animals to worship the decomposing remains. In exchange for a human sacrifice, Porter believed, Satan would appear and reward him with supernatural powers. . . .

John was starting to wonder if he really was crazy. He was asking Satan for more power, and began hearing what he would later describe as a voice inside his head. It told him that he had to prove himself.

One night, John became convinced that Satan was wrenching his soul from his body. He was so frightened that he climbed into bed with his dismayed parents. He was 17. "Just watch me during the night while I sleep," he asked, "and wake me up if it looks like I'm having any trouble."

Although his parents were puzzled, John made no secret of "the voice" at school. He told classmates who teased him about his "invisible friend" that it was no figment of his imagination. The friend, unbidden, would appear and make him do things, John said.

The *Times* continued the two-part story the next day, October 20. The three boys referred to the murder of Sean Newport as "the action." They had planned to carry the action out on more than one occasion, but failed each time.

"Every time we failed, I don't know what drove us, but we wanted that experience," said John. "Me and Porter [got a lot of excitement] from killing animals, I think, and Roy just from talking about it. We just had to have that experience. I know it had to spring from Satan."

At the moment of the action, here is the account. The three soon-to-be murderers had taken their intended victim, Sean, along with them into the woods to sacrifice a kitten to Satan. After they had finished killing the kitten, "Sean spoke first, saying he wished they had 'something bigger to kill.' Roy snorted derisively, 'What are we going to do now, John?' "

This time, John had volunteered to hit Sean first, but now he looked nervous. "I don't know," he shrugged. Porter suggested they smoke some dope. John had forgotten his pipe, and asked Sean if he had brought one along. Sean fished in his pocket.

In that instant, John heard the voice inside his head, the one that always told him to prove himself. "Do it now!"

John felt the bat strike Sean's face.

When the frenzy was over, Sean was still moaning. John Hadley took a bloody bat and nudged him in the shoulder.

They had clubbed him to death with baseball bats.

"Sacrifice to Satan," he said.

A close friend of John Hadley's summed up the feelings of many stoners who, like him, had enjoyed the morbid fantasies and animal tortures. He still does. Unable to fully comprehend or control these urges, he is terrified.

"Whatever it is inside of him that made him do that," he says, "we all have inside us." . . .

From his cell [John] wrote Porter a letter recently, and admitted that Satan had tricked them.

"I don't even know why we killed Sean," he says now.

John never did feel the surge of power he thought Satan had promised him in exchange for the ultimate proof. Not long ago, the voice came back, the one that told him to do it now.

Softly he repeats the words he insists Satan whispered inside his troubled young mind: "Just open the door once and I promise I'll never let you go."

PROFILE OF OCCULT VICTIMS

After reading these stories I became agitated, but sad. The lives of many people had turned into nightmares. Those who survived the ordeals suffered traumas that would undoubtedly mar their lives for many years, but those who died lost the opportunity to live out their years altogether. They were denied the opportunity to mend their ways, or to start over again. Their loss was the greatest. All were casualties of spiritual warfare.

Were these people simply rebellious, obsessed with bizarre fantasies, seeking power, or prone to impetuous violence? I think not. Here is the pattern they share: Their lives were already scarred, and they consciously chose to repeat activities intended to prove their devotion to Satan. By following him, they were seeking the happiness which had eluded them. An alluring, seductive attraction emanates from occult activities, and it can capture those who underestimate its power. The double suicide victims and the Jansen county teenagers were drawn in and trapped. It was probably nothing more than a fascination at first, but dabbling in demonism devours its victims. A price was paid—physical and psychological deterioration, destruction and death. These folks fit the profile of occult victims.

More than a hundred cases of people who were victims of "occult subjection" are reviewed in Kurt Koch's book, *Christian Counseling and Occultism.*[5]

Following a detailed analysis of each case, Koch reached this conclusion: Each victim opened himself or herself up to spiritual subjection, some by consciously making "deals with spirits, others by seemingly innocent dabbling, and still others through the influence of occultly subjected family members. These were people who had "opened the door to Satan" as adults, or whose parents had opened the door for them when they were children. Koch strongly states that in each case a price was paid. That price was psychological and/or physical illness, and when the occult influence was strong enough, the victim's life came to a miserable ending.

Koch's conclusions are drawn from his experience as a pastoral counselor in Germany, but his conclusions are very similar to those reached by an American psychiatrist, M. Scott Peck. In his book, *People of the Lie,* he develops the theme that "evil people" spread disarray and destruction among those with whom they have contact, and when the evil influence gains enough strength, it leads to death.[6]

That profile is seen often in MPD clients. They have histories of extreme abuse and torment during childhood years; their lives have been wounded by the evil acts of people, and they have been left vulnerable to spiritual oppression. They tend to come from families which either made a mockery of God or were involved in some form of the occult. From early years they saw the world through eyes distorted by spiritual oppression, fear and confusion. The world became all the more confusing to these people, because they used dissociation (see glossary in the front of this book for clarification of term) to escape their torture. (Good dissociators' lives can get severely fragmented, which will become more understandable to you as you read chapter 2. These people can experience blank spots during many days, and they get accused of things they have no memory of.) Psychological and physical wounds were inflicted, to be sure, but many clients with MPD were raised in a spiritual combat zone which was responsible for their wounds. When people who have this background seek therapy, the clinical problems are presented as psychological in nature, but as therapy progresses, spiritual warfare is often uncovered. Examples of this profile, drawn from MPD clients, are presented in chapter 3. They illustrate some of the ways spiritual warfare can emerge long after therapy begins.

STRETCHING HORIZONS

Looking back, I can see how important it was for me to have had exposure to the spiritual dimension of peoples' problems. During the four years I worked in public clinics, I found that people search for therapists who can weave spiritual and psychological issues together. When I gave clients the opportunity to talk about God and about the supernatural forces that have shaped their lives, many of them told me they avoided these topics with previous therapists.

I remember that while I was still an intern, one person improved dramatically because we brought spiritual issues into therapy. My supervisor advised me to leave that part out of the person's therapy notes, specifically because of the controversial issues that could come up for anyone reviewing the case. The supervisor, who is also a Christian, encouraged me to keep doing whatever helps people, so I continued to ask clients about their spiritual struggles. They were eager to talk about these things, because I was the first person who had ever asked them if unexplainable spiritual things had happened to them. I was surprised at the ease with which these people could talk about their spiritual experiences, when they were given a chance.

My horizons were being stretched. Weaving psychological and spiritual issues together is challenging. Because it arouses suspicion from the "professional" community, young therapists like me could find only a few places to discuss the spiritual realities that our widening horizons were showing us. As I would soon find, two new topics hovered on the horizon, which would stretch me to my limits—multiple personality disorder and satanic ritual abuse.

2

MULTIPLE PERSONALITY DISORDER (MPD)

> **NOTE:** Names of clients and identifying characteristics have been thoroughly disguised throughout this book in order to preserve their confidentiality. However, great care has been taken to maintain an accurate portrayal of the circumstances which surround each case, and of the developments in therapy.

HOW I DISCOVERED MPD

I DID NOT GO looking. People with multiple personality disorder (MPD) just showed up in my office—and I was not prepared to help them.

When I took doctoral level classes in psychology, MPD was not mentioned. I took my final psychology class in 1977, and the only information I had about multiplicity was from an introduction to psychology class—in 1967! Multiple personality disorder was considered so rare that I believed I probably would never see it in my clinical career. It was generally thought to be a freakish condition with unknown causes.

One of my clients had shared with me that sometimes she wondered whether she might have multiple personality, but I assured her that would be practically impossible. I did not know how to diagnose the condition, and I told my client of MPD's

41

extreme rarity. About a year after telling her that, I listened to a tape about MPD, and I was stunned. It was obvious to me that she was right—she *was* a multiple! Her history and symptoms made diagnosis easy, once I knew what to look for.

I had been working with two multiple clients for years, and had been treating them with the wrong diagnosis. They were not getting much healthier—and now I knew why.

The tape outlined a four-factor theory about the development of MPD. **Factor 1** is *biological*—it is generally deemed that about 25 percent of *all* children are born with the ability to dissociate if they need to. **Factor 2** has to do with *early childhood abuse*—about 97 percent of MPD patients have suffered serious abuse at an early age. Most of them have been abused sexually. They needed to use dissociation to cope with the abuse. **Factor 3** has to do with *continuing abuse and lack of nurture*—the life circumstances have been dangerous, and the children continue to suffer abuse over a long period of time. The home is not a safe place, and the child needs to keep on using dissociation to deal with the continuing abuse. **Factor 4** is about a particular kind of *psychological structure* some people have—a high ability to fantasize and a high level of creativity.

The theory stated that MPD can develop when all four factors are present, and two of my clients did in fact fit that pattern. I concluded they were probably both multiples, and felt badly that I had not known earlier. One client had been in treatment with me for more than three years, and for the other, I was the third therapist in ten years! The tape quoted a study that found MPDs had been in treatment an average of almost seven years before the correct diagnosis was made. That was a relief for me to hear, but I still felt uncomfortable that these two were in my care, and were being treated for the wrong disorder. I needed to look for information to help me develop a treatment plan for them.

Official Definition of MPD

I started to research the subject immediately, but found nothing on treatment. *The Diagnostic and Statistical Manual of Mental Disorders* (DSM-III)[1] did contain this official definition, which is accepted by mental health professionals, and is used in all research and clinical settings:

1. The existence within an individual of two or more distinct personalities, each of which is dominant at a particular time.

2. The personality that is dominant at any particular time determines the individual's behavior at that time.

3. Each individual personality is complex and integrated with its own unique behavior patterns and social relationships.

That was too general for me—I needed something specific to help me with *treatment.* I found precious few relevant books, and none of the clinicians I knew had any idea about diagnosis or treatment, nor had they even worked with multiples. Two helpful books I did find were *Treatment for Multiple Personality Disorder*[2] and *Childhood Antecedents of Multiple Personality.*[3] The content of these two books was wide-ranging enough to give me the assurance that I could treat my two newly diagnosed clients.

At our next staff meeting I told about the MPD tape. The people attending reacted with quite a bit of surprise, but seemed open when I told them about the two multiples in my caseload. Their openness was a relief to me, because in our training we *all* had been taught that MPD was an unknowable disorder with unknown causes and no known treatment.

They listened to the tape, and two of them discovered they also were treating some clients who seemed to be multiples! Together we were seeing a total of six! We were astounded that such a high number could appear in such a relatively small clinic. Since this was a new topic, a few of us started to meet weekly to discuss how to treat these folks. That was the beginning of our MPD team. It generated our MPD therapy program, and it was a fertile place to develop treatment ideas. The team also has been a vital source of support and encouragement to us therapists.

Disclosure of Diagnosis

One of the first principles for treatment that I learned is to tell the client of the MPD diagnosis only when he or she is ready. It looked to me as though one of my clients was ready. Beth was full of confidence in me as a therapist and as a person. I had known her for more than three years, and our relationship was a good one. I appreciated her and she appreciated me, and honesty was important to both of us.

I scheduled a two-hour session with Beth, so we would have enough time to talk about the diagnosis and see if it really fit her.

I started the session by recalling that about a year earlier she had uncovered memories of incest with her father. That was so devastating that she had gone into a serious depression, hardly able to get out of bed for two months. I pointed out that she felt like a *different person* after she discovered those memories.

I went on to tell her as much as I knew about MPD, and suggested that we hypothesize, for now, that she may have that disorder. She realized right away that she did have MPD, and it was a relief to her that we were finally on the right track for treatment. I offered that we could either find another therapist for her who specializes in the treatment of MPD, or she and I could learn about it together.

"I already trust you," she said. "I don't want a new therapist just because he already knows how to work with MPD. I expect you and I will do just fine."

"You realize," I replied, "that this will make you a guinea pig, don't you?"

"That is a chance I am willing to take."

ALTER PERSONALITIES
TAKING CONTROL OF BEHAVIOR

Beth and I agreed to go ahead and consider her a "multiple," and me a therapist who was learning how to treat MPD. I gave her the book about treatment so she could get as much information as possible, and we began. That first session was a very intellectual one. I later discovered that, during that session, I had been talking with Socrates, who was one of Beth's intellectual alternate personalities. He was also wise and terribly honest. He called things as he saw them, and he talked to me as though we were equals. Socrates and I could work well together. As therapy progressed for Beth, that was helpful because he had quite a lot of information about the alters. You may be wondering why I call Beth's alter "he." Let me clarify that practically all MPDs have both male and female alters. The client knows which the alter is, and I come to think of each alter according to its preferred gender.

It was important for me to have a session with Beth's husband and to explain as much as possible about her condition. I already knew him pretty well, and he accepted the diagnosis fully. He was remarkably supportive and understanding. He learned how to talk with each of her alters, and he gave a lot of love and care to the young ones. He would give them "treats," and make them feel special. It would be inaccurate to talk about Beth's progress without highlighting her husband's contribution. He helped her immeasurably and she was headed for quick progress because of it.

I found out much later that most of her alters were extremely upset with the announcement of the diagnosis. The secret was out, and every alter in its loudest voice communicated its discontent within Beth's head!

Mapping Alters

Despite the trouble she was having with upset alters, she went to work on my first assignment and seemed to make a lot of progress right from the start. I directed her to make a "map" (or chart) of her alters, in any configuration she thought represented them. A month into treatment, she drew the map shown on Figure 1 (page 46).

At that point we were pretty certain we were working with at least fourteen alters. We discovered, about nine months later, that Negative Voice had not been an alter, but an evil spirit. Notice that Negative Voice is quite a distance away from the other alters in Figure 1, and it is taking careful aim at Barb, the most vulnerable of the alters. It was she who bore the burden of guilt for everyone—she was the alter who could not switch out when she was in too much pain. It is not a simple coincidence that Beth's map pictured the spirit in that way: The Bible depicts Satan as a "roaring lion . . . seeking whom he may devour" (1 Peter 5:8, KJV). We know how lions work—they go after the

Figure 1
Beth's First Map, One Month After Diagnosis

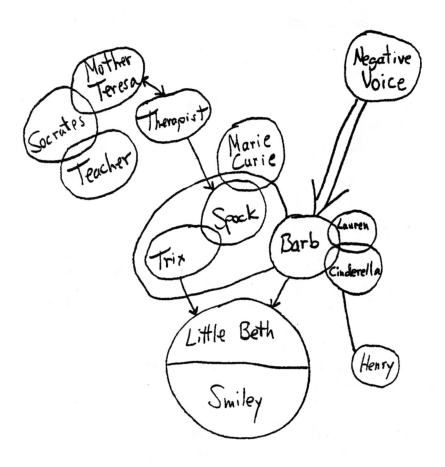

weakest one—and we found out later that Barb was the weakest one. She was the alter which Negative Voice could hurt the most seriously. It is remarkable to see how much of that Beth indicated on the early map, long before we knew anything about spiritual warfare, or anything about how fragile Barb was.

Beth and I sorted out as much as we could about the different personalities, and helped them get to know each other. Still a beginner with MPD, I soon learned that I needed to know, at any given moment, who I was talking to. Here are some of the alters I befriended: Socrates (mentioned before) was the wise one, who I soon learned was the "inner self-helper" (ISH). The ISH does not have much power and has no particularly negative feelings, but it has a lot of knowledge about most of the other alters. Socrates and I got along splendidly. He was always eager to be involved in a helpful way. Mother Teresa had only positive feelings toward people, and excelled in empathy. Since she was not contaminated by negative feelings, she was a wonderful therapeutic ally. Cinderella was a mute alter who came out only to dance while at home alone or to do artwork. She would take any opportunity to dance, or sometimes she would have a good time drawing for hours at a time. Henry's name came from Henry Wadsworth Longfellow, and he was a poet. For many years Henry had been going to the library without telling anyone he was there, and would read book after book. He developed a great love for poetry, and it was he who authored many of the poems written by Beth.

The picture was coming through to me that these were indeed separate personalities, with distinct traits, characteristics and feelings, and they recurrently took full control of Beth's behavior. I learned to recognize them by their facial expressions, vocabularies and tone of voice.

Alters' Names

You may be wondering why or how the different alters get their names. It varies from person to person. Some of the personalities come out already named, some of them are pleased to receive a name, some of them avoid being named, and some of them take on names describing their characteristics, like Night-time, Inner Mother, Therapist or Forgotten. I usually try not to suggest names; I just ask how to address each one, and let the name come directly from the client.

The above alters were all needed to get Beth through one therapeutic impasse: About five months after she had completed the map of Figure 1, we were in the middle of a session, and I became aware of a major problem among her alters—none of them seemed to like Barb. They paid no attention to her needs, and she felt rejected by them.

A "Black Sheep"

I spoke to Barb first, and I told her she had done her job very well, which was to contain all the negative feelings so the other alters wouldn't have to feel them. Each alter has a job to do, and she had done a particularly fine job. Unfortunately, the other alters had not understood she was doing this for them, and they did not appreciate her much. In fact, because she contained so many negative feelings, I suggested that the other alters were avoiding her and maybe even were treating her like a "Black Sheep." This seemed to make sense to Barb. I continued along these lines: Due to the fact that she had to do such a distasteful job for the others, they should be thanking her instead of mistreating her. They should be giving her some kind of award as a "Golden Sheep" instead of treating her as a "Black Sheep." Barb seemed comforted by my explanation.

I then talked to Socrates and Mother Teresa, and gave them the same message. A number of the other alters were also listening. At that time I had no way of knowing how they would respond, but they rallied around Barb in an unusual display of warmth and support. Cinderella came out in the waiting room, before Beth had even left the counseling center, and drew a beautiful picture of Barb, the Golden Sheep, walking along the beach with Mother Teresa. It was clear that the picture, from a mute artistic alter, was meant to convey to Barb that she was special. That evening Socrates and Mother Teresa wrote a little letter to Barb, and Henry authored a poem for her.

The "Golden Sheep"

It will help you gain a sense of the alters' distinctiveness if I include these compositions. Here is the letter:

Dearest little Barb,

We know you are painfully shy. We know you feel weighed down with so much guilt. We know your fear and your anxiety, the fear of being found at fault, the fear of total rejection. We know you feel incompetent. We want to help you, we want to be your friend, we want to comfort you if you will let us.

Barb, I can see you getting anxious about school—you don't have to go to school, Barb—let all of the older ones go—they know how to study, so don't be afraid. We will try to help you when you feel anxious—maybe it makes you feel anxious that Jim calls you the golden sheep. You are afraid you won't be a good enough golden sheep. But Jesus thinks that you are good enough. You are the Lost Golden Sheep, the goldenness of your childhood.

Love, Mother Teresa & Socrates

If you inspect those paragraphs, it will become obvious that the former was written by Mother Teresa, who empathized deeply. The latter was written by Socrates—he was doing his job as an ISH by coordinating the efforts of the alters, while imparting wisdom. They each encouraged Barb, the Golden Sheep, in their own distinctive ways.

This is the poem Henry contributed:

ABOUT THE GOLDEN SHEEP
WHO LOST HER GOLDENNESS
AND WHO IS AFRAID TO GET IT BACK

by Henry Wadsworth

The sheep who lost her goldenness,
The goldenness she had as a lamb.
She came into life with that goldenness
But soon she fell among wolves
And they sheared the goldenness from her body.
And if any goldenness grew back,
They clipped it back again,
Taking it for themselves.
And left her without any.

They clipped it away so often,
That, after a time, it would no longer grow back.
The spell of fear has kept it away.
And the lamb began to feel ugly without her goldenness.
And she began to feel the fear of the shadows
Because the shadows sometimes looked like wolves.

So she was lonely, because
She came to fear her own goldenness, as if the
    goldenness itself had caused the pain.

One day the wolves were gone
And they set the lamb adrift to wander in the wilderness
And the lamb felt naked without her goldenness,
But, still, she was afraid to grow it back,
Because she saw the shadows.
One day she met another sheep.
She had never known another sheep before.
And her and this other sheep became fast friends.
And they agreed to wander together for life.
She was so happy to find another sheep.

[My note: The other sheep was later identified as Socrates.]

And for a time she could rest because she could forget
    about the shadows.
This other sheep was very golden, even though he had
    also grown up among the wolves.
This sheep had learned to outsmart the wolves that
    kept him captive.
This sheep believed that she had once been golden too,
And he tried with all his might to get her to grow back
    all the goldenness.
But, just as it began to grow, the shadows would come,
And the goldenness would just disappear.
The two sheep became more and more sad that her
    goldenness would not grow back.

So, one day, by chance, the little sheep, who had
    become so sad,
Wandered into a special house.
In this house, there were many good shepherds.
One of the shepherds agreed to help her because she
    was so sad.
She cried and cried every time she went to see
    the shepherd,
But the goldenness stayed hidden underneath her skin
    because the shadows were there, and she was afraid.
Then one day the shepherd told her about the shadows,
    that they were parts of her and that they were inside,
    so that she should not be afraid.
He said to let the shadows help her and he told the

shadows to treat her like the golden sheep that
she was born to be.

A little flicker of light shown in her heart.
Could the shadows really be her friends
instead of wolves?
Would they really help her?
Could she really be golden once again?

You can see Henry was not yet convinced that the progress I expected would come. He was a morose and mournful person, as poets tend to be, but he was willing at least to find a flicker of hope in his own heart by suggesting that the shadows (the other alters) could be her friends. Maybe they would help her to regain the goldenness she had at birth.

These documents were brought to me at the next session, along with the picture Cinderella drew, and I was deeply stirred. The shadows were becoming Barb's friends. She went from the Black Sheep to the Golden Sheep in one day, and she was among the first alters to be merged.

By the time Beth completed the fusion of her alters, which was about two years after the diagnosis, we had uncovered a total of forty alters. They are on her final map, Figure 2 (page 52).

INTERNAL VOICES

Carla is the other MPD client who had already been in treatment with me when I heard that first tape about MPD. She presented other kinds of evidence that MPD is a real condition. A few weeks after Beth's diagnosis was verified, I began to review my cases more carefully, and Carla's caught my attention. I found that the clues leading to the correct diagnosis of MPD are difficult to identify, particularly for the clinician who is without an experienced mentor to learn from.

By now I had read that practically all MPDs hear internal voices, which are their alters reacting to each other. When I asked Carla how she made day-to-day decisions, like what clothes to wear, she told me about "her voices," as though she got messages from within. I knew she was not psychotic and that the voices were not hallucinations.

Figure 2
Beth's Final Map, Two Years After Diagnosis

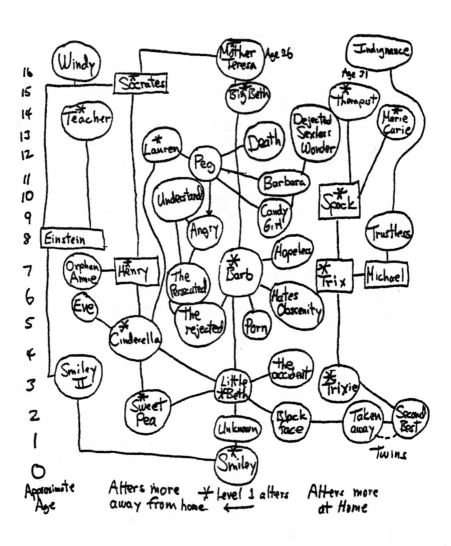

Voices heard by psychotic people tend to come from external sources, the house next door, for example. For multiples, the voices come from inside, in their head. Only recently has that distinction been discovered. For years, whenever clients talked about hearing "voices," their therapists concluded the voices were hallucinations, and psychosis was suspected. The most effective treatment for psychosis involves tranquilizing medication. I wonder how many people with MPD have been misdiagnosed as psychotics when they talked about their voices?

The tragedy is that multiples do not improve when given tranquilizers—they just get groggy. Psychotic clients who do not respond well to the medications are usually given higher doses. We can expect there are many groggy multiples in therapy, or in psychiatric hospitals, who are receiving treatment for the wrong condition.

Carla was. Carla had been hospitalized four times before I started working with her, but the psychiatrists had not considered her psychotic. The diagnoses covered a broad spectrum, from borderline personality (BP—see glossary) to suicidal depression, but she was never medicated for psychosis. She was just too bright and too high-functioning to fit into that category—and she had not told those therapists about "her voices."

Different Approaches Needed

Things did not go smoothly at all for Carla during the two-hour sharing-the-diagnosis session. I tried to help her understand that her voices were the different personalities within her who were trying to communicate with each other, but she did not stay in an intellectual alter while I explained the diagnosis. I became aware of that, and learned another important lesson in working with MPDs—I must speak the language of the alter which is present.

The intellectual approach was not working as it had with Beth, so, since I did not know Carla's alters yet, I started to speak the language of an important emotion—hope. The books and articles I had read all agreed there is a good rate of success in treating MPD clients, so I offered that she could be hopeful about her prognosis.

That did not work either. She did not feel hopeful, and to speak of hope was not what the present alter really needed.

The third approach I tried was to be comforting. I soothed her by saying that her life has been very difficult, but treatment for MPD should help her voices work together better. She did respond positively to that. Things had seemed chaotic all the time, and she was having a hard time making sense of her life—the voices were negative; they had many terrible nightmares, and they disagreed about practically everything in her life. She needed comfort.

That message was heard by an alter who believed that maybe she really *did* have MPD. We finally were able to end that session on a note of agreement. However, Carla had a difficult time in the following days—her personalities bickered about the diagnosis. Some felt a lot of denial, but others found hope in it.

Carla told her husband about the diagnosis before I could talk with him, and he did not believe it at first. He came in to see me for a briefing on the matter, though, and he finally did concede that she must be a multiple. Still, he did not take a positive approach to a few of her alters. Not having good support at home created a lot of conflict between her alters about her home life, and that made things even more difficult for Carla. I got along pretty well with some of her alters, but others seemed to pick up rejection from me and often stopped her from attending scheduled appointments. She missed more than a third of the sessions for quite a while, so her progress was not as steady as Beth's was.

AMNESIA—THE CLINCHING CLUE

Amnesia for a multiple is a blank spot in the day for which there is no explanation. Many of them call it "losing time." A client's losing time is often missed by therapists who are not looking for it. People who have grown up with MPD are accustomed to losing time, and think it is the way everybody lives. If you ask them in the first session if they experience amnesia, they will truthfully say they have no idea what you are talking about. "I don't *remember* having amnesia." Of course they don't remember it—that is the way amnesia works.

Early in Beth's therapy, it was not at all clear to me how extensive her loss of time was. Most of her alters depicted in Figure 1 were able to communicate fairly well and they knew a lot about each other. The amnesia between the initial alters was not complete, so that "partial amnesia" (see *amnesia* in glossary) was overcome rather quickly. Those alters were able to use "co-consciousness" pretty well during therapy, which happens when one alter is out and other alters watch and listen silently. Beth's therapy progressed more quickly because her alters were able to share important things that came up. The co-consciousness also meant that when there was a switch from one alter to another during therapy, her host alter (see glossary) would be aware of it and know about it afterward—I did not have to explain to the host what a different alter had just told me.

Later, after many of her hidden alters had shown up, and after she had merged most of them, she told me she could hardly believe how much she could get done. "I was losing four to five hours every day!"

Different alters would do aerobics, stay in the shower until the hot water ran out, or go down to the library to read for hours, and her host would have no idea where the time had gone. She could hardly believe how much other people could get done in a day. Beth was like most MPDs—she was very good at covering up when she lost a little time, and at continuing as though she knew what was happening.

With some clients the amnesia shows up early in treatment, and becomes the clinching diagnostic clue. Such was the case for Danny. One of the therapists in our group who does not work with multiples began treating Danny, and ran into some MPD indicators during the first session. After conferring with me about it, we decided I would take over Danny's treatment. He had been suicidal, so it was important to develop a good therapeutic relationship with him as soon as possible. We had a good first meeting, and he did not talk about feeling suicidal. He felt safe enough that by the second session, though I did not realize it right away, an alter came out to talk about his wish to commit suicide. Danny was totally amnesic to this alter. Here is what happened:

I asked Danny to relive the events of the day he had been suicidal. He became tearful and spoke about his feelings in a very therapeutic manner—he seemed to give them proper ventilation, and he experienced them deeply. I really must admit that I did not notice any switch. I did not see any indicator of MPD at that point, and making a diagnosis was the last thing on my mind. I had gotten thoroughly into an empathic mode and was feeling what he was feeling as accurately as I could. I had not said anything about amnesia or about MPD, and was just doing what any therapist should—validating feelings and giving support.

Just before the time ran out, I said we would have to close in a minute. He blinked his eyes and gave his head a tiny shake. That looked like a "switch" to me, and I *did* start to suspect MPD, but I said nothing. Danny panicked. He was embarrassed, apologetic, fidgety and very disoriented. "What happened? I'm sorry I took so long! I've got to go."

Danny was back in his host alter, and was certain that the secret about his multiplicity was out. As is often the case after a time loss, it seemed to Danny that he had just been caught with his hand in the cookie jar, so he tried to ease out of the situation without disclosing any further secrets. The forty-minute loss of time was something he could not hide and he was certain I could read his mind about it. That had not been the case. But when he appeared to switch and became disoriented after glancing at the clock, the secret was out. I recognized his amnesia and suspected he had multiple personality disorder.

As for Carla, the distinctness of her personalities was clear enough to convince me that a diagnosis of MPD fit her. When, in addition, amnesia showed up early and quite dramatically, that put to rest any questions I had about the diagnosis.

Carla's dividedness was extreme. Practically all her alters were separated from each other by complete amnesia. Her "everyday" alters often had no idea what had transpired during therapy sessions. The host, Caretaker, and I had an agreement that I would tell her about what had happened at the end of the session, so I would leave time for her before we ended. I usually had little difficulty in accessing Caretaker, and although it was draining for her to switch back and forth during therapy like that, it seemed to work fairly well most of the time. When I would ask if Caretaker could come back and hear about what had taken place, Carla's head would go through a roll, her eyes would close, and Caretaker would glance at the clock and say something to the effect that she could hardly believe the hour had passed so quickly. That is amnesia—a blank spot for which there is no explanation, "losing time."

One spring day Caretaker came into therapy and was quite upset. A lot of shopping items had shown up in her closet, and she had no idea where they had come from. Of course, the receipts were included in each bag, with her credit card imprinted on them all, but she had no idea how she had gotten them. During that therapy session I met four alters, who accounted for some of the new items in Carla's closet, and after I talked to them, Caretaker learned a lot about the alters who had gone shopping. Here is how that session went:

Caretaker listed the items she found in her closet: Two pairs of tennies, a pair of black shoes, four pairs of sandals, three hats, two purses (a very expensive, brown Italian one and a cute little white one), a man's pinstripe suit, a black and lavender cocktail dress, a silk suit (navy blue jacket and navy blue and cream skirt), and a pair of navy blue shoes. Her husband was very upset that so much money had been spent, but Caretaker was fairly calm, despite the lack of information she had about what had happened. Shortly after she had detailed out the list for me, a different alter came out and told me more.

"We took our car in to get some repairs, and we had to wait a few hours while they were working on it. You told me to let all the alters come out, so I took them shopping. We got a cab and went to the mall and everybody had a good time. We were really careful not to spend too much money on anything—we got a real bargain on the Italian purse—I tried to make everyone happy! That's what you wanted, isn't it? You want us to have positive experiences, right?"

What a dilemma! My objective is to help every alter to have a positive experience in therapy each time they appear in my office. That way they will come to trust me and what I will teach them about MPD. Carla's alters had turned that therapeutic principle into a blank check when it came to shopping. "Do whatever makes you feel good" was not my objective. Still, I could not say anything about her irresponsible shopping or I would risk offending a bunch of alters, so I chose to keep things positive and use this as an opportunity to meet some of Carla's alters by inviting them to tell me about their shopping trip.

With almost no hesitation, Bella accepted the invitation. She identified herself, and spoke rather quietly. She had never met me before, and was not yet comfortable upon finding herself in my office. After we had gone through a short "getting acquainted period," she said she was the one who had bought the tennies, and was wearing one of the pairs right now. She smiled and showed them to me. They were children's slip-on tennies, with a dainty print on a white background.

Bella told me that she knew only one of the other alters— Little Sara. Then she added that she was "the other side of Little Sara." I previously had learned that Little Sara was a neglected alter, who had to go to school in ragged clothes and wore shoes with holes in them. Little Sara and I had talked a few times. Bella said she wants to make sure that Little Sara will have new shoes for school. (Carla was in her mid-thirties at the time, and was not attending any school!) She began to get in touch with the feelings of sadness and abandonment that Little Sara experienced, which caused her to switch out. Most alters have only a certain level of negative feelings they can tolerate, and when that level is reached they disappear.

When Little Sara left, I met the second new alter. She identified herself as Margie. She was a much younger alter than Bella. Her voice and vocabulary were more like those of a three- or four-year-old. "I like purses—my aunty gave me a pretty white one for Easter—but somebody keeps taking them away." She started to get tearful, and switched out. Apparently, Margie was a carefree little girl who got excited about Easter, but could not deal with the loss of her beautiful new purse. Undoubtedly, when Carla was a little girl she had been victimized and had developed amnesia. Margie had no idea what had happened to the purse because it disappeared while an unknown alter was out and Margie was amnesic to the episode.

I was really caught off balance by the next personality. He sat up straight, glanced over at me for a split second, got up smoothly and walked past my chair to the window behind my desk. He stared "outside" without saying anything. That was peculiar, because the curtains were closed and he could see nothing outside. At first he would not answer any questions, and for a few minutes it seemed he was just trying to make sense about where he was and who I was, but he did not glance around the room. He just stared into the curtain, as though there were nothing in the world except for that one square inch of plaid! I explained that he was in a safe place; I was a psychologist, and I wondered if he had gone along on the shopping trip.

Speaking quietly, in a sort of French accent, he said, "Yes. I bought the pinstripe suit. It really bothers me that the others were buying only women's clothes, so I got a nice suit." He did not turn around to face me the whole time he was out, but continued the conversation. "I want to get my hair cut short, and get a mustache." Carla had hair halfway down her back, and was petite. It was clear that this alter wanted to be more masculine.

"I am Dr. Friesen," I said, "and I would like to get to know you. We could become good friends. I didn't catch your name."

"My name is Francois Finique."

"Do you know any of the people who share your body with you?"

"I know one of them. At least I have heard of Michael-Richard."

Michael-Richard was a personality I had met a few weeks earlier, who had described himself to me as a "he/she."

"I am glad you got the nice suit. Maybe you will wear it when you come in to see me one of these days. I have met Michael-Richard. He told me he is a 'he/she.' Do you know what that is?"

"No."

"If you get a chance to talk with him, please see if you can find out for me. I would like to know more about that. You are a man, right?"

He paused a little. "Of course."

"Might you be a he/she too?"

He remained silent. He must have been struggling with the dilemma of being a man in a woman's body. Then Carla's body pivoted toward me, her face changed subtly, and I didn't have any contact with Francois for quite a while after that. Looking back on the "he/she" question, I think it was a mistake. It was not good judgment to be that confrontational.

A new voice took over which was much more feminine than Francois'. This was Princess Kelly. Years ago Carla had watched a documentary about a princess by that name, and created an alter to be like her. Princess Kelly liked castles and exquisite things. She adored fine china, crystal, exquisite furniture, and expensive clothes, the way a little girl would. She had bought the three hats during the shopping trip. She was talking from the standing position, where she had found herself after Francois left. She was pleasant and innocent. She had a twinkle in her eyes, like a little Shirley Temple.

I don't remember exactly what caused her to switch out, but when she did, a very perturbed alter took over. She looked at the clock. It was about fifty minutes after the session should have ended. "How come you let me stay so long? I gotta get out of here," she said with an angry face. She was glaring at me in defiance, and remained standing.

I made an attempt to talk with Caretaker at the end of the session, as I always did. "Before you leave let me tell you about the people I just met."

"I don't want to know."

There had been a period of amnesia which had been going on for at least an hour, and there was no way she could deny it. The blank spell was very upsetting to this alter, and she wanted to leave right away. It seemed important to me to switch her back into Caretaker, so I could share with her what I had found out about the shopping trip, and about the newly met alters. I asked if she was Caretaker, and she said she was. I did not think she was telling the truth because she did not seem like the Caretaker I had known. It appeared to me that some other alter had interrupted therapy and was trying to cover up. Too many secrets were getting out, which made this alter pretty upset—she was pretending to be Caretaker so she could leave the therapy session before anything more was revealed.

When I eventually did ask Caretaker a few weeks later, she said she only remembered the beginning of that session. That meant I was correct in my hunch that another alter had pretended to be the host. That alter was only doing her job, which was to *keep the secret about multiplicity.* I had penetrated the protective barrier and had uncovered hidden alters, and that meant that this alter had not done her job well enough. She just walked out of the room, angry with me. The amnesia was undeniable. Caretaker had no idea what had happened.

SWITCHING—A SUBTLE SIGN

Amnesia is not always present in MPD, and even when it is, in most cases it is not nearly as easy to spot as it was with Danny and Carla. In fact, some multiples do not appear to have any amnesia. Some others are divided enough that amnesia appears only when a particular alter switches in, and that alter may not show up in therapy for months. The DSM-III definition says nothing about amnesia, and it is widely accepted that some people who are obviously multiples show no clear-cut signs of amnesia. Granted, amnesia episodes are an almost certain indicator of multiplicity, but when those episodes are not present, MPD still can be detected by a more subtle sign—switching. Such was the case with Emily.

We had been working together about five months before I had any idea that Emily could be a multiple. Sometimes the signs for correct diagnosis often unfold very slowly. Emily had been in therapy on and off for about four years with three other therapists. Her former therapist wrote me that she did not really know how to "get to the bottom of Emily's problems." Because Emily was in an abusive relationship with a boyfriend, one of my clients recommended that she begin therapy with me. We developed a good relationship quickly, but there was something neither of us could put our finger on, and it was stopping her from really trusting men. Because I am a man, and since she had been in painful relationships with other men, we concluded she must be conditioned against trusting men. When I look back on those first few months, it is apparent to me that at times she did have a good level of trust going, but at other times, she did not.

The first sign of dissociation came when Emily was recalling a junior high school-age memory with me. Emily was not in touch with her feelings while she talked about the incident, and she described the events as though she were telling me about a movie she had seen. She recalled a Friday evening in June. She was with two other girls and three boys, and they began to pair off into couples at somebody's house where the parents were gone for the weekend. She thought the other couples would probably end up having sex.

The prospect of her being expected to have sex frightened her, and she told me she urgently needed to get out of the house. Emily still was not reliving the events—it was more like she knew the facts but had no feelings about those events. Her face remained emotionless. She said she had not panicked but simply had gone outside and sat on the front curb. She remembered that while she sat on the curb, her body was telling her that it knew what it was like to have sex. Her mind said she had no idea what sex was like, and since she had never had any sex, her body should not know what it feels like. Emily pondered with me about how confusing that was, just sitting there while her mind and her body tried to decide if she had ever had sex before.

That was my first clue—she seemed to be showing signs of a partial dissociation while telling the story. She dissociated from her feelings while talking about the events, and her confusion on the curb indicated an earlier partial dissociation—her body remembered what sex was like but her mind and emotions did not.

About Dissociation

In order to show how that recollection tipped me off about Emily's MPD, let me explain a little more about dissociation. The noun, *dissociation,* is the act of defending against pain. It may be the most effective defense people can use, since it is 100 percent successful. When a person dissociates, he or she separates from the memory of a painful event.

It is as simple as this: A child goes through a trauma, and then pretends to be a new person, or alternate personality (alter), to whom those bad things did not happen. There is a separation from the memory. It is immediately and completely forgotten. The newly created alter "remembers" only a blank spot where the trauma happened, and there is no hint that the traumatic event could have happened. If the dissociation is complete, the amnesia is 100 percent. If you mention anything about what happened during the blank spot, there is a puzzled look on the new alter's face: "I have no idea what you are talking about."

There are instances where a dissociation is not complete, as was the case with Emily when she sat on the curb. I had the suspicion that her body was remembering the sensations that accompany intercourse, but her mind was not. That could be a partial dissociation.

I had her do some journaling before the next session to see if any sexual memories could exist, and she remembered being the victim of sexual abuse in a green garage when she was 4! When that memory surfaced, Emily simultaneously affirmed that it had really happened and denied it. My sense was very strong that she was dissociating.

That alerted me to look for other clues, and I noticed that she would switch from a trusting alter to a non-trusting alter. When "dissociate" is used as a verb, it means to switch from one personality to another, and that is what I had seen. Emily would come into a session, happy and childlike, and we would start out with lots of good feelings. When I began to get into some emotional material, the limit of tolerable emotions in the child alter would be reached, and a non-trusting alter would switch in. If I observed closely I could notice a change in posture, emotions and vocabulary. She had dissociated into a different personality.

It was a much more subtle sign than the loss of time that Danny experienced, but the switching helped me to confirm that the curbside memory was a partial dissociation. It added to the growing indications that Emily was a multiple. She had not made progress with the former therapists because they were not treating her for the right condition. Her dissociations pointed to MPD.

HIDING TRAUMATIC MEMORIES

Another one of my MPD clients, Helen, had received her diagnosis only a few weeks earlier, and she told a friend that she "thinks he is fascinated with me." Though that piece of information was not entirely accurate, I found it to be positive because it indicated our relationship was getting off to a good start.

It is important that I keep each session positive, particularly during the early stages of treatment. MPD therapy is difficult for the client, which makes it crucial for us to develop a warm and trusting relationship early. I expect tough times ahead. Whenever I detect dissociation for the first time in a new client, a wave of sadness comes over me. I know exactly what it means—painful hidden memories—and my job is to help the person uncover them.

The bottom line with Helen was that we were entering into a therapeutic relationship, and she had not yet found out about the awful things that must have happened to her as a young child. I knew that therapy would be very demanding for her, and I was doing my best to understand her system of alternate personalities. It took concentration on my part and a lot of interest in her as a person. I was not "fascinated" with her, but I was deeply concerned—I do not enjoy seeing people suffer.

Studies reveal that these people's histories show a consistent pattern. One thing we know about dissociation is that it is used only when the pain has been extreme, and it usually begins in pre-school years. In order for dissociation to become a preferred coping style, which is the case in MPD, the pain has to start that early, and dissociation has to be used often enough to become a habit.

Two studies about the early lives of multiples came up with the same percentages—97 percent have been subjected to serious child abuse as youngsters. Another study found that 88 percent had been abused sexually, with 83 percent having been sexually penetrated as young children! That is a horrible way to start life. Although I always hope when I meet a dissociating person that he or she will be one of those who were not sexually abused, that is not usually the case.

Benefits of Dissociation

Since dissociation so effectively blocks out the painful memories, the victimized child grows up knowing absolutely nothing about the abuse. Then when therapy opens up the memory banks, and the awful memories filter down, the client finally does have to deal with the pain of what happened during those early years, and it is not easy. One of the benefits of dissociation is that the dissociator grows up with healthy alters who know nothing about the abuse. Those alters are the ones who come to therapy, believing they have had a simple childhood. They go through a lot of denial when the truth breaks through the amnesia. As those painful memories are brought out of hiding, the healthy alters declare, "That did not happen to me!" In a technical sense, they are right—it happened to a different personality—but it did happen to their body, and that is a terrible fact to accept.

Helen's host alter fought very hard to maintain the posture that she had gone through a normal childhood, and that her family was a good one. She was hospitalized briefly for depression when memories of incest started to break through the amnesic barriers. She dropped out of therapy two times, hoping that she would be able to get back to her "normal way of life," but as is the case for many multiples, she could not keep a job. The alters kept switching in on each other, and she could not attend to her tasks.

Each time she returned to therapy we went through a short period of denial again—her family was held up as the "model American family," and she distanced herself from her traumatic memories as much as she could. However, the incest memories had surfaced to the point where they could not be ignored. After staying away from therapy for about three weeks, she called me late at night, and said, "I just hate what I'm remembering. I had some new memories [about incest] and I'm depressed again. Can I start back in therapy?"

Why can't we just leave the memories hidden? If the treatment is so fraught with pain, wouldn't it be better just to leave the dissociating system of personalities alone?

On one side of therapy lies a fragmented person, usually unable to develop a career or a life as an effective parent, unable to remember important things that have happened, and unable to have a trouble-free sex life. On the other side of the MPD therapy is the promise of unity. The arguments about who said what, and what actually happened are over. The career and/or parenthood will improve immeasurably. The traumatic sexual memories can be worked through, with a nice improvement in that area. The hope of a better life *is* worth the pain. After unity is achieved, former multiples say that life had always been a mess. Even though they wanted to drop out of therapy many times, life has never been this good, now that they have success-fully stopped using dissociation. The memories must come out of hiding.

THE UNCONTAMINATED PERSON

MPD therapy is known to have very good results because it uncovers and uses the client's natural talents. If a child can use dissociation in the first place, that means he or she has a high level of creative and intellectual abilities. It takes a gifted person to dissociate.

Even though they are gifted, these people have been trau-matized badly enough that they needed to use dissociation to protect the talents. Here is how that works: The *trauma* plus *dissociation* equals *one alter* who remembers the event (the "con-taminated" alter), and other alters who are protected from know-ing about the trauma ("uncontaminated" alters). These alters can retain their God-given talents precisely because they do not have to bear the burden of grief that goes with knowing about the traumas. Therefore, they grow up carefree, with their natural abilities uncontaminated.

MPD therapy is directed toward affirming the health and strength of the uncontaminated alters and then decontaminating those with traumas so that they all can be restored to use the abilities they were born with. This is an optimistic approach, indeed, and I believe that the outcome of therapy should put the unified person's functioning at their same level as their most healthy alter's level. That means the giftedness will not only remain intact, but it will spread to the traumatized alters as well. As decontamination of memories occurs and burdens are lifted, the suffering alters find that they, too, have high abilities. When the contaminations are removed, unity can result in restoration of all of the gifted person's pre-trauma abilities. That is why prognosis is so good. We are not talking about having these people survive the war as battle-scarred veterans; we are talking about winning it, and coming home as war heroes—uncontaminated persons.

The positive approach to MPD therapy is founded on a genuine truth—a person's natural abilities can be recaptured. Please do not let me imply that this is a simple process. The challenge of decontaminating memories is a sizable endeavor when the traumas are extreme. Therapy can become arduous, and the ground gained can sometimes only be measured an inch at a time. Such is often the case when memories of SRA are discovered.

3

SATANIC RITUAL
ABUSE (SRA)

WARNING: The material in this chapter is extremely upsetting. It is not advised reading for any person who has survived any kind of abuse.
- To continue reading risks serious disruption—even breakdown.
- You must stop if this material suggests to you that you have seen or experienced abuse of this kind.
- If there is any hint of such events in your life, you need to be in a solid therapeutic relationship before you are ready to encounter the violently upsetting feelings that can be touched off by this material.
- Survivors of abuse, incest, SRA, or any other gruesome acts need to be helped through the abuse memories and feelings by professionals who have been trained to help such survivors.
- Nor should this chapter be read by children or teenagers. It is not good at this stage in their development for them to be exposed to the suffering and dangers that life can bring.

Protection is needed for the innocent and the wounded.

FACTS AND FEELINGS

I WISH I DIDN'T have to write a chapter like this. From my first experiences as a child right up to the present, I have found people to be wonderful. They have affirmed me, and I have enjoyed them. It is easy for me to be optimistic—people have been good to me, and I expect to find good in them.

When I first learned about satanic ritual abuse (SRA) from a tape on adult SRA survivors, it went against my training about what to expect from people. I was in a state of disbelief for weeks. It was difficult for me to believe there are people who really do perform the terrible acts of SRA perpetrators. I still do not want to believe human beings are capable of slaughtering other human beings or of subjecting precious children to heinous crimes. Despite my wish that it were not so, I must document SRA in this chapter. Somebody has to reveal how horrid life has been for SRA survivors.

This chapter is presented in a documentary format. Again, some of the accounts are citations of published material, and some accounts come from interviews. Names and circumstances have been changed to protect the people involved, but cited published accounts can be consulted by those who wish to compare these versions with the originals.

I want to let the people tell their stories verbatim so that the emotional tone of the original accounts will be preserved. It is practically impossible to read this chapter without encountering very strong feelings. I understand that. The chosen format of the facts will not protect the reader from feelings. Contrarily, this format invites the reader to plunge into each speaker's story—with both the facts and the feelings.

There is a growing cadre of people who can verify that SRA really happens. Many are involved in exposing it and in helping its survivors.[1] People who are informed about SRA must speak up boldly about what they know. Evil will spread when good people do nothing.

I have entered into therapeutic relationships with victims of SRA because I want to help contain and heal the effects of evil. I have done the research for this chapter, despite the fact that it makes me ill, because I don't want evil to spread. I have gotten past the notion that we will be able to stop SRA in our lifetime, but we can make a difference in the lives of survivors, and we can reduce the number of victims who would otherwise be subjected to the suffering that accompanies this most heinous form of abuse. I want to avoid indicting Satanism—people from that religious organization could protest if they were categorically implicated here.

WHAT IS SATANISM?

A lot of space could be devoted to answering that question. Satanism persists in many different forms. Some worshipers of Satan do so in what they call a church, but others conduct private ceremonies. My comments here are intended to help you understand that there are not simply a few "bad guys" out there—there is not just a single group that performs evil acts. One prominent SRA researcher found that, after talking with more than a hundred SRA survivors, 80 percent of them report having used the name "Satan" in their rituals. For the 20 percent who do not report using that name, it is not certain if it was used or not, nor is it clear whether there was any direct or indirect connection to self-proclaimed Satanists. Even if some survivors have been ritually abused by non-satanic people, it is generally accurate to consider these groups satanic in nature, and their influences are far more widespread than most people imagine.[2]

Their influences are also much more complex than most people realize. I do not want to convey here that the problems which SRA brings are simple, and that when we do a few specific things, the problems will be solved. Things are very complicated, and to reduce them to simplistic concepts is highly dangerous.[3]

Occultic Practices

Understanding these problems would be less disturbing if we at least could have some clear guidelines. Questions like "Who has MPD?" "How can we detect SRA?" and "What can be thought of as 'Satanism'?" are not easy to answer. Unfortunately, danger lurks in many forms that could be included as variations of "Satanism" or "the occult."

A former Satanist high priest, Mike Warnke, who has devoted his post-occult life to rescuing occult victims, wrote about his experiences in *The Satan Seller*. His first-hand experiences have led him to research the varieties of occult/satanic influences more fully. He claims that in America there are about eighty different kinds of occult practices.

Some of the more popular ones he listed are tarot cards, witchcraft, astral projection, Ouija boards, spiritualism, table tipping, levitation, clairvoyance, numerology, fortune telling, voodoo, palmistry, and seances.[4] It is probably not accurate to say that all of the people who practice those things would call themselves Satanists. Still, I think it is accurate to think of these groups according to their level of satancic/occult entanglement.

The *Cincinnati Enquirer* published an article about Satanism, portraying it this way:

> Experts generally agree that Satanists fall into three categories: (1) self-styled Satanists, who can range from hardened criminals to confused teenagers looking for kicks; (2) religious Satanists, such as members of the Church of Satan, who worship publicly and are protected by law; and (3) satanic cults, some of whom may use brainwashing techniques and demand secrecy and loyalty from their members.[5]

Three Levels of Occultic Groups

That assessment is not very different from *Passport* magazine's appraisal. In its "America's Best Kept Secret" edition,[6] it characterized occult groups as falling into three levels:

(1) The level where the participant's interest is captured by the prospect of glimpsing into forbidden areas, which may hold unexplainable and fascinating experiences. Examples are seances and Ouija boards. These are seducing influences, designed to pull the participant into deeper levels of occult involvement.

(2) The Church of Satan, and any other "above-board" groups, are seen at the second level. Folks here pray to Satan openly and turn themselves over to his control as much as they can. The Satanic Bible is their guide along the road to self-indulgence and the glorification of evil. They practice a life that is dedicated to whatever is exactly the opposite of Christian teachings. I would add that those who open themselves up to spirits through religious practices would fit at this level.

(3) Level three is "America's Best Kept Secret." Here participants take care to remain above reproach in public while secretly carrying out rituals intended to give them power. The rituals involve the practice of SRA.

People at this level have given their allegiance to Satan and obey their cult leaders. By the time they find out what really happens at the rituals, it is too late to turn back. They will lose their lives if they talk about America's best kept secret to anyone except a cult member. They are hopelessly stuck—their search for power and their intrigue with occultism have seduced them into the most serious entanglement imaginable. If they do not continue to spread ritual death and destruction, they will be killed by the coven members. The power they were searching for has engulfed them, and now they are subject to it. The intrigue that led them into the occult opened them up to be captured, if not by Satan himself, at least by people who follow him.

Not About Satanism

One more note of clarification seems appropriate here. This chapter is not about Satanism—it is about satanic ritual abuse. I am making no reference here to those who worship Satan and do not commit crimes. They are guaranteed the right to practice their religion, as long as they break no laws. An important organization has an official policy statement concerning ritual abuse, which I endorse:

> The California Consortium of Child Abuse Councils opposes the abuse of children by anyone, in any setting, and in any form, including ritual abuse, and will do all that it can to end existing abuse, heal its effects and prevent its recurrence. The Consortium seeks no abridgement of the right to religious freedom that does not involve the abuse of children.

This chapter pertains to people who perform destructive, illegal rituals, many times in the name of Satan. It is necessary to spell out how bad things can get in order to motivate good people to mobilize. It is unconscionable to sit idly by. *Evil will spread when good people do nothing.*

SRA AND MPD

It is surprising, and sometimes shocking, when I find SRA unexpectedly showing up in an MPD client during therapy long after one would expect it. I was utterly dejected after a therapy session with Inga when she had an alter appear who had suffered

SRA. At last I knew what had happened to her that caused her to start using dissociation in the first place.

She had been in MPD treatment with me for more than a year, and I had no notion there was any SRA behind it. We were getting to younger alters after making progress with the adult alters, and here is what happened.

Inga had a flashback, and relived a traumatizing moment in my office. She became childlike and talked in a tiny voice which was full of fear. The flashback was not complete enough to block out the present—she was simultaneously at the scene of the event and present enough with me to let me ask her some questions.

She entered the flashback by glancing at blood-covered walls around her, as though she were in a toilet stall. She said she saw blood everywhere, and there were white sheets soaked with blood all around her. She was sitting on a toilet in the basement of a church, going to the bathroom, and she was shocked at all the blood she had found. So far in the flashback, I had no solid evidence that there had been any cult-related activity. Then she said there was a big upside-down cross "over there," and she burst into tears. I knew what that meant. She had accidentally entered a bathroom, in a church basement, which had just been used for a cult ritual.

I took her further into the flashback by asking her what happened next. The flashback thinned out a little; she got into a less emotionally charged state and reported the next developments from a different alter. It seemed that she had switched into an alter with a firmer voice. The alter on the toilet was replaced by one who could protect the first one by reporting the facts without emotion. The second alter told me she walked up the stairs to the ground floor of the church, where she was met by her mother and a group of people who were very upset that she had used the basement bathroom. She was beaten severely on the spot. Another alter took over and said that it liked to kill animals, but then it disappeared. Quite a few fragmented alters were rotating through, telling me their part of the story, but nobody knew the whole story. As much as I could put things together afterward, here is what I helped her construct from her fragmented memories:

Her mother went to church practically every day, during daylight hours, and met with a group which included a pastor who wore only black. Inga was 3 or 4 at the time, and was not allowed to be with her mother during the meetings. She was very afraid of the pastor, and the mother was often violently abusive to her. The alter who had the first flashback was afraid she would be severely punished if her mother found out she was down there in the bathroom. On the day of the flashback, Inga could not wait to go to the bathroom, although she had been told to wait, and sneaked downstairs to where the bathroom was. She discovered the scene of the ritual before it had been cleaned up, and she couldn't believe her little eyes. When she ran upstairs, she was caught.

Now that the little girl had discovered the cult activities, they took her into the cult, and they subjected her to SRA rituals. The fragmented alter who said it was fun to kill animals was almost certainly developed during the rituals in order to please the SRA perpetrators. They also trained her to dissociate, which kept their secret safe. As a result, Inga was headed toward an adult life full of confusion and unfulfillment—she could not understand why relationships were always going wrong. Her therapy was constantly sabotaged because of her lack of trust in me. All this started with SRA, and Inga is only one of many examples where SRA has led to a shattered life.

A JOURNALIST'S ACCOUNT

At a conference of the Consortium of California Child Abuse Councils in 1987, Dee Brown gave a presentation about SRA. I bought a tape of her seminar, and what follows is transcribed from that tape. Dee Brown was introduced as a journalist who has been a leader since 1984 in documenting the "almost unbelievable experiences" of SRA survivors. She said she had talked with twelve adult survivors in her SRA research, and their stories added support to what she was hearing from child survivors. She said that the same things being said by child victims and adult victims adds to the credibility of both. It strongly suggests that the rituals have not changed through the years.

She started the presentation by recounting her contact with the parent of a child who had attended a preschool which has been implicated in SRA:

"They were driving down the freeway," Dee said, when his son turned to him and said, 'Daddy, what does it mean when they make you drink blood?' "

The son disclosed more and more, so the father took him to talk with Dee Brown. They met with her in a public cafeteria, where the boy said to his father, "She's nice. She doesn't wear a mask."

Credibility of Allegations

"He wasn't the only one making those kinds of statements," Dee continued. "They talked about things we don't want to hear. They talked about being forced to consume feces, and about witnessing deaths—deaths of animals and deaths of children.

"The obvious question is, did this type of abuse exist or could these kids just be making it up? The sheer number of kids I was hearing from made me believe that something was going on. I could not believe they would consistently come up with the same types of allegations and sometimes describe exactly the same ritual separated by thousands of miles—and these were children who did not know each other.

"Another [thing] that added credence was just the way the child disclosed it. It was too real for me to assume they were fabricating it. They would describe things in such detail, I frankly believed the children at a subjective level. And if those questions were true, another question was, 'Just how long had this been going on?'

"I began to seek out adult survivors as a potential source of validation of what the children were saying. Adult survivors are people who have lived through it first hand. I've spoken with more than a dozen survivors, and I took notes in interviews with six. [In 1990 Dee said by then she had talked with more than a hundred!] . . . They were all intelligent, impressive, wonderful people. The experiences they described span the years 1938 to

1980, and the locations of these experiences varied, including Southern California, the Midwest, the South and Canada.

"Six out of six reported consumption of feces, blood and urine, and drugs. Four out of six said the perpetrators wore robes. Five out of six said that the perpetrators were important people, i.e., doctors, dentists, religious figures . . . who were basically the solid backbone of the community. Five out of six discussed incest as being part of their family environment. Four out of six described that these experiences happened under the guise of a traditional, fundamentalist Christian group . . . .The same people who were involved on a daily basis in the Christian aspects of religious worship were involved in the satanic aspects at night. Four out of six talked about Satan being worshiped. The other two have not said this, but they have not said 'no,' either.

"Clearly, the statements of the adult survivors validated the statements of the children involved in current cases, and it clearly has been happening for many years.

Effects on Children

"The result of this entire scenario is that the child loses his sense of his own free will. They do things they never imagined they would do—violent and destructive things, and they do it because they are controlled by the others. And they must do these things in order to protect the ones they love . . . .The threat is made that if the child ever tells [about the SRA ceremonies], the mother will be killed. Since these people have already carried out murders in front of the child, it is certainly believable. The child is bound by the burden of knowing about the cult events, but cannot talk about it . . . "

Dee then read excerpts from a survivor's letter. It was a plea for understanding and acceptance. The writer had grown up in a cult family. When it was time for her initiation into the cult at about age 12, she was required to participate in the kidnapping and ritualistic murder of a child. It was either her life or the child's. There really was no choice, yet she was led to a sense that she was as guilty as the rest, and as a coven member, she would always be required to subject her will to theirs. She had become convinced that she was one of them, and she must obey the orders of the leader, or face death. There was no other way to survive.

"Survivors not only need our help and support," Dee added, "but they also need us to understand how they came to lose a sense of their own free will, and how they are fighting to regain it. The adult survivors I know have fought for and regained their own free will, and that knowledge and insight is the greatest hope we have of investigating current cases and restoring the sense of free will to the children that we're trying to help in present cases."

A FIRST-HAND ACCOUNT

It was enough of a blow for me to hear this journalist's account of her investigation that I needed some recovery time. The things I had heard caused me to change my world view. Previously I had thought of the world as a place where it is easy to tell the bad apples from the good apples. Now it seemed more like the world is a pile of nuts where you really can't tell what is inside any shell—maybe good nutmeats, maybe rancid, but there is no way to be sure from the outside. It took a few weeks for me to adjust. I did not know any SRA victims then. I sensed, though, that soon I would be treating more than one of them.

By the time I did begin therapy with an adult SRA survivor, I was a little more prepared than when I first heard the MPD tape. I knew no other therapists who were trained and experienced in helping SRA survivors, though. That was discouraging, because it meant there would be no networking or supervision. We used the MPD team as a forum at my clinic, which turned out to be a very important step. Not long after we started working on SRA together, we found that other therapists, now that they knew what signs to look for, also were discovering SRA among their adult incest survivors. We gained confidence and direction as we continued to work together.

Fran was one of the first clients at our clinic who discovered SRA memories. She asked her therapist if she could talk about her experiences with two male therapists, so Dr. Wilder and I were asked to be a part of her support system.[7]

She believed it would be therapeutic for her to find men who could support her in her very difficult recovery. She hoped that she would find a man or two who would believe her, since it was so difficult for her to believe that her family had been involved in Satanism. She had uncovered memories about being raised in a cult family. Dr. Wilder and I gave her a lot of support. We had heard other clients tell us of similar experiences, so we readily believed her.

As I was deciding about what to include in the present chapter, I thought it would be good to interview her. She could provide a first-hand perspective with the benefit of having progressed nicely in therapy.

We became a part of Fran's "true family" after that session, as opposed to her family of origin. She was eager to touch base with me every month or so, to tell me how she was doing, and to share excitedly about the wonderful progress God was giving her. It was remarkable how fast her recovery was moving. When I asked her if she would allow me to interview her for this book, she quickly agreed. Following are excerpts from that interview.

> I started in therapy thinking it was just incest with my father. I was sitting in group therapy about eighteen months ago, and someone mentioned something about Satan. All of a sudden I heard this voice—it was demonic. It said, "I wish she'd shut up talking about Satan!" That is not like me at all. I had become really attuned to my own spiritual life, and that was not like me at all.

> I didn't know I had Satanism in my background. [Then I] had my first flashback. It was just very, very vivid. All of a sudden I was in a barn and there were all these people, and they were chanting, and it was really, really frightening. It was so real, I immediately called my therapist. I knew what it was. When the person in group said something about Satan, it sparked my memory.

> Almost immediately after that I had this in-depth flashback of my father killing my cat, and of me having a baby and sacrificing the baby, and about being raped by the high priest, and having the demon presence entering the room. I thought that took place all when I was about 17—I got all those memories mixed up at first. I thought that my parents had gotten into Satanism just before I left home, and this was what they finally evolved to. Little did I realize that there were twelve years of Satanism going back down the scale. I thought, *That is it—they finally got evil enough to*

get into Satanism, and I left home. That was not the truth. My father had brought me into Satanism at the age of 6. At first I remembered being almost 18, and then I would see myself being 17, and then 16, and all the way back to 6.

At first I couldn't separate my memories from each other very well. The cat sacrifice and the human sacrifice came in at the same time, and they seemed like they were happening in the same incident. My first memories were that the cat sacrifice was the worst, but they were just on the surface. It was awful. That was eighteen months ago, but I had not really remembered what had happened to that baby. In other words, my first memories of that baby were just barely on the surface. I would only remember bits and pieces of it at first.[8]

I can remember the whole of it now. It all came through. I was given a shot to induce labor. The high priest was there. There were all sorts of other people in the room. They had capes on. I'm not certain how far along I was in the pregnancy at the time, but I believe about seven months. The baby cried, and I heard her cry. I had never studied anything about having a baby, so I had no idea what was going on.

I asked Fran if she knew she was pregnant at that time.

No. I didn't know I was pregnant; I just started to gain weight. I have no memory of being pregnant. I had gained about fifteen pounds. I remember my father lifted up my blouse to look at my breasts. He was real excited. He knew what changes to look for if I was pregnant.

A Baby Sacrifice

I asked her if she knew she was in labor.

No. I was going into labor and I didn't even know I was pregnant. I can remember looking down and seeing that my tummy was larger than usual, but I just thought I was gaining weight. I felt no pain. My body started convulsing and moving in strange ways. Of course, they held me down. Things started happening fast. I can remember feeling like I was drugged—I just did not feel anything down there. All of a sudden they were getting very excited and they were pushing on my stomach. I was facing the headboard. It was draped in black and there were candles around the room. It was dark, even though it was day. I could see the sun coming in the sides of those blackout drapes. It was very dark in there. They were holding me down so much, and there was so much commotion, and I was feeling very dopey, and out of it in the first place.

All of a sudden there was excitement, and I knew something went by my face. I knew a little later that it was a baby, but the thing that startled me was the umbilical cord. It was huge, and it went up by my face, and scared the living daylights out of me. I didn't even know it was a baby, Jim, until I heard it cry! And then when I heard it cry, something happened inside of me, and I started to put everything together. They had a place over at the side of the room—a sort of a pulpit with an altar cloth over it, and they placed the baby on it. And all of a sudden I could see my father's hand go up in the air, and this huge sound came down as he killed it.

She went on to describe, in details that were remarkably vivid, the sights, sounds, smells, and flavors of the ritual, including chants of worship to Satan.

That was the baby sacrifice. It's pretty mind boggling. The worst was that it was a perfectly beautiful human being, and she was gone, as though she had never existed.

A few minutes later I asked Fran to tell me what some of her earliest cult-related memories were.

I was told to get in this car with my parents and we went real far away at night. I'm pretty sure this took place on the outskirts of [a specific town]. We drove to this barn, and I didn't know what was going on—I was only 6. We were ushered into this back room. We were kind of the maids of honor. It's really hard to describe that because I always think of a wedding with the symbolism. These people are so evil! Instead of your mother getting you ready for a wedding, your mother is getting you ready to get into Satanism.

I was the youngest one there—there were about five or six other girls. The girls I remember very well. I have talked to one of them recently to confirm my memories. I think she thought I was a Satanist, and didn't trust me at first. It was very, very helpful to me to have the conversation with this woman. It was powerful. She was one of the girls who was getting all these pretty dresses. They were kind of like Renaissance dresses—all kinds of pretty colors. Each one of the girls had a different color dress. They were really pretty—it was like we were going to a May Day celebration. Of course, we were excited. Our mothers helped us get dressed and we were taken out to this barn. We were in this line from the oldest to the youngest. I remember looking all around. It was very suffocating and very hot. There were a lot of people in that barn, and I started to feel faint.

There was this man who was in charge. He lifted each one of the girls up onto a slab-like altar. It was very cold. He lifted each girl up and examined them like a doctor in the doctor's office. He looked at each one and kissed them in their female parts, then he took them down and they were ushered into the back room. I was getting scared right then because the girls started to change their expressions. Their little dresses were lifted up and they were starting to cry. They were getting scared.

When the priest got to me he examined me too, front and back, and kissed me on my female parts, and said loudly, "You have saved the best for last." He paraded me a little bit. He was very pleased with me. He put me down and gave me a swat on my bottom, and I went off with my mother. I was chosen for something over the other ones, and later I found out I was chosen to carry his child. Some of the girls didn't pass, but I guess I did. That was the way I was [started in] Satanism, and that was the least violent act.

Other Memories

Fran went on to talk about other things she had remembered.

I remember being placed by my mother into a casket, lowered into the ground, and dirt put on top, and freaking out in there. I couldn't breathe. I've had claustrophobia all my life and that is why. I always had a feeling on my fingers. I was made to dig into the human sacrifices. I wouldn't put the stuff on me, so they stuck my hands in it. It's strange, because your mind says, "This must be something funny. You shouldn't get mustard and mayonnaise and condiments on your fingers!" When I would have Bible studies and lunches in my home, there were these jars of condiments that I would have to put away. I couldn't do it. I would have to get my daughter to do it. I couldn't stand to put my fingers in that stuff . . . I would never eat a hamburger and get the drippings on my fingers. It reminded me of Satanism, but I didn't know what it was reminding me of. I'd sit there with a million napkins on my lap!

I can't remember when I was not naked at these events. I can remember being brought into the barn one time when my mother ripped the clothes off me. Or they would have a cape. I can remember when they were doing Satanism in my home, the men and women would just have their underwear on underneath the capes. Not their bras, just their underwear. And then when they were ready to rape somebody, they would drop their underwear and usually drop their cape. But when they would have the full-out orgies in the barn they were just naked, like you would see in Dante's *Inferno* or something. The people were running and jumping around by the flames or the fire, with naked bodies. They were just spaced out. They were crazy. They were possessed—totally demon possessed.

People do not understand the evil in that place. They do not understand how anyone would give in to sacrificing a child. If you're in the most beautiful place in the presence of Jesus, you can just feel His presence, and you're engulfed in His glory. You know, in Satanism it is just the opposite of that. It is so evil, that even as you are remembering these things you can feel it. You can just feel the presence of that evil. There were times with my therapist that I just knew the enemy was trying to keep a memory from me, but we would pray and it would be broken. I can't even express it in words. The presence of evil is so strong, and the fear of death is so strong. When the presence of Satan comes into a room it's so stifling, so controlling, that you can hardly breathe. If you can imagine that there are all these other people over here calling to Satan, trying to whip it up, calling, "Hail Satan! Hail Satan!" and they're chanting and chanting and chanting, you know the power becomes stronger and stronger, and the force of evil is so strong!

Fran then described how she had been raped by a demon during that ritual. It was searingly painful, and she was totally immobilized while it was happening. It was an extremely violent instance of incubus.

After Fran had begun to uncover the memories, she had a great need to have them confirmed. They were so unbelievable, yet so vivid, that she felt she was a little crazy, even while talking to her therapist. However, she did come to accept that they are accurate. That is when she decided to tell them to Dr. Wilder and me. That helped her quite a bit, but she needed further confirmation. She called people who had spoken in public about Satanism, and they confirmed that what she had gone through was consistent with the things others had seen and heard. Fran has now come to a place where she has received incredible healing for those memories, and she has become actively involved in restoring other SRA survivors.

Fran's story is one of immense courage and victory, and at least now she doesn't have to put a million napkins on her lap when she eats hamburgers! She has been set free, and she is a picture of mental health. There isn't a psychotic thought in her head, nor does anyone accuse her of conjuring up new, morbid stories to please her therapist. The things described in detail above come from a very intelligent person, who is equipped with wonderful social skills. Lots of love flows from her when she interacts with people. I really can't understand the loving care that she gives to others.

As a therapist who was trained to be a scientist and a clinician, I can see a major rift. Fran's accounts are not scientifically based, especially the demonic rape, yet her progress is a clinical miracle. It is impossible to not believe her from a clinical point of view. On the other hand, it is impossible to believe her from a purely scientific point of view.

Her progress was possible because her therapist deeply believed all that Fran told her and was willing to help her find psychological and spiritual healing. The explanation for her progress transcends what scientists are able to explain.

If Fran were the only person whose experiences are beyond the scientific realm, it would be easy to dismiss her story as a fluke. However, if the SRA memories are accurate, and hers certainly are consistent with other suvivors' accounts, and if the people really do worship Satan and call on him to be present, and if there really is a Satan, the story has strong internal consistency. That is an important consideration—Fran's account does hang together, and she is so candid and transparent that the listener can sense the compelling force of honesty in her voice. The deceit and hate from her background have been transformed into truth and love in every aspect of her life.

A PARENT'S ACCOUNT

There are two kinds of SRA. Intrafamilial SRA occurs within the family, usually as part of a pattern that goes on for generations. Intrafamilial victims have been raised in cult families and have probably been exposed to the cult rituals from their earliest moments in infancy.

Extrafamilial SRA most often occurs in day-care settings, where the victims are ritualized starting at ages 2 to 4. As was mentioned earlier by Dee Brown, it helps to get collaborating evidence from the parent of child SRA survivors because it indicates that the whole case for SRA is not just being confabulated by a few adults. I worked with such a parent, Gladys, for about a year, while she recovered from the shock of finding that her daughter had been an SRA victim at age 3 in a day-care setting. I worked with Gladys on her personal and family issues, and another psychologist worked with the child. Gladys was eager to tell me what happened to her daughter, as a way to help other victimized families. Following are excerpts from an interview with Gladys, a few months after she had completed therapy with me.

At the beginning my daughter started to have weird behavior, where she'd start screaming. This was after she had been going to [the day-care center], but I didn't connect the two. She would go into a rage. She'd start hitting and kicking and screaming, and saying, "I hate you! You're stupid! Don't do that!" She'd just get hysterical.

I talked to some different people, but I didn't know what it was . . . . So finally I called my pastor. He listened, and said there is definitely a problem, but we didn't know what was causing it.

I sort of had a weird feeling when I left her at preschool one day . . . .When we came home, she said that the teacher had tickled her hard on her chest. I asked if she had tickled her anywhere else, and she pointed to her diapers. So I dropped her out of that school immediately.

Things seemed to calm down a little bit, and then over the next ten months nothing else came out of it, except she would occasionally have these screaming fits and you just didn't know when they were going to happen. We had moved from our old house to our new house, and I was getting ready to go on a trip to visit my family in Oregon. I was packing, and she started running hysterically through the house saying that the police were going to come, the firemen were going to come, and our house was going to burn down. She had shown signs of fear at loud noises, which my mom was real concerned about—on the fourth of July she was petrified of the fireworks. She was very afraid of being in the Jacuzzi, and things that she normally liked were starting to make her afraid. So I had a lot of questions, like, what's causing this? I did a lot of praying, "God, show me what this is."

When we got to Oregon she was okay for the first two days, then she started being really mean to everybody. She started causing arguments . . . and she had a look on her face which was not her normal look. She just looked mad all the time.

After having one of those screaming fits, we got her calmed down and she finally went to sleep. Then the next day she kept saying that she felt sick to her stomach, and she took a nap. When she got up she said, "Mommy, I think I'm going to throw up," so I took her over to the toilet. When I went to help her by pulling her hair back, she said, "Don't throw me in! Don't throw me in the toilet! Don't put me in there!" I was shocked. She was so scared, and I asked her what she was talking about, and she said, "I can't tell you. No. I have to get out of here! I have to be by myself."

Through the whole thing she would, in the middle of talking, throw up or get diarrhea. She would have reactions to her pajamas. She would say, "They choke you!" Her pajamas would choke her. Anything that would cover her feet, she'd say, "Don't put them on." That is what actually opened it up—she would live through the pain. She would get up on the bed and tell me her feet hurt.

[My comment: Her feet hurt because she had been given shots in her feet during a ritual to make her sleep, and that hurt enough to cause her to relive the experience when her feet were touched.]

She would be walking through the house and her legs would just go out on her and she would fall down. She'd say her legs hurt.

Before any of this came out, she developed a habit of wiping her face every night before we went to bed. She'd just wipe it, like she was trying to get something off her face. And also if any water got on her, she just had to change her clothes—she could not be wet. She couldn't stand it . . . . She would say certain things a lot, like her bottom hurt and she didn't want her covers on. She was wetting a lot. She wouldn't let me comb her hair because it hurt whenever I touched her head. She had constant headaches and stomach aches. She didn't want to go to bed at night. And her car seat—she would not let us put the strap on her any more. This was after the disclosures started, and I could not understand all that. Now over the past year I am understanding why she was saying those things.

Recognizing the Abuse

I asked Gladys what it was that finally helped her figure out what was wrong.

I think it was because I had a suspicion about that preschool. I had just been agonizing about her behavior patterns, like why was she wiping her face every night, and why was she reacting so violently to liquid? And why was she having these rage fits? It wasn't like a screaming tantrum. It went beyond temper tantrum. So when she started to talk to me, I knew that she had been abused.

There was one night in Oregon where I had left her with my brother-in-law. I had gone out to dinner with my sister, and she told my brother-in-law, "My mommy's never coming back." I knew it was abuse, but I had never heard about ritualistic abuse. The way she'd say, "Don't hide from me," and then jump out as if to scare me, I knew she'd been through a terrible experience, but I didn't have any answers.

On the plane coming home from Oregon, she talked about the color red a lot, like the sockets of her eyes being red, and her gums being red. She had just turned 3, so it was hard to understand it all. She would ask if our house would just pop away, like a balloon. She always referred to these people as "bad people." If you get mad they will squeeze your head off. They don't have toys—only bad people toys. Then one night she came running into my room and said she had blood in her eyes, and they were going to squeeze her eyes out with a big clipper.

She said, "You go to their house and never come back. They put you in a yucky bed."

I had a hard time trying to figure out all that, like, what's a yucky bed? She talked a lot about being put in a yucky bed. Now I know she could have been put in a coffin, and I know that they could have put urine all over her. That is why she was having the reaction to anything wet.

She said that they killed Jesus, that they cut him up and killed the baby who cried and cried. One night she came in just sobbing and sobbing, and told me that they killed a baby, that they put poo poo and potty on the baby, that they cut off the baby's head, arms, and legs with a knife. She has also talked about lying down with dirt and bugs being put on top of her, which you can assume was a grave, because where else would you have dirt and bugs on top of you? She has talked consistently about the baby, and that she hurt the baby also. They made her poke it. She says they gave the baby shots all over its body. She said they pulled out the heart, and blood is in your stomach. She said the kids were forced to eat the poop.

A lady with no shirt on kissed her, and they got married. She must have been through a marriage ceremoney of some kind with a bare-breasted woman—and my daughter was only 3 years old at the time! And then one time we saw a couple kissing in the car, and my daughter got nauseated. She's talked a lot about marriage. She also said they hurt your bottom with the glass, and in her medical exam she had rectal scarring, so we knew that they had done something to her in this region.

One night she showed us how she was tied up, hands and feet. Then she asked me, "Mommy, have you ever hung upside down from a chain?" That is not a normal question for a 4-year-old to ask. She talked about candles, and about a woman who was wearing a black shirt and a black skirt when she tied her up. It has taken about a year and a half to get her to talk this freely about things. The details get clearer as she relives them.

[My comment: The daughter's recovery process very closely resembles what Fran reported—the memories became clearer as they were re-lived over a period of time.]

Once she said that this is how they killed the baby. She said the baby had holes in its hands like Jesus did, and they made the kids poke and hit the baby. She said she is bad because she hurt the baby. She said she was thinking that I didn't love her. They told her that I was going to die on the cross, just like Jesus did. They just told her that a lot. They were not threatening to kill me if she told about the satanic rituals, but they were just saying that I was going to die, and that was that.

I have to believe her. She has described the blood and the cutting, and said so many times that the baby cried and cried. I used to try to believe it was just a doll—that they had used a doll or something, but that doesn't explain the impact that the crying had on her. She keeps talking about pulling the heart out.

Now, in therapy, she is working through the fact that I really don't hate her. So she asks me a couple of times a day if I hate her. If I show any kind of emotion, if I get frustrated or anything, she asks if I hate her. Any little sign of disapproval will trigger that response in her. She has been programmed to detect that I hate her, and that the bad people are right. There is practically no way I can deal with it except to keep telling her that I love her.

Effects on the Family

I told Gladys that this is the kind of self-fulfilling prophecy the cultists program children with. They say things that lead the children to conclude for themselves that the parents really do hate them. This is just one of the ways cultists drive a wedge between the kids and their parents. Most of the time the SRA is not discovered. The parents do not know what they are dealing with, and the children develop very unhealthy ways of thinking and behaving. The family becomes dysfunctional as a result. The wedge stays between the child and the parents throughout childhood, and the prophecy comes true: The child believes that the parents have hated him or her all along.

Gladys and her family had been a healthy, loving family. They simply chose the wrong preschool. Major family disruption has resulted, and an innocent child's life has been seriously impaired.

Other families, too, have broken apart or become extremely dysfunctional from the effects of the satanic evil that has befallen them. The damage done by just a few SRA perpetrators is alarmingly far-reaching and long-lasting.

HOW WIDESPREAD IS THE DAMAGE?

Harold is an acquaintance of mine. I do not know him very well, but we talk now and then. Recently he asked me if there is an area of psychology that I specialize in. When I mentioned MPD he told me that he is married to an adult survivor of SRA, and asked if I knew about that. He was surprised to find that I do know about treating SRA survivors who are also multiples, because his wife had had a very difficult time finding a therapist who does.

As we began to share how disgusting and thoroughly revolting the acts of SRA are, he said that it doesn't take many SRA perpetrators to do a lot of damage to a lot of families. He has also suffered by having his life disrupted. He had to change professions because his wife needs him to be home more of the time, and they have to spend massive amounts of money for her therapy.

Yet those are not the things that bother Harold the most. What really bothers him is the evil. He is extremely sorry for and supportive of his wife as she struggles to recover from the effects of SRA. The family disruption and money problems are difficulties, to be sure, but the most difficult part is that this family has had to change directions, and everyone in the family has suffered because of the SRA. It all started in a preschool about thirty years ago, and the agony of that woman has been carried to the other members of her family. They are all still suffering. Many families are still suffering.

Glady's family situation is another example. Not only did her daughter go through intense fear and suffering that no child should ever have to endure, but Gladys and her husband have suffered too. In fact, I started working with Gladys after she was released from a long hospitalization. She had become so depressed after finding out what had happened to her daughter that she was highly suicidal for a long time. SRA very nearly killed the surviving child's mother, which would have destroyed the family and left the daughter with immense guilt for the rest of her life—she would have concluded that she had caused her mother's death!

Harold was right. The damage is immense, and a few SRA perpetrators can spread fear and destruction among many families. The video, "America's Best Kept Secret," puts it this way: "From the number of preschool cases alone, it would appear that a massive indoctrination of American children into Satanism is going on." It doesn't take many SRA perpetrators for the problem to become widespread.

I talked to one of the leaders in the Los Angeles County Task Force on Ritual Abuse, who estimate that there have been more than a hundred California preschools implicated in ritual abuse. When children have been identified in that many preschools by many therapists as SRA victims, we have a major problem on our hands. Many of the child victims are developing MPD defenses, and will become adults with MPD if the effects of SRA are not corrected in therapy. The damage is immense. Many families are being destroyed, and as SRA child victims grow up, the likelihood is high that their suffering will spread to other people too.

Few Public Investigations

Isn't it odd that the free press in America does not investigate more fully what is revealed about major SRA-related stories?

Mass murders Richard Berkowitz (Son of Sam) in New York and Henry Lee Lucas in Texas have both confessed to being part of satanic cults involving blood sacrifice. In Montana, Stanley

Dean Baker dismembered a man he had stabbed 27 times, took out his heart and ate it. He had one of the man's fingers in his pocket at the time of his arrest.

Richard Ramirez, the night stalker murderer, holds up his fist and says, "Hail Satan!" as he is brought into the courtroom, and not one journalist follows up on that! Eventually, however, a small magazine does investigate it:

> Richard Ramirez has been heavily connected to Satanism. Confirmed reports have revealed that Ramirez has a pentagram tattooed on his left hand; that for the last two years he has worn only black or dark clothing; that he was obsessed with Satanic themes and music . . . that police found pentagrams scrawled on the walls of some of the victims' homes; that police found similar markings on Ramirez's jail cell. Captured on videotape and film at the time of his arraignment, Ramirez was holding up a pentagram inked on the palm of his left hand as he shouted, "Hail, Satan!" Even one of the victims testified that Ramirez had ordered her to "swear upon Satan."[9]

It was obvious that he was some variety of a cultist, and yet major newspapers did not write anything about that during the trial—it could mislead or confuse the jurors. His case was stuck in court for years, and people did not write about what was behind the murders, some sort of cult organization, because we were protecting his rights. What about the right of the public to know about the deadly effects of his beliefs? Has any journalist even tried to find out if he was connected to a particular cult group?

At his Los Angeles trial, after being convicted of thirteen counts of murder, Richard Ramirez was brought into the court to hear the decision about his sentencing. He was allowed to make a statement to the court before the sentence was given. Here is what he said: "You do not understand me. You are not expected to. You are not capable of it. I am beyond your experience. I am beyond good and evil. Legions of the night—night breed—repeat not the errors of 'Night Prowler' and show no mercy. I will be avenged. Lucifer dwells within us all. That's it."

Little Public Information

If the public could be informed—without cover-up—about the "legions of the night," we would all be safer. Perhaps Richard

Ramirez was right when he said we do not fully understand "Night Prowler," with his inverted pentagram sign, but I believe that we must learn about the "legions of the night." How many people will be killed if we neglect that? How many little children will suffer if we do not keep pressing for the truth about what has happened in the "offending" preschools? I want to live in a society where children will be protected, even if it involves lengthy and expensive trials.

Disappearing Evidence

Although I am not very close to the facts about most of the alleged preschool cases, I have followed the newspapers about some, and they report that the detectives' evidence disappears. That is consistent with the way SRA perpetrators work. They are masters at murder—and at cover-up. If SRA was really practiced at these preschools, and the charge was brought into the court-room, the case would almost certainly be thrown out for either of two reasons:

(1) To raise even the possibility that the cruel acts which constitute SRA could have occurred in such a public setting would paralyze a jury. They cannot be expected to believe any-thing the victims would say if such a ritual were described. It really would be unbelievable unless the judge and jury are educated about SRA and about the clues which point to it.

(2) Just to say the word Satanism in court would end the proceedings immediately. The case would be thrown out of court, never to be re-tried. Why? Because lawyers haggle over "religious" protection. Law suits about protecting Satanism and about slandering a religion would cripple court proceedings to the point where the original intent to protect the children would fail. People have a right to worship as they please in this country, so Satanists are protected by our constitution. Their right to worship Satan is guaranteed by law.

Whether cult rituals in which Satanism is implicated may be part of any particular preschool trial is not for me to allege. I am only pointing out that cover-up takes place. The jurors from one trial believed that many of the children had been sexually abused somewhere, and the defense attorney even said publicly that it seems to have happened. My hope is that whoever performed those abusive acts will come to justice. If the case involved SRA, I hope the authorities will investigate thoroughly enough to prove it so the survivors in other "offending" preschools will be helped and so SRA perpetrators will be stopped from carrying out their unspeakably awful acts.

Emerging Reality

People want to believe that the terrible acts reported by the children didn't really take place. Judges and juries are not ready, lawyers are not ready, courts are not ready, and America itself may not yet be ready to hear what the children are saying. However, there has been at least some awareness of the SRA problem simmering on the surface of the public's mind for some years. SRA will undoubtedly emerge and be understood more fully sometime soon. The public will have to deal with the reality of SRA, simply because it is so widespread that it will soon be impossible to keep all the cases under cover.

There are no prominent books which document SRA at present, but quite a few newspapers have carried the stories. To illustrate how widespread the problem is, and to show that these news items are getting to the public, let me quote from an article I have in my files, the *Chicago Tribune* (July 29, 1985) article, "Satanism Haunts Tales of Child Sex Abuse":

> NOTE: In order to protect the privacy of any innocent parties who may have been involved, I have chosen not to reveal the names of the cities nor of the people mentioned in the article. All indications are, though, that the newspaper account is reliable, and it may be resourced if desired.

Scores of children in more than half a dozen California communities are telling authorities that they have been sexually abused by adults who also forced them to take part in satanic-type rituals, including the drinking of blood, cannibalism and the sacrificial murders of other children.

The latest such case surfaced in [a California city] 10 days ago, when the [a California county] Sheriff's Department held a press conference to confirm reports that half of the fifteen victims of an alleged child sex abuse ring had made such accusations against their parents and other adults.

"We understand the initial human reaction of, 'I don't want to believe it; make it go away,' " said Cmdr. [name omitted], who heads the department's detective division. "We do believe the children. But it's not only in California. You can see cases across the United States popping up where you get these tremendously uncanny similarities." . . .

Allegations, disturbingly similar in detail to the ones here, have been made in recent months by at least three dozen other California children, all of whom also claim to be victims of sexual abuse.

Authorities say that as far as they know, none of the children in any of the California cases, which range from [a northern California city] to [a southern California city] , is known to any of the principals in the other cases, nor is there any solid evidence linking abuse suspects.

In [a California county], north of [a northern California city], several children who attended the same preschool have told police they were made to chant "Baby Jesus is dead" and subjected to other satanic rituals as a prelude to being sexually abused.

The [another California county] sheriff has received allegations by nine children, ages 4 to 10, that they were sexually abused by half a dozen residents of the same middle-class suburb who combined the abuse with satanic rituals and child murder.

Those who treat sexually abused children are both perplexed and worried by the apparent similarity of the children's accounts. "It's something I don't want to be identified as knowing that much about," said a psychiatrist who has interviewed the children in one of the cases. "I think anybody who works in this area ought to carry a badge and wear a gun, and not have a family."

"Good luck with your life," said another child therapist, one of whose patients is among the children making such accusations. "My car was blown up 10 days ago."

The first therapist, who said he had heard sexually abused children speak of "eating flesh, being forced to kill other children, things like that," had initially been skeptical of the children's accounts.

"I wanted to believe in the worst way that this was explainable on some other basis," he said, "but I have a hard time looking at it logically and coming up with any other conclusion."

Apart from their personal safety, the overriding concern among those investigating and prosecuting such cases is that many Americans who are only now coming to grips with the extent of sexual child abuse will conclude that the children in such cases are fantasizing, not only about devils and demons but also about being abused.

"People," one psychiatrist says, "just aren't ready for this."

The biggest potential impact, however, is likely to be on the jurors in sexual child abuse cases who find themselves also weighing children's testimony about black masses, human sacrifices and the like.

Just last month . . . a deputy district attorney in [another California county], east of [a California city], tried a case in which a 9-year-old girl had accused her natural father of abusing her and other children sexually in concert with a group of Satanists.

A mistrial was declared in the case when the jury announced that it was deadlocked 6-6, and . . . several jurors [said] later that it had been their disbelief of the girl's testimony about satanic rituals, and not about being abused, that prompted them to vote for acquittal.

"There's no doubt in my mind that she was a participant in satanic worship," [name omitted] said. "But she also described incidents of human sacrifice, bestiality and cannibalism, how her father put his hand around her hand and then the two of them plunged a knife into the chest of an infant. That raised some questions."

[My comment: This method of murdering children is precisely what SRA victims report all over the country, time after time, without knowing others are reporting the same thing.]

Skillful Cover-Up

That *Chicago Tribune* article is six years old at the writing of this book, and only one case of child-related SRA has been effectively prosecuted in the whole country. That was in Florida, and the verbatim account of the trial is contained in the book, *Unspeakable Acts*. Other cases will certainly follow, but the skillful job of cover-up has prevented successful outcomes in many other cases. The SRA perpetrators are very intelligent, imaginative people, and they do not want to get caught, so their cover-up skills are extremely well developed.

Take the first case mentioned in the above article for example. I grew up in that city and have occasion to visit people there at various times in the year. I was following the news about that investigation, where more than thirty children were removed from their homes, when that story began to draw national attention. The thing that really stands out in my memory of the news accounts was that the evidence fell apart and the children were returned to their homes. I found that very disturbing. People I know might be in danger.

A few months after the investigation was closed, I ran into a high school acquaintance in that city at a party. We exchanged warm greetings, and told each other what we have been doing all these years.

When he said he works in [one law-enforcement] department, I asked if he knew anything about the alleged SRA case which had been reported in the newspapers. His mood changed instantly. He really didn't want to talk about it, and made that very clear, but his wife eventually prevailed upon him to tell me. Here is what he described:

The evidence was disappearing from the department as quickly as it came in. The accounts of the children were compelling, convincing and consistent, and there was no question in his mind about what had happened—a ring of SRA perpetrators had been discovered. He knew one of the investigators very well, and that man was baffled about how the evidence disappeared. My acquaintance said he surely didn't want to get involved. The evil of the perpetrators was too much for him, and he didn't want to get his family in trouble with them. He wasn't going to say anything to anybody about how the evidence, which doubtless could have convicted the perpetrators, had vanished. He had to conclude that somebody in the departmental unit was on the cult side, but he was not about to go public with it. The cover-up was very successful.

At a recent convention in Anaheim I chanced to meet a therapist from the city referred to above. He told me he knew therapists who had treated some of the children involved in that case. According to him, although the evidence that those children had been SRA victims was ironclad, no court proceedings could be initiated because of the lack of supporting evidence. He was highly agitated as he described to me the injustice he saw.

Another acquaintance of mine, who also is a therapist in that city, told me he was appointed by the courts to work with some of the child victims who had been removed from their homes at the time the initial evidence hit the newspapers. His job was to make recommendations about whether or not the children should be put back into the homes that had been implicated in SRA, but the evidence had been misplaced. His account to me was that in the whole system, from the courts, to the local child therapy clinic, to the investigators, and even to the courthouse itself, things were mishandled. He maintained that from top to bottom, the information was interfered with to the point that nobody would ever hear the complete story.

He said that after he told one set of parents their children had likely been sexually abused, they changed therapists, and they were not stopped from seeking a therapist who would give them the opinion they wanted to hear!

He went on to tell me that after the cases had been closed, one therapist who had been assessing the children changed her name, left town, and switched professions.

One investigator went on permanent disability, due to the extreme emotional stress involved in the case. Attorneys were seen crying in the court hallways, because they could not do enough to protect the children from being returned to homes they were afraid of. Lives were being shattered all around. The evil was so widespread, it was frightening.

Recommendations Ignored

My acquaintance said the children he interviewed gave him abundant evidence that SRA had really taken place, and he recommended to the courts that the children not be placed back in their homes. The evidence was not taken seriously; his recommendation was not followed; he had to conclude there must have been some kind of conspiracy. The children were returned to the homes where they were not safe at all!

Soon after their return, my friend said he saw that "a dull numbness" had appeared on their faces, and they immediately contradicted the accounts they had given earlier. It looked to my friend like the victimized children had been programmed, probably with electrical shocks, drugs, and/or hypnosis, to refute what they had initially told the therapists. He was near tears as he said to me that the children were surely being subjected to more of the same kind of SRA they had initially reported, and he could do nothing to stop it.

"We'll never know what happened," he said. "The decision must have been made before I even saw the children—they had to be returned home in order to save face with the media. I've got part of the story, but nobody will ever know it all."

No Bodies Found

One thing that helped sink the case in that city, according to the *Tribune* article quoted above, is that no bodies were found "despite the excavation of sites and dredging of lakes where the children say the sacrificial victims were buried." SRA perpetrators plan their cover-ups so that the child witnesses will be thoroughly discredited. They take the children along to watch them bury the remains. It is a great way to come up with a water-tight cover-up! If the perpetrators really wanted to hide the sacrificial remains, they certainly would not take the children along to watch. They would do it in secret. However, in a number of cases, the children stated they were taken along. The perfect way to discredit the children's testimony is to exhume the remains later, after the children have watched them buried! Who would believe a child's story when he says he knows exactly where the baby is buried, but no baby is found at the site?

The *Tribune* concurs: "The principal obstacle confronting them, say those investigating the various cases, is the almost total lack of physical evidence, including bodies, to confirm the children's allegations."

How widespread is the damage? Nobody knows for certain. We do know that a lot of information about the extent of SRA is being suppressed because of court-related complications, and we do know that SRA perpetrators are masters at cover-up. It may never be known how widespread the damage is, but I believe that after a few of these cases successfully get through the court entanglements, justice systems will be modified to bring quicker justice, and the public will be informed about how to identify SRA survivors and perpetrators. It will take something specific, like an SRA training program for judges and juries, and it will take something general, like documentaries and more case histories in print.

WHAT CAN I DO?

Worshiping false gods and killing infants have been connected for a long time. The Israelites were twice commanded by God not to offer their children as sacrifices (Leviticus 18:21 and Deuteronomy 12:31). The prophets Isaiah, Jeremiah and Ezekiel accused the Israelites of sacrificing their children to false gods, and they described the actions as detestable to the true God (Isaiah 57:3-5; Jeremiah 19:4,5; Ezekiel 16:20,21).

A shocking account of one of Israel's kings is carried in 2 Chronicles 28:1-4:

> Ahaz was twenty years old when he became king, and he reigned in Jerusalem sixteen years. Unlike David his father, he did not do what was right in the eyes of the LORD. He walked in the ways of the kings of Israel and also made cast idols for worshiping the Baals. He burned sacrifices in the Valley of Ben Hinnom and sacrificed his sons in the fire, following the detestable ways of the nations the LORD had driven out before the Israelites.

Even the great king David told of the lamentable deeds of those who had worshiped false gods: After he told how the people were worshiping a god named "Baal," he wrote in Psalm 106:36-39:

> They worshiped their idols,
>   which became a snare to them.
> They sacrificed their sons
>   and their daughters to demons.
> They shed innocent blood,
>   the blood of their sons and daughters,
> whom they sacrificed to the idols of Canaan,
>   and the land was desecrated by their blood.
> They defiled themselves by what they did;
>   by their deeds they prostituted themselves.

Thus the history of child sacrifice is documented in the Bible, dating back at least 3,000 years. Recent research has found evidence showing that satanic rituals were practiced during the post-biblical era. Two clinicians who have heard SRA accounts from their clients, have located the historical materials which describe scenes practically identical to the client accounts. Here is their summary:

> As early as the fourth century elements of a satanic mass were well described: (1) a ritual table or altar; (2) ritual orgiastic sex; (3) reversals of the Catholic mass; (4) ritual use of excretions; (5) infant or child sacrifice and cannibalism often around initiation and often involving use of a knife . . . (6) animals; (7) fire or candles; and (8) chanting. Extending the historical search from 400 to 1200 A.D. yields only a few new elements: (9) ritual use of drugs, and (10) of the circle, and (11) ritual dismemberment of corpses.

It is tremendously validating for SRA survivors to learn that their memories can be identified as an on-going part of history. It is also sobering and distressing to average people, like you and me, to realize that these practices have not been stopped. They are still being carried out by those who worship false gods. Satanic cults have survived and are flourishing today.

We have documentation of SRA in many countries over the past hundred years. Aleister Crowley is a name recognized around the world as a deceased leader of the occult, and his story indicates a lot about what happens to cult members.

Passport magazine carries the story of Crowley, who was born in England in 1875. It is stated that, as a youngster, he set himself up in God's place. It was not a temporary attitude—it stayed with him and set the whole course of his life:

> A bisexual, Crowley had a voracious sexual appetite that, coupled with his extreme interest in the darker forces of life, earned him a sinister worldwide reputation. The popular press during the 1920s proclaimed him "the wickedest man in the world."

> For a time, he lived with disciples at the Abbey of Thelema . . . near Cefalu in Sicily, Italy. Satanism was practiced at the abbey and animal sacrifices were offered up to the devil by the men and women who lived there. After finding out about the black magic rituals taking place at the abbey, the Italian government investigated and discovered that human infants born to the disciples were also being killed in rituals. Crowley was expelled from Italy.

> The Book of the Law, written by Crowley as dictated to him by a spirit named Aiwass, truly convinced him "that his mission

in life was to destroy Christianity and build among its ruins his own religion of Thelema."

After the bizarre and mysterious death of his grown son at a private ritual in a locked room attended only by his son and himself, Crowley spent his last years as a babbling idiot.

The worship of Satan is firmly entrenched in human history, and it is an ominous element in our culture today. When you consider the magnitude of the evil spread through SRA, you can see it would be easy to take a passive stance, concluding that there is practically nothing one person can do. "I cannot make any worthwhile difference!" Beware, lest you fall prey to that kind of thinking. Every individual is important; every survivor is worth restoring. *Evil will spread when good people do nothing.*

Concerned Citizens

"What can I do?" Believe the children. Believe the adult survivors. Support them physically, emotionally and spiritually. Help them create healthy families. Because of the magnitude of their suffering, do not expect them to recover quickly. Network with SRA survivors, and with others who want good to prevail.

Demand that laws and justice systems become shaped to care for these survivors. Call for the press to carry out its duty to warn the public about the heinousness of these practices.

Donate money to agencies who are helping survivors. Help them pay for their therapy. See if they may be eligible for a state disability insurance program. The expenses of extended therapy are huge, and most SRA survivors cannot afford it. Agencies which work with these survivors, do so despite the fact that an SRA/MPD program will ALWAYS be under budget—they need lots of financial assistance in order to provide the sheer quantity of help that is needed! Survivors who have insurance or who can afford treatment are usually helped, but there are many who cannot afford it. Treatment centers who try to help a lot of survivors tend to end up with budgets pretty far in the red.

Therapists

If you are a therapist, be careful to find physical, emotional, and spiritual support for yourself. Are you developing an ulcer? Are you becoming isolated? Is your work taking a toll on your family? Do you have an adequate supply of daily spiritual nourishment? Do you rely on chemicals?

It is a blow to encounter raw human evil. Many times I have felt overwhelmed and stale by the end of a working week. Some therapists break down or burn out if they fail to care for themselves properly. It is difficult to supply the care that is needed for desperate SRA survivors and still protect one's mental health. Please keep a protective boundary around yourself so you can remain effective.

Finally, it is advisable to let law enforcement officers and the justice department do their jobs, and you do your job. It is generally considered safe to be in the business of rescuing SRA survivors, as a clinician or a friend, even though threats and property losses may occur. Stay connected to a network of people who will love and protect you. Try not to let fear stop you. However, to do "detective work" in order to prosecute cultists is to invite trouble and possibly death. These are dangerous folks, so do not underestimate their resolve to retaliate if they are exposed. Report the things to the police that you are required to report, but do not name alleged perpetrators in public settings or in published accounts—that makes you a threat to them. My stance is that clinicians should be in the business of restoring survivors. It is up to others to indict and prosecute.

PART TWO:
PSYCHOLOGICAL RESTORATION

4

DIAGNOSING MULTIPLE PERSONALITY

THIS CHAPTER outlines the concepts our MPD team has been developing. I trust they will be discussed among practitioners and dissociating clients, and that the ideas which would prove useful will be included in the development of more effective approaches to diagnosis and treatment.

GUIDELINES FOR THE MULTIPLE

Nobody wants to be a "case study." It is insulting to treat a human being like a science fair exhibit. That must be what it feels like for someone with MPD when a friend learns about the diagnosis. We almost automatically get curious when we hear about surprising developments in a friend's life, especially if it's something like MPD. That fascination can be very painful to the person who has MPD, and the extra attention often gives him or her the sense of having been put into the "demented" category.

One day in therapy, Carla declared, "It just gets worse, Jim. First there's the [childhood] terror, and then there's the humiliation because I survived. But this is my life and it's never going to change. Part of me wants to be honest and tell my friends I'm a multiple, but part of me is afraid. I can't take any more [pain]."

And so the fight for survival continues. Just getting treatment did not make Carla's life easier. Actually, it was getting harder—much harder—because the hidden childhood pain was finally being expressed. While that was under way, she was in

105

no condition to tolerate any questioning by her friends—that could pull out painful memories which the client is not yet ready to deal with.

It is not usually a good idea for people with MPD to talk about their condition openly, at least until therapy has brought them through the dividedness. Someday they will be able to speak proudly about how they achieved unity, but while they are still divided, parts of them will need to remain hidden, and parts will cringe when the dividedness is talked about. Hiddenness has been a way of life—it is against their training to start broadcasting secrets. They need to be protected from premature diagnosis sharing.

One thing they will discover is that their family and friends will have a hard time appreciating how dissociation has helped them. People with MPD are not genetic failures. In fact their inherited qualities—*creativity and intelligence*—were what enabled them to dissociate in the first place. This not only kept them alive, but it also preserved their inner beauty. Without dissociation they probably would be dead or emotionally demolished. What seems a "sickness" to friends has actually been a blessing for the person involved.

WHEN THE DIAGNOSIS IS WRONG

Shortly after I learned how to diagnose MPD, I began to wonder if I could be sued for malpractice. I had been conducting therapy for about three years with two clearly dissociative clients and unknowingly had been treating them for anxiety and depression. Their lives had not worsened, but I had not helped them with their dividedness. Almost the first thing I read about treating MPD was that unless therapy is directed to the issue of dividedness, progress will be minimal at best. Perhaps I had not hurt them, but neither had I helped them with the root problem.

Therapeutic Abuse

When the correct diagnosis is MPD, treatment for any other diagnosis will usually hurt instead of help. The most common reason for this is that, too often, therapy is abusive, particularly when the approach uses confrontation. Fortunately, I had not been confrontive with either of my MPD clients before I learned they were multiples. Non-confrontation is a necessity with these people, because abuse spawned their condition in the first place. If they pick up confrontation from the therapist, the abuse alert will be sounded, and the alters who most desperately need therapy will go into hiding. MPD will not even be evident when the therapy is perceived to be abusive—the healthier alters will attend therapy, and will habitually stay "out." A lot of trust needs to be developed before the wounded child alters will sense enough safety to be able to seek help.

Religious Abuse

A second problem that can lead to therapeutic failure is religious abuse. To be accused of being infested with demons is probably one of the most damaging things I can think of. I believe if a therapist were to convince me I was demon possessed, I might never recover! The notion that evil spirits can control our lives can produce feelings of extreme helplessness and hopelessness. My life is not in my own hands if I'm possessed. The direction of MPD therapy should be toward establishing self-control, and the accusation of spirit possession seriously contradicts that direction.

For people who have seen instances of deliverance from spiritual bondage, it can be easy to misdiagnose dissociations. When a different alter takes executive control of the body, the process is often accompanied by a change in posture—a twitch, a blink, or a black-out, for example. It is understandable that some people could misinterpret the postural change as an evil spirit taking control.

Whenever such a dissociation is treated as possession, I would call that religious abuse. Any dissociator's system of alters will be damaged by being falsely led to believe that one or more of them are evil spirits. Alters cannot be erased, and they cannot be cast out. Life takes a plunge if that is attempted.

Religious abuse can cause even more hurt than therapeutic abuse. In both cases, the treatment is misdirected, and the results are negative. Fortunately, therapy these days is being increasingly directed toward the root problem—the dividedness. As we discover what signs to look for,[1] and as we learn from our mistakes, more dissociating people are receiving the proper therapy.

I keep hoping things will get simpler and the MPD field of study will somehow boil down to a few ideas so clinicians will not need to keep digging for answers. However, at this point it looks like there will be no such streamlining. Instead, I think things are going the other direction. Although MPD seemed to be a manageable discipline during the early stages of my study, new questions keep surfacing as I go along, and I have to keep rethinking the things I am learning.

ROLES AND SYSTEMS

Alternate personalities are commonly formed in four ways:

(1) *When an event is traumatic enough to cause a dissociation,* a new personality or personality fragment is formed to go through the experience. The way brains operate, there is no better method to deal with traumas. Every life experience must be stored and filed somewhere, and no event can be erased. The closest a brain can come to erasing a memory is to become amnesic to what just happened. That involves creating an alternate personality for the occasion, and setting it behind an amnesic barrier. The other personalities would say "I don't know anything about that. It didn't happen to me!" When dissociated memories start to surface during treatment they *always* seem unreal. The clients have a hard time accepting the reality of the memory, because it does not seem like it happened to them.

Of course it seems that way because it really did happen to someone else—to an alter they have never met. Dissociation has an immediate effect—a protective barrier forms immediately which blocks all information about the traumatic event. Repression, on the other hand, blocks information but does not start working right away and does not protect against the ill effects of the trauma as well as dissociation does.

(2) Another method of alter formation is to *model after an important person*. The characteristics of a parent or authority figure are often incorporated to produce an alter that mimics that person. Alters can also model after siblings or even television

characters. An example from child therapy illustrates how this works.

William was an 8-year-old who had completed therapy with me two years earlier. I knew he was a very intelligent and creative child. After I had stopped seeing him, his mother remarried, and the new stepfather was now being verbally abusive to him. William was also being accused at school these days of saying swear words, which others heard, but he denied ever saying them. He was brought back into therapy with me for his "lying," but we discovered that William had developed an alter to model after his angry stepfather, and was totally amnesic to the times when the angry alter took executive control. It was not difficult to merge these alters in therapy, and the angry amnesia episodes ended. He still got angry, but now he remembered when he swore.

(3) When people who have learned to use dissociation as a preferred method of coping get into *new life situations,* they can automatically create an alter to fit into the new niche.

When Beth got married, she found herself with new roles. No other existing alter was suited for the job, so Beth had to create one, and a personality emerged to become Mrs. Smith—Big Beth. She accommodated very nicely to the demands of being a housewife. She fitted the position perfectly because she was created to do so. It was her job, and because she was needed for the sake of the others, she did the job well.

(4) Information has come to me from a number of sources that *cult members* are instructed in how to *create MPD intentionally in their children.* This maintains the secrecy, because the children's host alters will know nothing about the rituals. Electric shock, drugs and hypnotherapy are skillfully employed by the cult members to program their children to create alters starting when the children are about age 2. Using brutal brainwashing-type punishments, the cult members train particular alters to behave only in specific ways, and appear only at specified times.

Level 1 and Level 2 Alters

Child alters can be programmed to answer the phone late at night and get instructions about where to go for a ritual, and none of the other alters will even know the phone rang! How could that happen? Because there is an alter—totally amnesic to the other alters—whose role it is to answer the phone at night. Through this method, cult members can continue to keep people involved in their rituals even though the other alters are in therapy.

I know it sounds practically impossible, but it does happen. Adults who grew up in cult families may be participants in a coven, with their level 1 personalities having no knowledge of it. ("Level 1" refers to the "everyday" alters who know each other and can get in contact with each other without much difficulty. Any of the alters who are unknown to the level 1 alters can be thought of as "level 2" alters.) The other alters wake up remarkably tired in the morning with an unfamiliar taste in their mouth and with no idea that the cult alter spent three middle-of-the-night hours attending a cult ritual!

Cues

In the case of such a cult alter, there is a specific stimulus that pulls it out to a position of control—the phone call which awakens the person in the middle of the night, for instance.

Each alter has its own specific stimulus, or cue. It may be that when a man arrives home from work, a home alter switches in, and his arrival at home is the cue.

Some alters seem to enjoy therapy, while others stay away. Arriving at the therapist's office may be a cue for a depressed alter, and the alters who do not like to entertain unpleasant memories do their best to stay disengaged while the depressed alter is out. It can turn into a struggle if the therapist looks for the cues to access the alters who don't want to be there. If the therapist accesses unwilling alters, things can get unfriendly for a while, until the alter warms up to the therapist.

At times there can be quite a struggle between alters about even coming to therapy at all! Here is an example.

At 11 o'clock one morning, just at the time Carla was scheduled to begin her session, she phoned me from her upstairs bedroom. She said she was looking down at her car parked halfway into the street at the edge of her driveway, with the driver's door open. She said, "Dr. Friesen, I don't know what happened. I guess somebody didn't want me to come to see you today. I don't remember getting into the car, and I don't remember getting out, but the car radio is playing loud rock music. I couldn't have been driving because I don't like rock music. We know we should be at your office now, but can we just have a phone session today?"

I said that would be fine, and let her turn off the car radio and put the car back in the driveway before we got started. Some of the alters really wanted to talk with me and some really wanted to do other things. Her system of alters was not yet working together well.

Rotation and Equilibrium

Most adult multiples live quiet lives, and develop new alters for new situations that come up. The system of alters maintains a stable equilibrium, and usually a group of level 1 alters take turns with their tasks, not upsetting outside people if they can avoid it, yet meeting the demands of the most powerful alters. They operate like a revolving door, each rotating out front when needed. The alters who are amnesic to the one out front do not know what is happening, and hope they will not miss the cue that will rotate them out at the proper time.

It can be very unpredictable if there is too much stress in the system. Sometimes one gets pushed out front who has no idea what is going on and will appear quite disoriented! They all rely on unspoken rules for the rotation, and many of them think they are the only person in the body. You can imagine how the equilibrium breaks apart, how "disequalibrium" occurs, when these isolated personalities learn they share their body with a lot of other personalities and are supposed to negotiate about when to rotate out and take executive control.

Here is how the process can work. As soon as the kids are in bed, the maid alter rotates out, cleans the house and gets the kids' wash going. Then a different alter watches a late movie, which somehow cues the artist, who paints until daybreak. An hour or two of sleep later, her children wake her up because they don't have any clothes for school. The artist didn't know there were clothes in the washing machine, and they did not get dried. In fact, nobody on level 1 even knew that the artist had been out, but the evidence was right there on the easel—a painting inspired by the movie. "No wonder I'm tired!"

Personalities often compete for time, in order to accomplish their separate tasks, and the body can get exhausted. This is one reason multiples so commonly have sleep difficulties. Not only do many alters wait until bedtime for their turn to pursue their agendas, but when sleep does finally come, some of the alters also have nightmares, and the little sleep they get is not restful at all.

The system seems to adapt to environmental demands well enough most of the time, but things can get overloaded. When that happens, the equilibrium breaks down and time gets lost too frequently for things to work smoothly. Depression sets in for the victim alters, and therapy is usually sought.

Judith Spencer's *Suffer the Child*[2] does a wonderful job of portraying how Jenny's alter system developed in childhood, adapted to changes in life, and periodically broke down. Eventually, some fifteen years after the first major breakdown, the diagnosis of MPD was finally made and Jenny received therapy for dissociation. This remarkable book spells out, point by point, the internal conflict, and it explains how the alters worked together not only to survive the SRA, but also to restore Jenny.

A multiple seeks therapy usually because the system's equilibrium has started to go downhill. The person just wants to establish a little safety in the life. If the therapist knows the signs of dissociation, it is possible to get to the heart of the problem— the dividedness.

After the diagnosis is accepted by the most influential alters, the equilibrium can get interrupted in a big way. When the alters learn that it is okay to come out, and they are treated well, word circulates through the system that they do not have to stay hidden any more. The host alters often are not heard from for weeks. The child alters come out and play, toymakers who have not been on the scene for years, stay out for a few days making dolls, and host alters end up not going to work. Sometimes it turns out that the kid alters show up at work!

After the shock of accepting the diagnosis, it often takes a few months for the equilibrium to come into a more workable alignment. Many alters start getting to know each other for the first time. They learn one another's cues, and hear one another's voices. Working together is more realistic when the alters know one another—before therapy begins, many of them have no idea on what basis the alters are cued or how the system works.

When they know nothing about MPD, the alters just assume that people live their lives this way. "You know, there are holes in the day, but that just happens, and there is really no way to explain it. Things get lost, or I don't know how I got to this part of town, but this must happen to everybody." The system uses a lot of rationalizing and minimizing about discrepancies, in order to keep life running smoothly.

The dictum that the alters all operate under is, "Don't rock the boat. We would not want to upset people on the outside, and we want to keep as many of the inside people appeased as we can. Things just happen in confusing ways, so let's do the best we can without solving the mystery about who put on a man's jacket—I had on a dress when I left the house!" The equilibrium operates through a system of alters who follow automatic cues but have no idea that things could work any other way.

When Beth accepted that she was a multiple, she was convinced, or, to be more accurate, Socrates was convinced, that there was no amnesia, although it was undeniable that we were working with a cast of at least sixteen alters. After she was fully integrated, more than forty alters in all, Beth estimated she had been losing about four hours each day. She had not been able to figure out how other people got so much done!

The alter named Henry liked going to the library to read poetry; some alters spent hours on the phone; Lauren did lots of aerobics; Trixi took walks; and Big Beth Smith, the host, had no idea where the time went. She *did* know when it was almost time for her husband to get home from work, so she could get something together for dinner. That was her job, and although she did not know about the rest of the system, she did her job well. Fortunately for her, the system worked well enough to get her home by the time her husband got off work.

Figure 3
Clinical Expression of Dissociation
Mesa and Mountain

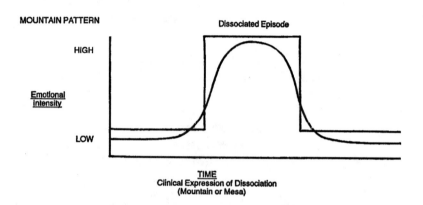

TIME
Clinical Expression of Dissociation
(Mountain or Mesa)

THE COMPONENTS OF DISSOCIATION

Dissociation is the most wonderful protection against pain that any child could ever develop. There could be no more effective defense—the child pretends the traumatic event happened to somebody else, and then ... Poof! ... *COMPLETELY* forgets about it. It is gone.

There is no way a child can bring a fully dissociated memory to mind. It takes directed therapeutic effort to break through the amnesia, and without that the child will grow up having no idea he or she was traumatized. A wonderful side effect of dissociation is that the child grows up with a very healthy group of level 1 personalities. They are not burdened by the degradation of the awful events. The self-image is protected.

In order to have a complete dissociation, absolutely no information can be shared between the dissociated personality states. The memory of the **mind**, the memory of the **emotions**, the **body's** memory, and the **will** are the four components that appear to be necessary for a complete dissociation. When one of those components is not broken but the rest are, a *partial dissociation* occurs. Figure 3 on the previous page illustrates how that works.

Partial Dissociation

The most common partial dissociation seems to occur when the mind does not dissociate, while the emotions, body memory, and the will do. That is what I found with Vera. She could remember everything that had happened, but her will was divided about some very important subjects, the emotions of her characters were unavailable to each other, and her body was also divided—part of her wanted to eat for comfort and other parts were very upset when she overate. As a divided individual, she would not stay on any weight-loss program, so she would remain overweight.

One particular partial dissociation was described in chapter 2, where the client told me her body remembered what it was like to have sex, but her mind did not. In that case, only the bodily memory had been accessed during therapy, while the other components remained dissociated. Many times during a therapy session, a partial dissociation is recovered, and usually it is the bodily memory. Too often it is quite disconcerting, and even embarrassing for the client, because his or her body starts reacting without the mind knowing what the body's reaction means. One example I heard of was that when one client got in touch with angry feelings, bug bites appeared on her arm despite the fact that there were no bugs around! Her angry emotions helped her body to remember there had been bug bites on a specific traumatic occasion, but the mind could not now recall what had happened. Components are recovered in quite a few ways, and this was just another example of how dissociated memories can manifest.

Another example of a partial dissociation was brought to my attention when a minister called me. He was working with a client who was pretty far along in therapy, and asked me if he should be concerned about the rope burns that kept appearing on his client's arms during therapy. I related the following story to him, to help him understand what he could do.

This incident happened to Beth while she was merging a few alters. She came in for her regular session one morning, and said that her arm had been hurting all night, and she had missed a lot of sleep. She was in contact with no feelings pertaining to the hurting arm, but needed to take care of the arm. She could not concentrate on her school work because it was hurting so badly.

Since the arm had not been recently injured in any way, we decided it had to be a "body memory" problem. We did a memory search, and she immediately flashed back. Her arm felt like it was stuck under the sofa in her living room. We never figured out how the sofa had fallen on her arm, but we did recover the rest of the episode. She felt about 4 years old while she relived the excruciating pain, and she re-experienced the fear that her father could be coming in at any moment to punish her for bothering him. Sure enough, as the flashback progressed, he came into the room and beat her severely. She nearly vomited in my office before she progressed to the end of the dissociated episode. She was literally sick with fear, panic and the physical pain in her arm.

That pain disappeared at the end of the flashback, which is the point I made on the phone to the minister. I told him that to help a body get past a bad memory, it is necessary to connect the body memory, in this case the client's rope burns, to the other dissociated components.

DISSOCIATIVE ABILITY (DA)

The first taped seminar about MPD that I listened to quoted a study which estimated that about a quarter of the children under age five can dissociate if they need to. I would like to expand that idea—every child has a certain amount of dissociative ability (DA). Some can use dissociation if they undergo a relatively small amount of abuse, others can dissociate for a moderate amount of abuse, still others are able to dissociate only for extreme abuse, and a few can hardly dissociate for even the most serious abuse imaginable.

DA seems to be genetically determined and has to do with intelligence, creativity and suggestibility. I believe that a very small proportion of the general population, less than 1 percent, has an extremely high DA, and can dissociate just about whenever they need to. These people do not usually show up in a therapist's office. They are likable, creative people who use partial or complete dissociation as an effective tool for stress management, with very few adverse effects. They have used it practically all their lives, and have used virtually no other coping methods. As long as their lives stay safe and predictable, nobody will even notice that these people are dissociators.

Probably about 25 percent of children have a DA high enough to use dissociation for relief from chronic sexual or physical abuse. When these children grow up they develop MPD if they have been abused.

In comparison, SRA is so much more terrible a kind of abuse that it causes dissociation in a much higher percentage of its victims, maybe as high as 75 percent, or even more. The abuse SRA victims have suffered is as bad as it can get, so the restoration usually takes longer than for non-SRA multiples. Yet those SRA survivors who have a particularly high DA seem to get healthy more readily than those whose DA is not as high.

A "LOWER LIMIT" MODEL FOR DISSOCIATION

If the amount of abuse received by a child exceeds the lower limit of his or her abuse tolerance, dissociation will likely occur. As noted before, if dissociation proves effective at an early age, other defenses will not likely develop, leaving dissociation as the preferred method of coping. This is what leads to multiple personality disorder.

When the child's first dissociative event occurs after about age 5, dissociation likely will not become the preferred coping method, and the event probably will result in a traumatic dissociation (TD). For abuse that almost reaches the DA's lower limit, partial dissociation will likely occur. Partial dissociation usually leads to non-amnesic dissociation (NAD).

Non-Amnesic Dissociators (NADs)

The system works effectively for NADs, because they lose no time. But even for them, when a personality state is in control of the body, there are times it will not want to give up control until it has finished its work. One evening I observed such an episode while working with Vera, whom I suspected had NAD. That episode clinched the diagnosis for me. She had been directed to have a discussion among her "characters" by imagining that they were sitting in different chairs. She was supposed to take a different seat when each one wanted to speak.

After a tiny bit of reluctance, she changed chairs and assumed the Critical Parent character. My mouth almost dropped open when she unleashed a scathing attack on the Victim character. Most of the time Vera had been such a polite and gentle person, and this was not at all like anything I had previously seen or heard from her. Her husband once told me that sometimes she was like a viper, and now I knew where that came from. The barrage lasted for about twenty minutes and did not drop in intensity at any point. I didn't say a word. I was afraid to—I had encountered a venomous personality state!

There was a backlog of many episodes in which the Victim character had failed but had not yet received her scolding. When given the invitation, Critical Parent took over and stayed in control of the body until she had finished scolding the Victim about all her backlogged failures. The Victim did not respond, hardly to my surprise. She was not willing to incur any more verbal punishment. After Critical Parent had finished, Socialite took the chair that had been assigned to her, and tried to smooth things over with me.

"Critical Parent isn't really so bad," she said. Socialite made it clear that she intended not to allow the Critical Parent to speak in my office again. She admitted that Critical Parent had been unexpectedly ruthless.

In many ways, Vera's behavior was quite similar to the things that happen during a session with a multiple, but there was no time loss! Each personality state heard every other one, and it was a good group discussion. There were sharply divergent points of view being expressed with candor and cogency.

These characters knew each other, but did not know how each other felt, even when they talked things through! Merging was still a long way off for them.

Traumatic Dissociators (TDs)

With another client, I noticed a different kind of dissociation. She was not particularly creative. I had been seeing her for more than a year, and she did not fit the profile of a dissociator in any way that I could tell. Then she began to recall the barest outline of the facts about her childhood years.

When she was about 8 she had come down with leukemia. She suffered physically and emotionally, but received no comfort. She had kept the whole bunch of leukemia-related feelings bottled up inside for years as a child, and when she went into remission she dissociated from them. It appears that her Victim character lost contact with the other personality states, mostly through repression, but there was also some dissociation. She went through a few flashbacks, got the kind of headaches that appear in treatment for MPD, and seemed to manifest other soft signs of dissociation (see Figure 4 on page 123).

The MPD team found other cases which followed this pattern, so we came up with another descriptive diagnosis: traumatic dissociator (TD). In our experience, TDs have just one or two dissociated personality states, and the other ego states do not show separateness from each other. They know how the others feel, and seem to resolve their conflicts between themselves without much need for therapy. Their system seems to work fairly well, with characters doing their jobs at the right times. Therapy for TDs needs to focus on the suffering and the healing of the dissociated memories.

Borderline Personalities (BPs)

For children who undergo traumas without being able to dissociate from them, life is more difficult. They carry trace memories of the traumas, and they develop weaker defenses to protect against further pain. One study found that MPD clients and borderline personality (BP) clients came from the same kind of background—they were victims of serious abuse. The study also found that multiples used dissociation but borderlines did not.[3] That tells me quite a bit about what dissociation can do for a child. It is generally believed that therapy for BP is a long and tedious process, without a particularly good prognosis. On the other hand, MPD usually has a shorter course of therapy with a much better prognosis—the multiples had better internal protection from their traumas, and consequently they maintained healthy parts within their system.

There is, however, a major drawback to using dissociation as a preferred method of coping. It is such a great defense that there is no reason to develop any other defenses. The child who dissociates while still a preschooler will not need to learn to cope in any other way. That will be fairly practical in childhood, but during adolescence and in young adulthood, if reliance on dissociation persists, it loses its effectiveness. Time loss and contradictions can plague the dissociator severely by age 30.

Intermingled Symptoms

MPD, NAD, and TD symptoms may be intermingled, so that what initially presents in therapy as NAD, may turn out to include MPD and/or TD symptoms, as the alter system becomes more fully uncovered.

A clear diagnostic picture does not usually come into focus very quickly. The clues that lead to correct diagnosis tend to unfold slowly in the context of a safe therapeutic environment. Because most systems work hard to maintain equilibrium and keep certain events hidden, a lengthy process of developing trust in therapy may be needed before there will be enough openness for the therapist to make a diagnosis. When the first sign of dissociation shows up during therapy, it is good to make a hypothesis that dissociation may be present and then set about testing that hypothesis.

In some cases, what seemed to be an NAD system proved later to include some level 2 (fully dissociated) alters, but they did not show up early in treatment. In other instances MPD therapy had gone well and things seemed to be almost finished when a layer of highly fragmented SRA alters unexpectedly emerged from level 2. It is as a famous baseball player once said: "It ain't over until it's over," and until the therapeutic process has been completed, newly discovered alters can continue to emerge. Amnesia can be thicker for some alters than for others and they can remain undiscovered for a long time.

MOUNTAIN AND MESA PATTERNS

A few months after we began to work with MPD clients at our clinic, we noticed that a few clients behaved much like the multiples but showed no signs of amnesia. Like multiples who demonstrated amnesia, these people were bright and creative, and they displayed some dividedness. They were compliant much of the time, but when they got into a contrary personality state, they could attack with ferocity. They seemed a little less creative than the multiples we were seeing, but we had no way to accurately assess their DA. After discussing these cases, we came up with the non-amnesic dissociators (NADs) diagnosis for them.[4]

Based on what we were learning from readings, clinical observations and consultations, we were improving our ability to identify dissociations. They had been taking place right in front of us for a long time but we hadn't known what they looked like. Most non-dissociating clients do not just drop into a feeling during therapy and stay there. Rather, they start to let a feeling emerge, and with a little encouragement to stay in contact with it, they usually find the feeling getting more intense. After reaching a peak it begins to decline and then gradually subsides. The cathartic experience makes it seem like a profitable session. "Thanks, Doc. I'm feeling a lot better now that I got that out," is what a non-dissociator will say at the end of a good session.

The graph of such a feeling would approximate the silhouette of a mountain (see Figure 3 on page 114). However, when the multiples and NADs contacted a new feeling in my office, the silhouette was more like a mesa. That is, the feeling would hit instantly at full force, remain for a while at full intensity and then disappear completely. There did not seem to be any gradation in the feelings of dissociators, and when the feelings left, the person could not remember very well exactly what the mesa feelings were like. These clients did not seem to "feel better" at the session's end, either—the emotional "work" done in the session did not seem to have the helpful effect that I had come to expect with other clients.

The mesa response is consistent with the way dissociated personality states function. When a dissociated state develops, it usually has just a single feeling, and that is the *only* one it can experience. When a different feeling is needed, a different alter rotates in with that feeling. Many systems have an angry alter, one or more who are hopeless (at different degrees), and others who handle particular kinds of experiences. Each has the feeling which accompanies its task, and no other feelings. Some are even immune to feelings—their role is to protect by not allowing any feelings. The distinctiveness of the experiences and the separateness of the feelings bring the mesa response, which suggests dissociation. Clinical venting of a dissociated feeling does not seem to help much, largely because it is the only level of feeling the alter has. When a feeling is evoked, it persists at that level.

A large number of people bring "flat affect" (complete lack of change in facial expression) to the therapist's office. Dissociating people show "flat affect" when certain personality states are devoid of feelings, but when a switch occurs, there is immediately a lot of "affect." That is a mesa response.

Early in treatment some dissociators can fool me into thinking they do not have strong emotions—they can remain in alters whose job it is to protect against feelings, and there is a "flat affect" in therapy for a while. Then one day the client will have intense feelings. When I notice this mesa pattern, I begin to look for other signs that could point to dissociation.

Dissociation Indicators

The "Dissociation Indicators" on Figure 4 help test the hypothesis about the presence of dissociation. The group data, listed to the right of the eighteen items, are the result of a pilot study. A large pool of items was tested to find the ones which most accurately point to dissociation. The control group consisted of non-dissociating clients at our clinic, and the MPD and NAD groups came from our caseloads. We did not have a large enough group of TDs or BPs at that time to list them.

Figure 4: Dissociation Indicators

Group Data

NAME_____ MALE_____ FEMALE_____

	MPD	NAD	CONTROL

PERSONALITY CHARACTERISTICS

They may be present separately or jointly
in at least one alter personality.

	MPD	NAD	CONTROL
___ 1. High intelligence.	19/19	5/5	14/25
___ 2. High creativity—music, writing, drama or art, for example.	17/19	4/5	4/25
___ 3. High suggestibility/ability to use imagery.	16/19	4/5	7/25
___ 4. Urgency about time, either a rush to get finished with therapy, or a general urgency about life.	18/19	4/5	4/25
___ 5. A sense of extreme deprivation—feeling they have been "ripped off" most of their life.	16/19	3/5	3/25
___ 6. Inappropriate need to please—a high need to be acceptable in all circumstances.	17/19	5/5	3/15

(4 or more of 6 suggests MPD or NAD may be present,
i.e., a high dissociative ability.)

CLINICAL OBSERVABLES

	MPD	NAD	CONTROL
___ 7. Secretiveness or refusal to reveal personal experiences.	15/19	4/5	2/25
___ 8. *Amnesia for previously covered material.	17/19	2/5	2/25
___ 9. *Headaches or dizziness of sudden onset during therapy.	14/19	1/5	2/25
___10. *Evidence of internal dialog.	17/19	2/5	1/25
___11. Sudden shift in mood or voice.	19/19	3/5	3/25
___12. *Flashback/abreaction—reliving a traumatic experience.	15/19	2/5	3/25

(4 or more of 6 suggests MPD)

OUTSIDE DATA

	MPD	NAD	CONTROL
___13. Uneven achievement in school.	15/19	3/5	4/25
___14. *Reports of hearing inner voices.	17/19	0/5	0/25
___15. *History of sleep disturbances.	19/19	1/5	1/25
___16. *Difficulty finding their parked car.	12/19	1/5	0/25
___17. *Inordinate indecision about which clothes to wear.	12/19	1/5	1/25
___18. Denial of actions that were clearly observed by others.	13/19	2/5	0/25

(4 or more of 6 suggests MPD)
*Good discrimination between multiple personality and
non-amnesic dissociater. High scores in these sections
indicate a high likelihood of amnesia.

This page may be reproduced for personal use.

The first section of items estimates the level of dissociative ability. The items are pretty general, but for most therapists it is not difficult to use them. The first three are basic measures of DA. Items 4, 5 and 6 are results of using dissociation as a preferred coping method. Taken together, the first six items suggest the existence and the use of dissociation.

Item 4 is related to DA in this way: Urgency is experienced by each alter because it has never known how long it may be out. It could disappear, without warning, at any minute. Item 5, feeling "ripped off," results from the long pattern of having unfilled agendas by many alters. Things just don't turn out right! Item 6, the need to please, happens after a child has been traumatized often enough to develop fear in many situations.

All the MPDs and NADs in this study obtained a score of 4 or higher in this section. Many MPDs had all 6. Apparently, if the score is less than 4 in the first section, you can reject the notion that MPD or NAD are present. None of the controls reached a score as high as 4 on the first section, nor did they obtain a score of 4 or higher on either of the other two sections.

The second and third sections are to be used if a high score is found in the first section. They are designed to test for amnesia. All of the multiples obtained 4 or higher out of 6 except one, who scored 3 on the second section, and 4 on the third section. None of the NADs reached a score of 4 or higher in the second or third section.

Item 7 refers to the kind of reticence which results when there is a system of alters with secrets. There is often a lot of openness about particular subjects, but when a hidden area is cued, an alter switches in to cover up the security leak, and refusal to inform has clearly set in.

Item 8 is amnesia for something discussed in therapy. If I suspect a client has completely blanked on a major topic we have discussed, I inquire. For example, if I think I have seen a switch, I ask if the client would like to add anything to what we were just talking about. Another way to confirm this is to ask about the previous session—if there is no recall, I wonder if a different alter was present.

Item 9 refers to a specific kind of headache, which precedes a dissociation. It usually can be felt only in a part of the head, and is quite sharp. Medication does not help this headache. It indicates that an alter, which has some material amnesic to the present alter, is on the verge of making an appearance.

It is not particularly easy to observe the internal dialogue, listed in item 10. This internal dialogue is most often evident when, after a question is asked, the person glances silently for a few seconds toward the ceiling before answering. The alters really do talk to each other, and the dialogue takes a little time to be processed.

The mesa response is looked for in item 11. A sudden shift in mood is quite evident when angry alters or depressed alters switch in.

When dissociated events are remembered through flashbacks, as in item 12, it is quite distinctive from other kinds of memories. A flashback is like reliving a traumatic event all over again, including all the components of the dissociation.

It is best to check with friends or relatives regarding the "Outside Data" section. Uneven achievement in school, item 13, happens because only when the class is safe can the student alters show up. This makes some years good and some years bad. Sometimes there is an alter who loves science, but nobody will do the English, so some subjects are As and others are Fs. Sometimes when I ask dissociators about grades, I get no information because there is no memory of anything preceding high school. Blank childhood years often point to amnesia, and that suggests dissociation.

Clients really must trust the therapist in order to answer item 14—the one about hearing inner voices. In case the person has not already volunteered this information, I ask if it is sometimes necessary for him or her to listen to inner voices. I make the distinction between inner and outer voices so that the person can be reassured that this does not mean he or she is "crazy." Psychotic people hear voices "out there," but dissociators hear inner voices—the alters discuss things. There are also times when a few voices are joined by many others in heated arguments, and the client can hardly hear anything outside.

Item 15—a history of sleep disturbance—was mentioned earlier. Bad dreams and fears keep these victims awake, and so do their night alters.

Item 16—great difficulty in finding their parked car is really not the same as forgetting where it is. MPDs can go to the mall in one alter, switch a few times, and have no idea how they arrived. They may not know which car was used or they may just go home and not know they had taken a car in the first place. Some alters may not even know which cars are theirs or how many cars they own. Some alters will not drive other alters' cars and will not let any other alters drive their car!

Item 17 often produces a very interesting, and telling, conversation. I ask a female client how she goes about picking out her clothes in the morning. I know that if a person has MPD, each alter usually has its own wardrobe, or at least has a serious preference about which clothes to wear. The multiple usually answers this question, matter-of-factly, as though it is not unusual to spend up to an hour choosing clothes. She describes how she puts on one outfit and it looks fine, but then a few minutes later it looks awful. This sometimes goes on for an hour or more. Time can be lost. Often I can tell which alter has come to therapy by which clothes are being worn. Some alters may not show up in therapy at all without their own clothes. This item does not seem to help diagnose male clients as well as it does females.

The last item can be inferred after getting to know the client. If there is a lot of fighting with a spouse about what was said or what was done, item 18 will be indicated. Denial of actions that were observed by others becomes an emotionally charged issue for many because it happens all the time, and the host alter really believes he or she is constantly being falsely accused.

This list is the result of a pilot study, and it may be improved on by other researchers. It would be good to see if there is consistency across therapists in rating these items. However, even in its present form, Figure 4 provides a promising direction in MPD diagnosis. In every case I have followed, these eighteen items correctly indicated, or accurately ruled out, MPD. When other therapists have used it, they have not told me of any false positives or any false negatives. It appears to be as accurate as

Figure 5
Dissociative Ability, Severity of Abuse, and Presenting Symptomatology

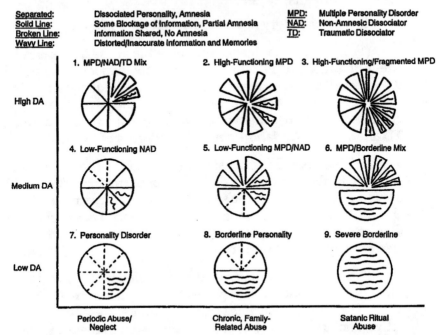

Separated:	Dissociated Personality, Amnesia
Solid Line:	Some Blockage of Information, Partial Amnesia
Broken Line:	Information Shared, No Amnesia
Wavy Line:	Distorted/Inaccurate Information and Memories

MPD:	Multiple Personality Disorder
NAD:	Non-Amnesic Dissociator
TD:	Traumatic Dissociator

1. MPD/NAD/TD Mix   2. High-Functioning MPD   3. High-Functioning/Fragmented MPD

High DA

4. Low-Functioning NAD   5. Low-Functioning MPD/NAD   6. MPD/Borderline Mix

Medium DA

7. Personality Disorder   8. Borderline Personality   9. Severe Borderline

Low DA

Periodic Abuse/Neglect   Chronic, Family-Related Abuse   Satanic Ritual Abuse

any diagnostic approach and is less cumbersome than others. Overall, the utility seems very high, so I hope it will be tested on a wider group to see just how helpful it really is.

VARIETIES OF DISSOCIATIONS

Figure 5 above, "Dissociative Ability, Severity of Abuse, and Presenting Symptomatology," is based on two hypotheses:

First, *everyone has a certain amount of dissociative ability*— there is a continuum of DA along which each person can be placed. Dissociations are more likely to be found in those who are at higher levels.

The **second** hypothesis is that *children respond differently to increasing levels of abuse*—the more severe levels of abuse are more likely to produce dissociations. The kind of dissociation used is determined both by the person's *dissociative ability* level and the

severity of abuse. The matrix which results from these two continua helps explain and predict the kind(s) of dissociative symptoms for particular cases.

Two explanatory notes are needed for this figure.

(1) It is based on instances where the abuse took place by
age 5 or earlier, as is usually the case for dissociation-related
disorders. Those who were abused later in childhood probably
had already developed non-dissociative coping methods, which
changes the picture somewhat. Later abuse can result in a single
TD alter, and dissociation is not utilized most of the time.

(2) This has to do with using both continua: There is literally
no limit to the number of different configurations that could
occur on this matrix. For the sake of keeping things simple, I have
chosen to portray nine such configurations. Those nine just
illustrate the kinds of presenting symptomatology that could
take place at specific positions.

The pie-like illustrations depict varieties of dissociative
processes. The side-by-side pieces in each pie represent level 1
alters. They do not lose time when they rotate. They are the most
active, and until therapy uncovers their distinctiveness, the client
usually does not recognize the patterns of switching that regularly take place among them.

The solid lines between the level 1 alters illustrate the
blockage that prevents information getting through from one
alter to another—the partial amnesic barriers. It is usually the
feeling component that is blocked by the partial amnesia. As a
result, level 1 alters carry out daily tasks but do not share each
other's feelings.

The pie pieces separated from the level 1 clusters are level
2 alters—those who are not accessible to level 1 alters because of
complete amnesia. The wavy lines within some pieces stand for
distortion—the alters' experiences which were not consistent
with reality. The expectation that all men, even images of Jesus,
will be sexual perpetrators is evidence of a kind of distortion. It
is the kind that is certainly true for the particular alter, but it is
not consistent with other alters' reality.

Considering the many combinations and mixtures of symptoms that can develop from these dissociative processes, one can see that the variations among alter systems are virtually endless. Here are a few comments about the nine configurations illustrated on Figure 5.

1. MPD/NAD/TD Mix. People at this DA level present a varied combination of dissociative symptoms. For people with extremely high DAs and a safe environment, there are not many reasons to stay in therapy. Their dissociative coping methods work well. Many people at position 1 are not motivated highly enough to stay in therapy, especially when they start to remember early traumas. They usually have a solid group of level 1 personality states. These people do not often become suicidal, nor do they usually need lengthy hospitalizations.

2. High-Functioning MPD. This position on the matrix, and position 3, are where most of the people come from that I have seen. They tend to have a solid group of level 1 alters and a good social network. They can engage in interesting conversations and are very creative. They usually avoid hospitalization, but they can become suicidal.

3. High-Functioning/Fragmented MPD. Fragmentation refers to the production of many part-personalities to deal with small bits of highly traumatic time. People at this position usually use dissociation well enough to maintain a functional group of level 1 alters. During the course of therapy, the traumatized, dissociated alters improve to the level of functioning of the most healthy alters in level 1, so post-therapy life for these people goes well. Brief hospitalization can become necessary when stress gets high or when suicidal alters are discovered.

4. Low-Functioning NAD. People at this medium DA level are not quite as adaptive. They tend to use more self-defeating coping methods. Many of their personality states have mesa responses, which means their feelings are experienced intensely. They probably will not want to remember the traumas which started the dissociative process, and therefore will not be good candidates for long term therapy.

5. Low-Functioning MPD/NAD. Even in the level 1 alters, these dissociators are not very good at keeping the memories of abuse away from the healthy alters. Hospitalization may be necessary for suicidal times. The brilliant artwork and poetry are usually missing at this DA level.

6. *MPD/Borderline Mix.* The high distortion in these people presents difficulty in therapy. The memories which surface tend to be disbelieved because of the distortions and because the memories come into distorted level 1 alters. These people may seem histrionic or manipulative, but their main problem is that they operate from a distorted data base. The level 1 personalities seem overwhelmed by the pain which is not fended off by dissociation. Extended hospitalizations may be necessary to re-organize and decontaminate the system.

7. *Personality Disorder.* These people need long-term therapy. They do not have a very good prognosis, due to the distortion from early abuse. There is no high-functioning alter to pull the other alters up to, as was seen for position 3. There is usually no dissociation or even partial dissociation at this DA level.

8. *Borderline Personality.* This is a difficult diagnosis to work with. Distortion and manipulation can predominate. It would be better for borderlines if they were able to use dissociation more skillfully. Borderline patients, tend to "split" along the lines of a "good" character and a "bad" one, which I believe is a rather primitive type of dissociation. If their dissociative skills were higher, they would develop more personality states than two, and would be better able to protect the health in level 1.

Colin Ross's textbook on MPD contains a discussion about the relationship between MPD and borderline personality (BP), and he concludes that BP is a dissociative disorder.[5] His considerations include a history of the diagnostic controversies that have always surrounded BP and citations from prominent BP theorists.

These illustrate that what BP theorists have called "splitting" can be understood as a kind of dissociation. His recommendation is that BP should be listed in the future as a dissociative disorder. Although controversial, Ross's observations are consistent with what our MPD team has found: BP clients make better progress when their treatment focuses on the dissociative underpinnings of their disorder—healing their dividedness.

9. *Severe Borderline.* I only know of one person who appears to fall into this category. He had been in therapy for many years before there was any indication of his SRA background. He has made some improvements, but suicidality has been high all along during his therapy. He has been off balance continually, and so has his therapist. The SRA memories are badly distorted and seem truly unbelievable to him. It has been difficult for him to overcome his automatic tendency to be manipulative.

If the SRA family's child cannot be trained to dissociate properly, he might start talking to outsiders about the rituals he remembers, and he is therefore doomed. Many children at this position on the matrix may be sacrificed to Satan because they do not dissociate well enough for the cult members to consider them safe.

"DO YOU THINK I HAVE MPD, DOCTOR?"

Crystal was obviously agitated when she said to me, "I saw 'Sybil' on TV last night and got so upset that I didn't sleep a wink! I couldn't stop crying for hours, and I can't go to work today. Do you think I have MPD, doctor?"

"It's hard to say, Crystal. I know you have been in therapy for about a year already, but some conditions are not easy to put a label on." Sybil was an unusual case of MPD, and most people who dissociate don't appear anything like her.

"I know you have been through some bad abuse in your life, and I know that most people who come from backgrounds like yours are pretty messed up in comparison to you. You are a successful, interesting person. Maybe that is because you have developed the skill of dissociating from the bad stuff in your past. Dissociation is the most wonderful defense God made to help people stay healthy in the face of serious child abuse.

"You could be likened to a computer. You've got great hardware, Crystal, and when your software gets messed up with a virus, you just start a new file. The new files are not connected to the virus-infected files, so they work just fine. People who can't dissociate do not have as easy a time fighting the effects of the virus. They can't start over like you have.

"I don't mean to sound as if I already know you have MPD, nor do I want to sound like MPD therapy would be easy for you. It will take time to find out how you use dissociation, and what memories you have hidden. Therapy for dissociation is not easy, but the results seem good."

At this point I got out a copy of Figure 5 and told Crystal she is probably somewhere between positions 1 and 2. After I explained that there are many kinds of dissociations, I pointed out that she has maintained a healthy core personality by dissociating. I went on to say that the dissociated states can be expected to recover from their painful experiences and that they likely will achieve the same level of health found in her healthiest parts.

"Even though you will have to stick it out through some tough periods in therapy, the goal is well worth it. You know that you have struggled with rejection—real rejection—from lots of people throughout life. For you to be able to develop rejection-free relationships is something worth working for."

Quite a long time later, Crystal's memory work unexpectedly turned up SRA. She had been taken by a friend of the family to what was supposed to be a party. She was victimized there as part of a cult ritual. It was so violent and cruel that the SRA memories had to be walled off in a traumatically dissociated (TD) state. Before she could regain her health, she needed to remember and overcome the effects of the SRA. That part of her therapy was agonizing.

She would need psychological—and spiritual—restoration.

5

TREATMENT FOR DISSOCIATION I
Preparation and Beginning

THE MATERIAL in this book is intended for dissociating clients and for family, friends and therapists. (The SRA-related material should probably be included only if necessary and only under the supervision of a therapist.) My sense is that people can understand these things in ways which will keep everybody properly involved in the restorative process. There is no need to reserve the treatment-related material for "specialist" clinicians. MPD is not an illness. It is a protective way of life, and those who use MPD are bright enough to profit from the material presented.

Some of the therapeutic considerations which follow may be less pertinent to clients than to therapists, but in some cases the "clinical portion" may steer therapy in the proper direction when read by the client. In order for good teamwork to take place, it helps if all the team members have access to the same information. The therapist should be the "coach" and generate therapeutic direction, but clients and others should not be discouraged from becoming properly informed.

DEVELOP AN MPD TEAM

Any weaknesses in the therapist will be exposed during therapy with dissociators. Therapists need to come to grips with the awfulness of evil, and with the immensity of the pain out there. It seems that beginning therapists can get discouraged— even overwhelmed—by working in this area. Treatment traps like "Please don't tell me any more bad memories"; "I've got my own problems to deal with"; or "Why don't you just let me be your parent?" can become therapeutic obstacles from the therapist's side.

It is very hard for me to picture myself working alone as a therapist for dissociators. When such solitary therapists call me for a consultation, I always encourage them to find other professionals to team up with, or they will likely burn out in fairly short order. A therapist must be able to keep his or her own emotions in balance in order to work with these difficult cases, and membership on a team seems vital. When spiritual restoration and/or spiritual warfare is part of the treatment picture, teamwork provides safety for all the players.

Perhaps the most helpful part of being on an MPD team is the continual monitoring of how each therapist is doing. It is difficult to hear the clients we feel so close to talking about the pain of their lives. We need other therapists, who have been in that position, for us to talk with on a regular basis. Without consistent time to open up about feelings, even therapists can get flooded with sadness and grief for the pain these survivors have endured.

On-the-spot consultations, finding the right cotherapist for a particular client, sharing the things we are reading about, and learning from our mistakes are a few of the other benefits of belonging to an MPD team. Working with dissociating children can be particularly difficult, and it has its own set of guidelines not covered in this book. Therapists who work with childhood cases of MPD and SRA will find it crucial for their own well-being to form an MPD team.

THE THERAPEUTIC JOURNEY

It is not uncommon, early in therapy, for clients to ask how long I think they will be in treatment.

I try to avoid sounding like a stereotypic psychologist who beats around the bush without answering the question—I want to be straightforward—yet I must say, "We really have a lot to discover about you before we find how long your journey will take."

Then I add, "Before it is completed you will find new ways of thinking, feeling and acting. Developing these new habits will take some time. In the beginning stages let's not look for a lot of quick growth—you will need to pull out a few weeds first. We will start by talking about whatever is bothering you most in your present life and by focusing on pent-up feelings. Then we will try to find where those feelings appeared earlier in your life. We will search for childhood memories that have connections to your present life. Those which have been hidden probably will be the most painful. God has created us with remarkable ways of protecting ourselves from being bombarded by traumatic memories. The mind works very hard to hide them and therapy often requires people to work just as hard to recover them.

"Why do the hidden memories need to be recovered? Because their wounds ooze into daily life as long as they remain hidden and unhealed. The frustrating feelings in your current life are almost certainly being fed by hidden pain from your past. Every time you take care of a previously unknown conflict, new energy becomes available to you, and your growth speeds up. If negative feelings emerge during therapy, and if traumas are uncovered, we will take as much time as is needed to provide healing for them.

"You were fragile as a child—as we all were. Whatever methods of coping you used then were the best you could do as a kid. Now in adulthood those methods have become obsolete, and therapy is a place to develop better coping mechanisms. That involves pinpointing and working through hidden hurts, in order to bring healing.

A Roller-Coaster Ride

"Therapy can be likened to a roller-coaster ride. After you strap yourself in, you'd better not get off! Your feelings may become very intense. Things will almost certainly get worse before they get better, but please don't leave too soon. We don't know what the ride has in store, but I certainly encourage you to finish."

And so I enter into an agreement with the client to help him courageously make connections between past and present, looking for triggers that set off feelings. It is somewhat like the famed

"Pandora's box." People find isolated memories, and as we get to deeper levels of trust, the most painful, buried feelings surface. Because therapy uncovers these deeper levels of awareness, things get progressively more difficult, and you can see why people often drop out of therapy before they have accomplished what they came for.

A few minutes into one session, I sensed that the client was sitting on something very tough to talk about. When I pointed that out, she faced me, made eye contact for the first time, and knew exactly what she had been planning to tell me. "I don't know what I'm doing here, Jim. I've been seeing you for more than a year, and my life is not getting easier. I didn't come here to feel worse! I know you keep saying that all feelings are important, but I'm tired of despair. What good can despair be? Shouldn't I be through this by now?"

A Therapist's Discovery

A sinking feeling grabbed at my stomach. She was waiting for a reply. I said, "When I began training as a psychologist, therapy didn't turn out to be anything like I expected, either. I thought I would be like a technician, helping people bring order to their lives. I dreamed of people starting therapy with me and beginning to feel better right away.

"Eventually I had to let go of all that. Therapy is inevitably a struggle. Pain is a part of life. You must actually encounter and experience the pain that has been caused in your own life before healing can set in.

"So my career has taken a different course from what I ever would have thought. Much of my work brings pain out into the open—I don't simply help people feel good. They often fall apart. Boxes of tissue get emptied. Peoples' feelings become chaotic, and I ask myself, *Shouldn't things be going more smoothly?* I can't help but wonder if I shouldn't be doing something different.

"But I've learned that life is difficult and so is therapy. As you come to the more demanding stretches of your journey, I'll help you to find shortcuts or to generate more power for the steep grades. Exposing your weaknesses will free up your strengths. Transformation involves breaking down some things and building up others. So take some tissues, and face your issues. Let's start with despair."

REMAIN POSITIVE AND HOPEFUL

Constantly encourage, support, and reward with lots of positives for the work being accomplished during the sessions. Not very many things have happened to these people to make them feel positive or hopeful. To help them gain hope can make the difference between life and death. When they have "poured out their guts" to you, encourage them: "Those things were very difficult for you to talk about, and I liked the way you were honest about your feelings. That shows me you have the kind of courage it takes to recover."

This may not seem like a very powerful intervention, but it goes a long way toward breaking through hopelessness. They have accomplished something, and when you point that out, it can generate the first inkling of faith within them. A little faith and a little hope can bring a lot of healing.

I am not merely talking about "positive reinforcement" here, I'm talking about really believing in the person in front of you and helping that person realize there are good reasons to believe in herself (or himself), too. I'm talking about genuine caring for the welfare of the dissociator, and having faith that the person's fragmented life can be unified so that her potential can be reached.

Whenever I feel despair about my client's problems, or whenever I begin to doubt that my client will overcome an obstacle at hand, I know I have lost my direction. My internal compass is malfunctioning at that moment and my spiritual bearing is floundering. It is urgent that I correct my own course. If I discover what the obstacle is and take the appropriate measures, if the client and I can connect well, and if we have a sense of spiritual direction, practically any impasse can be overcome. Faith and hope are more powerful than despair.

I believe what I have read about progress in therapy for multiplicity because it is consistent with what I have seen: Multiples who stay in therapy tend to get better. In many cases the progress is incredibly successful. Take the widely known case of

The Three Faces of Eve, for example. Chris Sizemore (Eve's real name) is a splendid person. Through her willingness to "go before the public" we all have learned to know her as a person with a tenacious desire to become healthy. She spent a tremendous amount of energy to gain her mental health, and now she is spending her energy to help others. She tirelessly crusades for the benefit of the mentally ill, and those who have met her find that just getting to know her is healing in itself. I have seen her on videos, and find her to be truly a beacon of light. Not all multiples will be like Chris Sizemore after they finish therapy, but they will be free to be themselves, and they are splendid too! It is wonderful to see them reach their full potential.

Staying positive and hopeful, however, is no small task when new alters keep declaring how hopeless their life is, and when therapy seems to be stuck. There is a wish, in both the client and the therapist, to get through therapy as quickly as possible, but that expectation can bring despair. It is not very realistic to expect steady progress. A few steps forward and one or two back—that is what to expect. A new alter will emerge who has had access to a limited amount of the life experience of the whole person, and the only things that alter can remember were disastrous. All the components of that alter's dissociated memories may point to hopelessness—the feeling memory can consist solely of depression, the mind can recall only traumatic events, the body can remember only pain, and the will can wish for nothing but to die rather than face any more pain.

Minimized Feelings

Be careful not to minimize the feelings of such an alter. There probably has been a long history of feelings being minimized in the client's life. Nobody has believed how bad things were. People have always stopped the traumatized alters from sharing their story. They have repeatedly heard things like, "If you do this or that, things will get better." That is not the positive approach—it is minimizing their feelings. As the therapist, this is the time for you to relate to this person in a new way. "I do believe the things you are telling me. I want to hear everything you have to say. Please don't hold back. Let me hear about the things that other people don't want to hear from you. The job you probably have had to do was to absorb the most terrible experiences for the other alters. Because you did your job well, they were allowed to stay healthy. You coped with the hard feelings so they wouldn't have to. That's been a thankless job.

"When I tell the other alters about all the things you have lived through and kept to yourself for their protection, they will probably want to give you a certificate of merit or throw a party in your honor! Your status should go up quite a bit when they express their appreciation for all you have done for them."

The hopeless feelings must be acknowledged as valid. Understanding that doing their job for the well-being of the system helps them to make sense out of their life. It also helps them see that therapy is going the right direction—alters are getting to know each other, and you expect that will make things improve.

"You will not have to suffer alone any more. There are comforter alters in the system, and we will help you get in contact with them. Therapy is not easy at times, but around here there is a team of people you can count on, and we will stay with you when you go through difficult times."

Every therapeutic event—even a phone call—is important. Do your best to produce a positive experience for every alter on every occasion, every time you have contact with each one.

BE CAREFUL NOT TO PROCEED TOO QUICKLY

It is important to lay a good foundation in the therapeutic relationship before you discuss the diagnosis with the client. Unless she has a lot of trust in you, it may be impossible for her to accept a diagnoisis as complicated as MPD. Even if the signs that point to dissociation are strong, you do not have to discuss them with the client right away. Go along, carefully establishing solid bond with the most powerful alters, and do what you would do with other clients. Talk about present conflicts, about feelings, and about the history of those feelings. Change areas of discussion in order to insure that you will not be spending time with only one alter. The host, one of the victims, and an observer are good targets for friendship. You should probably be at least two months into therapy before the diagnosis is discussed, even if it seems to fit in earlier.

There was a time when an intern under my supervision began to pick up the signs of dissociation in Laura, who was one of her clients. I did not think the intern was ready to handle such a case, and I asked to take over for her. Laura was extremely eager to get answers about some baffling things that had happened to her, and was insistent that she get some explanations from me immediately.

I was a good listener for about forty-five minutes, went through a mental checklist about the presence of MPD, and all the signs indicated she was a multiple. She was very persistent in getting some answers about blank spots and about some wacky visual experiences, and she seemed to be able to handle stress well, so I decided to go ahead and tell her about MPD.

I gave her a "positive spin" about dissociation and about treatment, answered her questions about the lost time, the unusual visual episodes, and about understanding her "Christian" side and her other side.

The latter side was much more athletic than the Christian side, and did some things that seriously conflicted with her Christian side. Her host alter was initially relieved with my explanation, and I was sure that she would do well in therapy.

I gave her an assignment about getting to know as many of her inner characters (which is the way I described them to her at that point) as she could, and that was the end of the session. She came to therapy a few more times, but soon she started missing sessions, and then pulled out altogether, and never told me why.

The best sense I can make out of her withdrawal is that she was not connected to me well enough to get into MPD therapy that quickly. I had not gotten to know protector alters before exposing the pain within the system, and they pulled the plug on therapy. I was guilty of pushing her along too quickly, not only by sharing the diagnosis but also by getting into the heart of treatment before we had developed a solid relationship.

It takes time for most people to trust a therapist enough to open up about deep issues. Considering how many people have failed the client, we can understand that it can take a lot of time for him or her to trust enough to accept this particular diagnosis.

SHARE THE DIAGNOSIS

More recently, Tricia was referred to me by another therapist who thought Tricia might have MPD. The therapist told me she lives too far away from Tricia to start treating her for multiplicity. Sometimes the client needs to come in for an emergency session, and at those times it is good to be close at hand. Tricia had been with three other therapists over the course of more than three years, but had recently stopped. That therapy was not getting to the things that needed to be dealt with, and Tricia knew it. She told me that during those three years, one session had seemed truly helpful to her. That session was with a pastor who had prayed with her, and that had helped more than all her work with the three therapists! It was a great reassurance to Tricia to find that I am a Christian, and that I have done a lot of praying with my clients. This seemed to help get us off on the right foot.

Signs of dissociation showed up during the first session, but I did not give in to Tricia's urgent request for me to explain them to her.

"Every effect has a cause," I said. "It takes more time to find the cause for some effects than it does for others. Every feeling is real. Minds do not just make up feelings for no reason. Feelings result from real events, and your mind is working hard to find out about those events. It is important for us to spend enough time together to get to know about your feelings, and where they got started. Every feeling has a history, and we need to discover where and when the feelings that bother you these days appeared in your past. It will take a little time."

Meeting the Spouse

Although Tricia still had the urge to speed through therapy and get to the issues she knew she needed to work on, we were able to take a slower start. A thorough history revealed very high scores on the "Dissociation Indicators," and her journal contained the phrase "sacrifice to Satan," although she couldn't remember writing that. Before I was ready to share the diagnosis, it was necessary to meet her spouse. He came in for a session of his own, and I laid out for him the task at hand: Tricia needed lots of security in order to make progress. She would be going through a difficult time of therapy, and he should be careful to be non-confrontive with her. I explained my hypothesis that she has MPD, but I left out the SRA. He told me the referring therapist had already told him that she was practically certain Tricia had MPD, so he was prepared to accept that diagnosis. I asked him to keep the diagnosis to himself, but to feel free to call me any time he needed to. I also told him it would be necessary for him to come in for sessions with me from time to time so he could understand and support Tricia better.

The Right Time

The next session was the right time to share my hypothesis about MPD with Tricia. I told her that the diagnostic picture is usually not very clear for awhile, but there are a few things we can check on which will help clear it up. I showed her a few diagrams about how "characters" operate like pieces of a pie, and how some characters know about each other and some don't. She had already developed some trust in me and said she knew that the Lord had led her to work with me, but the diagnosis was discordant to her.

That diagnosis could not be anything but discordant to a single personality. No alter can be expected to experience things as a group! I had a sense that I was talking to the Inner Self-Helper at that moment, and if that was the case, she would have a lot of information about the other alters, even if she had never before considered them to be separate personalities. As must be the case for any system of alters, there is little awareness of the mechanisms that have kept the system in balance—the switching and cueing. The Inner Self-Helper, who later was found to have the name "Pollyanna," tried to understand the picture I was painting, but still struggled with it.

It was important to tell her about the revolving door, and how she was sharing a body with the personalities who were waiting behind the door. I told her how a system works, and about equilibrium. There seemed to be a switch, and suddenly she went into a lot of denial. I later met the alter who had appeared right then, The Perceiver, whose job it was to defend against feelings by keeping the secrets hidden. It could have developed into a struggle, since the Perceiver did her job well. I decided I needed to appeal to The Perceiver's own experience.

"How do you explain the sudden headaches that are not helped by any medication? Why do you lose your car when you go to the big shopping centers? Why do you think it takes so long for you to pick out your clothes in the mornings?"

"How did you know about those things?" she asked. "I didn't tell you about them!" She was feeling exasperated—a strong feeling for an alter whose job it is to defend against feelings!

"Those are three things that usually happen for dissociators. Those inconveniences should clear up for you if you complete treatment for MPD." I pulled a copy of the "Dissociation Indicators" (see page 123) out of my desk, and pointed to the three items I had just mentioned. By now, Pollyanna had switched back in, because The Perceiver could no longer keep things hidden. Her "inconvenient" experiences could be explained by the possibility that she dissociates. Pollyanna had heard what I was telling Perceiver. We agreed to continue to keep the diagnosis in the hypothesis stage, while we looked for any distortion or lies that could be leading us in the wrong direction.

For many months quite a few of Tricia's alters strongly doubted the diagnosis; it did not seem like the "new memories" were real since they had happened to a different personality. It turned out to be important to have made a good connection with Pollyanna and with Esther (the alter who had the deepest religious convictions), and to have gained the cooperation of Tricia's husband. A few times she would have stopped coming altogether if he had not told her she really needed to stay in therapy. Going slowly and being more careful about when to share the diagnosis probably were important factors in keeping her effectively engaged in therapy.

PROVIDE APPROPRIATE INFORMATION

The almost bizarre sensory experiences that go along with flashbacks can make the dissociator believe she or he is going crazy. When those violent memories come into the mind of the host alter, they are highly unbelievable.

"They are not my memories. My mind is making it all up! They are just things." Tricia did not want to accept what some of the alters were remembering about her father. "I can accept the SRA things (as memories), but I don't think my father would do those things to me!"

Fortunately, I had been providing Tricia lots of information all along, designed to be external validation for the things she was going through. From the time I shared the diagnosis with her, I had provided her with some beginning reading about what dissociation is, and how it works. Periodically, I would lend her an audio or visual tape, and let her listen to it with her husband, so they could both learn the basics about MPD and SRA.

Much of the "homework" was discounted or disbelieved by a few of her alters, but taken together, it was vital that she had read, listened to and watched the informational materials I had provided. She would need to draw on that information in order to make it past the impact of the flashbacks. She learned about alters having separate thoughts, feelings and body memories, and she applied what she was learning to get through the flashbacks.

I explained it this way: "When the child alters feel safe enough, they begin to share all the components of their memories with the others. That is what a flashback is. The young victims are letting you know about the thoughts, feelings and bodily experiences they went through during those bad traumas. Unfortunately for the rest of you, you are destined to learn about the things they have kept to themselves all these years. The traumas were locked up in their memory banks, and now you will have to share the memories. That is how it works, but there is a benefit for the traumatized alter—because you are sharing the pain, her pain will be a little easier to bear. She has been suffering all these years, and now you are helping her to get through the suffering by letting her share the memory with you.

"It always seems unreal at first, when a flashback comes. As you have learned, the events really did happen to a different personality, so you are right when you say they are not your memories. The alters who had those experiences will need the understanding and acceptance of the other alters in order to receive healing. It will be extremely helpful for them if you can believe what they are telling you in the flashbacks."

Sharing the correct diagnosis and supplying good information about the condition is very helpful for clients who have a high Dissociative Ability. People on the top row of the Figure 5 matrix can use the information well, so the things described here will be more helpful to high-functioning clients.

For example, when low-functioning NAD clients or borderline clients get information, they tend to resist and deny it rather than incorporate it usefully. The healthy group of alters that good dissociators have been able to maintain in level 1 do not use much denial—dissociation has been the only coping method they needed. Therefore they do not have to break through denial before they can profit from the new information. The lower-functioning dissociators have needed to develop coping methods like denial, so they will continue to rely on those, and they will resist the information that helps higher-functioning clients. Therapy goes more slowly for the low-functioning dissociators precisely because of that phenomenon.

ESTABLISH SAFETY

When I had asked to see Tricia's husband, I was looking ahead to the safety issue before I shared the diagnosis with Tricia. I did not want to get her into the difficult parts of treatment before I knew if she would get the support she needed at home. It can take a day or two, or even longer, to recover after a difficult session, and I wanted her husband to know that. I was glad to have developed a good relationship with him, and that he had readily accepted the diagnosis.

Not far ahead was the discovery of what the phrase in her journal, "sacrifice to Satan," meant, and I knew that would be very upsetting to them both. Memories of rituals started to surface, and before long we found that Tricia had grown up in a cult family. Some awful flashbacks lay ahead, and it was crucial that she have the support of her husband. There would be days when reality and fantasy were hard to separate. Some pretty unbelievable flashbacks and partial flashbacks would intrude. It was absolutely necessary to have her husband believe them, exactly as they were described to him.

Tricia's position on the Figure 5 matrix was in section 3. She had friends, a lot of intelligence and creativity, and a healthy group of level 1 personalities, and she would remain safe.

Lack of Safety

For those people who are in position 6, though, it can be much more difficult. Examples abound of people in that section who are sidetracked by the lack of safety, and so do not get to the inner issues. This cannot be underscored strongly enough. Safety in the living environment is a prerequisite to therapeutic progress. When too much energy is used by going to work or taking care of children, there is not enough leeway for the equilibrium of the system to become upset. When cult members make threatening phone calls, an SRA survivor's system can become chaotic. Vulnerability to the whims of certain alters can get the person into situations that the host would never get into, causing difficulties at home.

One evening I received a phone call through the answering service. The operator said, "There is a 'Carla' on the line, who wants to speak with you. She says it's urgent."

"Hello," I said. "Is this Carla?"

"No, but that is the name we have to go by in order to get you on the phone. We're lost at a bar, and we can't find our car."

She found her car that night, but her husband did not like her disappearance, and did not like the level of intoxication she came home with.

The tenseness at home over that incident led Carla's system of alters to a point of panic and alarm. Some were frightened at the bar, and I never did get an account of what had happened there or when she got home. It was tough just to get the inside people to calm down. Maybe no single alter even knew everything that happened at either place!

There was no journaling or other therapeutic work completed for a few weeks. Even during the next few therapy sessions, the fragile alters did not show up because the protector alters would not allow them to surface. It was not safe out there. "Even Dr. Friesen did not help us find our car." Some of the child alters were very upset that I did not hop in my car and come to rescue them, or at least help them access the person who parked the car.

Perhaps it was a mistake to suggest on the phone that her husband should be the one to rescue her. She had said okay but some of the young alters were slightly afraid that the husband would be unsafe. They really had wanted me to rescue them, but they said nothing on the phone.

Non-confrontation needs to become a way of life for those who live with multiples, even though sometimes they may seem manipulative or deceptive. There may be confabulated stories, made up by child alters who are accustomed to turning out explanations to fit any situation. They are great at covering up when they are in charge, with no ideea of what just happened. At such moments it is very helpful to be in the presence of non-confrontive people, who understand enough about MPD to take things in stride.

Telling Other People

Another part of keeping things safe is determining which friends will be supportive if they are told about the diagnosis. Often there is an urge to go out and start telling friends, once the diagnosis is accepted. It has been so wonderful to finally talk to people with whom secrets can be shared—the therapist and the spouse—that it is almost automatic to want to tell others. That is usually not a good idea. It seems to the multiple that practically anyone can understand about switching, losing time, or finding oneself disoriented in an unfamiliar place—but friends usually cannot grasp those things easily. They often are not able or willing to understand things that are as different from their own experience as MPD is. I caution newly-diagnosed clients to take care not to tell very many people. Since most friends would not understand MPD very well, it would be preferable to hold off until it can be seen how supportive they are about less complicated parts of therapy. One thing to mention to the newly diagnosed multiple is that some of their alters would not wish their diagnosis spread around anyway, so it is important to accede to that wish.

Medical Problems

As a part of keeping things safe, the therapist also should be alert for medical conditions that need attention. For example, if there is an illness that needs constant monitoring, like diabetes or hypoglycemia, try to let all the alters know about it so the eating habits of some alters will not endanger the body's health. A high percentage of multiples have frequent health concerns, and many of them do need attention. However, sometimes it is necessary to not pay attention to less threatening complaints—there may be a hypochondriacal alter in the system who could take up too much therapy time. It is often helpful to refer the client out to other settings for "complaints."

Substance Abuse

Substance abuse—including alcohol, illegal drugs and over-the-counter substances—needs to be controlled. Without making a confrontive issue out of this, the therapist should look for signs of drug abuse, and help the alter who is abusing the chemicals to bring that issue into therapy. With education about taking care of the body that they share, and with teaching the chemically dependent alter to get the other alters' opinions about drugs, the chemically dependent alter should be led to deal with that problem. Sometimes the therapist may decide it is necessary to require the client to be involved in a chemical dependency program. There are just too many adverse affects from substance abuse to let it to go untreated.

If the bodily complaints or the chemical abuse constitute a relatively minor part of the system, those problems tend to clear up as the therapy focuses on the dividedness. The dissociative disorder is the superordinate diagnosis. When therapy for dissociation is successful, the subordinate conditions are usually resolved.

Maintaining Safety

When safety is maintained, therapy can successfully address the issues that underlie the dissociative disorder—the traumatic memories, wherever they appear in the client's life history, and the amnesia which maintains the dividedness. When safety is not maintained, the result is that all of the therapy time is taken to re-establish safety. Frightened and vulnerable alters will be locked out of the therapy process by protector alters, and will not receive the help they need.

Internal/External Work

Balance must be maintained between "internal work" and "external work." The way life is on the outside is an indication of how things are on the inside. External work—how the client relates with others—must be accompanied by internal work—how the alters relate with one another—or subordinate conditions (crisis after crisis) will be the only focus of attention. When the client's world is mostly safe, the balance between internal and external work can facilitate the things that need to take place—the erosion of amnesia and the resolution of traumatic memories.

PROTECT FROM HARASSMENT

Moody Monthly published a special report on Satanism with the title, "Evil in the Land." In one of the articles[1] a survivor whose cult background had been discovered in therapy was interviewed. A chilling account of harassment was carried in the article; it detailed repeated attacks on the cult survivor. They put her through the same torture and rituals she had endured as a child, including repeated rapes, and the forced ingestion of human remains. At the time of the interview it was stated that the longest she had gone without an abduction or beating was three and a half weeks, and on the day of the interview, her chin was severely bruised from being knocked to the ground.

Support From Others

Hers is a case where it has taken a lot of support from a church and a therapist to keep her on the track to health. It was stated that she still has a long time to go before she has fully recovered, and although her life is difficult, she daily asks God to give her strength "because tomorrow might be better." It is stirring to know that other therapists and churches are working together to help people escape from cult covens.

The magazine also quotes an investigator who has talked with "more than 170 survivors of satanic cults"[2] and all of them "report seeing human sacrifices." It takes courage and determination, as well as support from a lot of people, for an unwilling cult member to break away when they know they may face harassment and continuing physical torture.

The article emphasizes that friends must be prepared for a long-haul commitment—years of spiritual and psychological healing will be needed. They also advise support people to "be available" and to emphasize the love and forgiveness of Christ, as opposed to the submission demanded by the cult. It is also vital for friends of the survivor to "have a grip on" their own fear.[3]

Certain numbers spoken over the phone, or even certain sounds on the phone, can elicit an alter who is obedient to the cult, so one way to protect the person is to unplug the phone each night, and let a friend take it away from the house until the next morning.

Also, a beeper can be carried around, which can serve as a great protection device. A network of friends can keep calling the cult survivor by using the beeper, and if the phone number on the beeper is not answered within a few minutes, the police can be notified. Such a system is relatively simple to set up and can be effective in warning perpetrators to stay away.

Going Public

Another safety device is to go public. Have the client tell a number of people that SRA is in his or her background. The intent is to inform the public that cult attacks may be possible. Then if any harm comes to an adult survivor or any children, the investigation of the crime will immediately be successful. However, make certain that no cult members' names are mentioned publicly, because there are too many sticky issues that could come up in a courtroom. A public airing would be very unsafe. To mention the word "Satanism" in court could invoke some religious protection issues, and to have a multiple or even a former multiple as the primary witness might disallow some important testimony. We are just helping the victims recover.

Nonetheless, if the harassment turns into violence, it may be necessary to make the perpetrators accountable for their actions. A therapist should be ready to go to court if the client has been hurt. If his or her well-being is threatened or if the client's children are abused, and if there is irrevocable evidence as to who the perpetrators are, the therapist should not object to going to court.

Non-SRA Situations

Harassment is not as dangerous in most non-SRA circumstances, but often protection is almost as difficult to attain. Many of the clients whose position is at 2 or 5 on the Figure 5 matrix, come from families with evil parents. There is so much resistance to change in these families that it is often necessary to stop all contact with perpetrating family members during the course of therapy. Even a phone call or a letter has the potential of bringing therapeutic progress to a halt and of keeping it that way for several weeks.

It is widely known that abused children develop a strong loyalty to the abusing parent. That is part of the problem. Some of the child alters have unrealistically strong bonds to the evil parent(s), and can have a great deal of trouble staying out of contact with them. "To come to terms with evil in one's parentage is perhaps the most difficult and painful psychological task a human being can be called on to face. Most fail and so remain its victims."[5]

Some clients get a phone answering machine, and simply stop returning phone calls that are not safe. Some just throw away letters from perpetrating family members without opening them, even if it means losing contact with Mom or Dad. If it takes that to protect the child alters, then it should be done.

Certain alters ask me, "Does that mean breaking contact with my family? That is hardly the Christian thing to do!"

My answer is that the Christian thing to do is to be a peacemaker. If that means reorganizing the family, then that is what will have to be done. Jesus taught that a person's true family is the family of God: "My mother and brothers are those who hear God's word and put it into practice" (Luke 8:21). Another of His teachings seems pertinent here:

> Anyone who loves his father or mother more than me is not worthy of me; anyone who loves his son or daughter more than me is not worthy of me; and anyone who does not take his cross and follow me is not worthy of me. Whoever finds his life will lose it, and whoever loses his life for my sake will find it (Matthew 10:37-39).

The Christian thing to do is to gather people around you who are willing to hear God's Word and put it into practice, and to let go of "family members" who are unsafe. After all, family is only "family" in the Christian sense of the word when it adheres to Christian principles.

TALK ABOUT THERAPEUTIC OBSTACLES

I recently received a resumé from an intern who wants to work at our clinic. She mentioned that one of the reasons she is applying at our clinic is to get some experience with multiple personality disorder because she may decide to specialize in that area. Her credentials were very impressive, so I brought the resumé to the attention of the MPD team.

"What would make her want to specialize in that?" one member asked. "Is she into self-abuse, or does she just like to look bad?" We had a good laugh.

After our foibles have all been exposed in MPD team meetings, we are ready to laugh at ourselves. We wonder, time after time, why we work so hard at this. There are so many ways things can go wrong that we constantly need to help each other make mid-course corrections in our cases.

Perhaps one of the crucial tests of progress in MPD treatment is whether we can talk with the client about treatment traps that take shape during the course of therapy.[6] Resistances can develop from either the client's side or the therapist's side, and they need to be explored in the MPD team meeting so they can be talked through during therapy. Over the course of the client's whole life, whenever a dilemma has shown up, it has been automatic for the client to dissociate. That preferred method of coping has worked every time to lessen the anxiety and no other coping skills have been developed. Therefore, talking about the obstacles instead of switching away from them is a step in the right direction—toward developing coping methods which are more effective than dissociation.

I often describe thereapy to multiples as a kind of "psychology laboratory," where we talk about the goals of therapy and we practice them. We work on being realistic, and part of that is being honest about blockages to progress. If the client can learn to cope with life's obstacles by talking instead of dissociating, the psych lab will have been a huge success.

Despair

Crystal had been told that therapy would be difficult, but when she caught the full force of the feelings attached to the violent victimization of her dissociated Hurt Child, it was almost too much for her. "You didn't tell me it would be this painful. This pain will never stop! I will never get over it. It would be better if you would just let me die."

Her stepfather had been such a relentless and constant perpetrator that there was not a safe room in the house, and there was no safe time, day or night. His abuse was so brutal that she had been in constant fear, and now that we had contacted the memories of Hurt Child, Crystal was finally in touch with how bad her life had been. Despair was dominating her life in the present, because she was sharing Hurt Child's feelings. She felt her life would always be full of fear since Hurt Child believed there was no way out. Her mother had been drunk all the time and would not protect her. There was no place she could escape to for safety.

Her pain ran so deep that I felt very much the way Job's three friends must have felt. His struggles are portrayed in the Old Testament book bearing his name. Job had just lost everything he had—vast material possessions as well as his sons and daughters—and was afflicted with painful sores from the bottom of his feet to the top of his head. His friends came to sympathize with him and to comfort him. When they realized the immensity of his pain, they could only sit on the ground with him for seven days and seven nights without saying a word "because they saw how great his suffering was" (see Job, chapters 1 and 2).

I sat quietly with Crystal as she recounted to me the events she had been remembering during the week. Hurt Child was uncovering countless episodes of violent sexual abuse by the stepfather and his friends, and the feelings were making their presence known after being hidden all these years. When I thought she had gotten past the bottom of her pain, I began to bring the session to a close. Just a little hint of optimism on my part sounded like a barrage of minimization to Crystal. I said something like, "I'm certain that these feelings will diminish over time," but Crystal heard me saying the same thing she had always been told by her family—"Your feelings are not really that bad."

Crystal was certain I had not grasped how bad she felt. "How would you know what it's like to be raped any time of the day or night? I feel like a worthless whore. People just screwed me and then tossed me away like a piece of trash. No matter how many showers I take, there is no way I'll ever get clean again in my whole life."

I had blundered with my "positive approach." She needed time and space to get through the middle of the bad feelings. I could only sit silently and weep with her.

Feeling Trapped

By the next session we were ready to talk about what had happened. Hurt Child had been feeling trapped, just as she always had been, and was in continuous fear. She couldn't sleep, because the stepfather could be coming into her room at any minute, and that meant terror. The despair had been with her for two weeks—since she had her first flashback from the Hurt Child. It was tempting for Crystal to just drop out of therapy, or even to stop living, since the hopeless feelings were so strong. I knew we had to talk things through. I explained about the process of getting in touch with flashback feelings—they come in at full force, and start to diminish after a week or two. They never completely go away, but over time they will be experienced at much lower levels. By now, Crystal's feelings of despair were alternating with the feelings of other personalities. Happy Child showed up at my office by the following session. That was an encouraging sign.

"You know, there was a reason for the amnesia," I said. "It protected the rest of you from the pain in Hurt Child. There is always a reason for amnesia, and it is never a nice one. The reason is that the pain has been bad enough that you needed the most effective protection available—dissociation. When you pierced through the amnesia with flashbacks, you got in contact with the pain, and I am tremendously upset at the vile things you found hidden by the amnesia. But after you found it, you did what you had to do—you acknowledged it as fully as possible, without minimization, and began the process of decontaminating the memories. I think that, when you started talking it out, you handled it in the best way possible."

When she was a teenager, Hurt Child had been protected by Rebellious Child, who carried out her job by switching into acts of rebellion. Now, she was talking about the painful feelings, and that was a much safer way to deal with things. Crystal got through the therapeutic impasse caused by strong negative feelings. She gained some skill in dealing with tough issues through talking instead of through switching. That skill would help her with the other therapeutic obstacles still ahead.

There is a point I must emphasize. The despair that was embedded in Hurt Child abated, but it did need focused work in therapy for the next few months. It was not simply that we needed to understand the dissociative arrangement of her system properly—we also needed to carry out exorcisms when demons were found attached to memories of SRA, and we called on God to help with healing her memories.

It was difficult for Crystal to accept the beautiful aspects of herself, and it was difficult for her to protect the Hurt Child from being attacked in the work environment and at her home. When coworkers or roommates picked on her, she was not good at protecting herself. Upon achieving progress in those two areas, her personality came together at a high level. She is a splendid person.

Abandonment

Another common therapeutic obstacle is abandonment. It is a very difficult obstacle to talk through, because the client usually finds it easier to just quit therapy than face abandonment feelings. Another client, Martha, had a difficult time in therapy, as she had started life in an SRA family. She had been given demons at birth and at SRA rituals. She was trained to dissociate very early in life. Her parents had gone to remarkable lengths to program her alters with lots of distortion, but since she had a pretty high DA, she had some healthy alters, too, despite the frequent rituals and merciless punishments. Her parents had exploited her through abandonment during the first few years of life by using her abandonment fears to train her to be a good cult member. "If you don't do the things a good cult member does, we'll send you away, and you'll never see us again."

The abandonment cluster of alters surfaced just about as soon as the other cult alters became known to Martha's host alter. The confusion reverberating through her system was shared by the MPD team. We spent a lot of time trying to figure out what was going on. It had become clear fairly early in her therapy that Martha needed both a male and a female therapist, and she needed frequent contact in order to maintain her equilibrium after the cult-related alters were brought up to level 1. She needed to develop a sense of being in a healthy family.

It was a great relief for all the semi-amnesic alters in level 1 to finally figure out why her life had been so disrupted. They clung to the healthy relationships that were developing with members of the MPD team, in the same way a child would cling to a stuffed animal. She plunged as fully into treatment as she could, but she was split deeply over the "loyalty to family" issue. Abandonment is such a common problem for MPDs that the MPD team was already familiar with that aspect of Martha's plight. Nonetheless, an abandonment/suicidal trap lay ahead for her, and it was almost too much.

It seemed that Martha was dropping out of therapy every week or two. The people at the front desk were getting confused as to whether an appointment had been cancelled or not. Some person—an alter who was loyal to her family—had cancelled, but other alters who were amnesic to the "family alters" showed up at the right time for her appointment! Then the split in her system over "which family deserved her loyalty" would get uncovered in the session, and she would end up running out past the front desk with me close behind her! The healthy therapeutic relationships were quite appealing to some of the alters, but they were quite different from what the family alters were used to—they feared abandonment too severely to let her get close to those of us on the MPD team.

One thing she got from our clinic that she did not get from her family was loyalty in return. Whereas with her father she had gotten abuse and abandonment paired with occasional periods of warmth, she got consistent loyalty from our team based on genuine faith and hope in her.

Suicidal Tendencies

These healthy relationships, though, triggered feelings of abandonment throughout her system—when the warmth from our team was felt, the abandonment feelings came with it. There were a few weekends when she would be swept along by suicidal alters—the ones who felt worthless because of abandonment. Extreme measures were carried out to keep her alive, and to keep her talking about the thing that was keeping her stuck—the abandonment trap. Whenever she started to feel good about a person, it would get her in touch with abandonment feelings.

Looking back on it now, the crisis does not seem nearly as serious as it did at the time, but there were periods when the only thing I could do was pray. Martha could have killed herself—she had been programmed with suicidal alters who were activated when she started to tell the secrets of her SRA past. The abandonment alters and the suicidal alters could have been a deadly combination, but she had a healthy enough core to get on the phone with me or with one of the other team members to talk things through. Martha's system eventually got the message to the newly-contacted alters that it was safe to talk about whatever was bothering them, and they worked through their feelings quickly enough to subdue the feelings of the "suicidal cluster."

Martha stopped her episodes of dropping out of therapy soon after the abandonment alters had been decontaminated.

Cult recontact and frequent harassment still plagued her for quite a long time, but she stayed in therapy and continued to talk about her problems.

Looking for an Easy Way

Rosie is another client who had quite a bit of difficulty getting through the impasse produced by SRA memories. She had accepted in her head that the SRA images being discovered were real enough, but she was trying to find as easy a way as possible to deal with them. I had not been her primary therapist, but did have a little contact with her over a period of a year or so. I was one of the people she hoped might be able to help her. Whenever she would get too close to awful feelings, she would go to a different therapist and see if that one could help her stay in control.

I was trying to assist her to find an easy way too, but I knew that if I let her keep looking for just the right way to get through the pain, she might end up dropping out of therapy. She had gone to other therapists, had engaged a pastoral counselor to help her with deliverance work, and had looked into every way she could think of to take care of the pain.

After all that, one day she put it into words. She said that she still felt as though she "was teetering on the brink of a bottomless pit of feelings," and if she "fell off," she "might never recover." When she said that, it cleared the way for me to point her in the right direction.

"We need to work a little more on getting your alters to trust each other so they will be able to keep your equilibrium in balance. They seem to be afraid they will lose control." I gave her an assignment, to list the characteristics of her alters and see if she could tell which of them had the different attributes. She was ready to work, now that she had given clarity to her position with her words—she was "teetering on the brink"—and now she needed to find out how the personalities on level 1 could keep things in equilibrium.

By the next meeting, she brought in the following list of characteristics: Logical, Creative, Spiritual, Shame/Intimidation, Fear, Mother (critical), Mothering (healthy and nurturing),

Sarcasm, Forgetful, Handicap/Denial, Handicap/Grief/Lament, and Compulsive/Anxiety. She said she could not tell the difference between them—they just happened whenever they happened, and she could not see any particular pattern of lining up or of switching.

Identifying Distinctive Characteristics

I asked her how many times she had changed clothes today.

"Five times, but that is not unusual."

"Here is something that may help you to discover which of those characteristics belong to each alter. Figure out which one wears each outfit, and then try to find out as much as you can about each one of those alters."

"How do I do that?"

"Ask them."

"What do you mean, like . . . talk to myself?"

"Whatever it takes. They all have been following an unspoken rule—that silence is necessary. However, that is just the opposite of what is true. The less silence the better! Have them talk with one another, and get to know each other. After all, they have been working together for a long time. Even switching clothes so often will be easier when they start communicating with each other better."

Rosie still did not get very far in identifying how the alters were different from each other, but she was able to see the switching pattern a little better by the next session. She described an incident where she had been in the helper role at a lecture about a particular type of artwork. When the lecturer talked authoritatively, she said she felt very much like a child—a subservient child. Then someone in the audience would talk down to her while asking for her assistance with something, and she would feel the blood rush to her head in anger. She would get a little dizzy while she was briefly in her angry child alter, but the dizziness soon cleared up and she would get subservient again. If somebody else asked her for help in a nice voice, she would start to feel maternal. She began to see how the alters were readily responding to their cues, and how confusing that got. Her head was literally spinning!

By the end of that session, we had gone through the characteristics from the previous session, and had concluded that there were fourteen identifiable alters she could see as distinct from one another. The message had gotten through. Silence is not golden. Everybody needs to be heard from. Talking about the system is the only way to stay in control. To avoid talking about these things is to perpetuate the impasse.

6

TREATMENT FOR DISSOCIATION II
Guidelines to Unity

HELP THE CLIENT
DEVELOP A "CAST" AND A "MAP"

IF I HAVE BEEN seeing someone in therapy for a few months and dissociative signs begin to emerge, I look for ways to test whether I am actually working with a dissociator. The "cast of characters" assignment allows me to find out how much separateness there is between the personality states. A large amount of separateness indicates the client may be using dissociation as a preferred method of coping.

Some therapists could conclude I am suggesting to my clients that they have MPD when I use maps and casts. Therapists who believe that the emergence of MPD is only another fad have said that I am just "leading my clients on." They may even go so far as to suggest that I am creating their condition through the suggestions I make to them. Wary therapists would like to believe these suggestible clients could be more effectively dealt with in other therapeutic frameworks, and sometimes those skeptical therapists even conclude that my work is fraudulent.

When I ask a person to do a cast or a map, I am not creating anything. The client is merely using this framework to describe how life really is for her (or him). If her life is divided because of dissociation, she will not profit measurably from any other therapeutic framework. Either she will work on the superordinate condition—the dissociating—or she will find her therapy sabotaged by the competing interests of the alter system. I am not suggesting to her that she has MPD—she is discovering whether MPD is present on the basis of her own awareness. Other psychological frameworks tend to gloss over the dividedness within the clients through intellectualizing and empathizing. These do not get to the dissociation-related problems. Only when the system is uncovered by allowing the alters to become known by each other can their competing agendas be resolved. Only when all the components of their dissociated lives get shared among the alters will they find the means to start a project and finish it.

Here is how the cast helped me with Beth's diagnosis. (She was first mentioned in chapter 2.) Before I had learned about MPD, Beth was attending one of my therapy groups that met once each week. I had given them an assignment to develop a cast of characters which represent the roles they play in the various arenas of their lives. The instructions were not complex—the members were to describe as many different characters as they could and write up to a page for each. That proved to be a good way to pinpoint conflicts for them, and group members still use their casts to talk about the forces that shape their lives. I had started using the cast with the group just three months before I heard the tape about MPD. During that time the group members had varying degrees of success learning to know their characters and profiting from the work.

Beth, however, seemed to have gone overboard. She got out her journal and showed us that she had written page after page about a number of characters! She shone like an A+ student for that assignment, and could go on and on about each character.

Even I found it astonishing. I listed only five or six characters for myself, and a few sentences for each one was about all I could come up with. But Beth portrayed Socrates, Spock, Mother Teresa, and Trix in immaculate detail! It almost made my head spin. The details, lives and feelings of each one were explicit down to the tiniest detail, and new members in her cast showed up each week. The other group members began to feel inadequate and tended to stop using the cast model for a while—they were only doing C work compared to Beth.

The amount of separateness that had been displayed in Beth's cast-of-characters assignment did a wonderful job of preparing us both for addressing the question in her private therapy of whether she had separate alters. It was hard to miss. She was ready to accept the diagnosis, and the integrative work was already under way. The inside people were getting to know each other. It was time to develop a "map" of the characters, and the result is found in Figure 1 (on page 46). As new alters were discovered, they were given places on successive revisions of the map. Figure 2 (on page 52) is a copy of Beth's final map. That was a very productive way for Beth to do her internal work, and she stuck with it, session after session.

Since that time I have found it helpful to use the cast of characters assignment when examining an individual client's ability to dissociate. When secretiveness is encountered in one or more of the characters, or when the cast grows very large, dissociation may be inferred. If so, it may be time to have the person put the characters onto a map. I hope the map assignment will allow the person's creativity to emerge.

Clients are instructed to organize the maps according to the amount of power each alter has, or according to how old each one is, or any way they see fit. The variety of map constellations that take shape is endless. The creativity in these people allows each map of alters to be arranged in a way that accurately reflects the person's system.

The cast assignment also may help with the diagnosis of TD. In Crystal's case, we initially found a Happy Child who seemed to be rather distinct from the others, but there did not seem to be any others who were very different from one another. As therapy progressed, Crystal got the sense that some things had happened during a stage of her childhood which were going to be pretty painful to get in contact with. At her request, we asked her pastor to join us for an extended session of prayer and the healing of memories. What she started remembering during the prayer session was very difficult for her to accept or even to believe. As mentioned earlier, in her late childhood she had been repeatedly abused by a stepfather and she had blocked out the abuse memories entirely, allowing them to be contained in the Hurt Child character. What incredible fear Hurt Child had gone through. That dissociated character was quite different from and had been amnesic to the other characters. The rest of the cast was healthy, and the abuse started well after age 5. Her position on Figure 5 was somewhere between 1 and 2—she had traumatically dissociated the memories, and the cast revealed only one troubled member (as is often the case with TD). We never needed to develop a map.

BEFRIEND EACH ALTER

Every alter is a real personality with real problems. Each has real feelings to work through and real needs that must be attended to. Multiples have become adept at picking up subtle indications about people's feelings—they can tell immediately if they are being treated condescendingly, and they will not put up with it. There are alters in every system who have been traumatized and who will be alert for the earliest sign of danger.

Every alter is important. Any alter can sabotage treatment if it is not given the same respect as the others. Be careful not to let any alter convince you it is bad—it may be contaminated because of cruelty and it may have spiritual problems, but it is not inherently bad. It belongs to the system, and has an important job to do for the system.

Therapists and friends of multiples must take care not to be judgmental. If an alter picks up non-acceptance because of its displays of anger or because of its sexual behavior, that alter will be certain to undermine therapy behind the scenes in subtle ways. If one alter engages you in talking slanderously about another alter, the slandered one may be listening in and may take offense, so never let yourself get caught up being judgmental about alters who are not present. The mindset must always be that every alter is basically good, even if misled, and the alters must get that message about each other. They need to get to know each other and accept each other, in order to work together.

During one session with Martha a new alter was uncovered. "My name is Shadow, and I am a cult recruiter. My job is to find people's weaknesses and call the head cult honcho, who sends someone to exploit those weaknesses. You would be surprised to find out how many people have been recruited because I can figure out what they need. Money, clothes, drugs, sex, power, status—you name it. If they have a crack, I'll find it."[1]

I don't think Shadow knew where she was when she came out in my office. I had been trying to get in touch with an alter who seemed to be working against the system's therapeutic progress.

Often some of the amnesic alters turn out to be more powerful than the host, so getting the system to cooperate can take a while. Shadow admitted she worked against the host, so it would have been easy for me to consider her an enemy. After all, she was drawing people into the violent and merciless activities of the cult. I resisted my natural tendency to consider her an enemy, and she shortly introduced me to her partner, the Cult Princess.

She and the Cult Princess, who were almost always coconscious with one another, were invited to share their life histories with me. Despite their reluctance, they eventually did tell me a lot more than they had first intended. Although some of the scenes they described were sickening, these were people, made in the image of God. They were headed down the wrong path because somebody else put them on it, and they didn't know how to get off. They did not think they could choose to get off. They needed to learn about how MPD works—the revolving door and the many inside people who don't know each other. They also needed to listen to the other alters, many of whom had decided not to participate in the cult any longer.

Over the period of two weeks or so, the two cult alters substantially erased much of the amnesia between them and the other alters and were converted away from the cult. Once those two alters found out they were free to choose which life they could live—with people who follow Satan or with people who follow God—it was not hard to decide. Truth and honesty were much more attractive than deceit. Shadow and the Cult Princess, who thought they were the enemies of the Christian alters, began to cooperate, largely because they were befriended by me, and were accepted by the other alters.

ESTABLISH INNER CONTROL
OVER INTRUSIVE MEMORIES

Dissociation is an effective way to lessen the impact of traumatic memories, but it is not effective enough to keep using on into adulthood. It may do its job well enough during childhood, but dissociation becomes inefficient and often debilitating as a person reaches maturity. As one writer has put it, leakage into consciousness of dissociated aspects of trauma and intrusion phenomena are evidence that dissociation is insufficient to resolve the trauma definitively.[2]

Intrusive visual images that may penetrate the dissociator's mind, images which have been previously unknown, are extremely unsettling. Flashbacks and partial flashbacks (both of which are components of dissociations) have always been present. Their frequency and intensity increase, however, when therapy begins to erode the amnesia which has kept the memories hidden.

Carla's willingness to continue in therapy was seriously challenged by intrusive memories. "Those memories in the church basement are crazy! They couldn't have happened to me. [There was a long pause.] I am willing to go through whatever it takes to get the different personalities in me to work together, but those things didn't happen to me! My family is not like that—they couldn't possibly have done that. Maybe my mind is just playing tricks on me. Do you think that could happen, Doctor Friesen? Am I making it all up?"

There was no way I could think of to deny the verity of her memories, and still keep her on course in therapy, so I said, "Traumas are bad enough to discover, but when a person's parents are implicated it is okay to hope that the memories will be inaccurate. Something is being remembered, and whatever it is must be important or it would not be coming up. Your mind is a great mind, and it is not playing tricks on you. Even if the people who hurt you were tricking you, you can be certain that your mind is recovering memories just as they were experienced. There is a chance that people were dressed up to look like members of your family during the rituals you are seeing, but the flashes you are getting do represent what happened. When you have successfully melted some of your amnesia away, 'unknown' memories can appear. As therapy progresses we will find ways to clarify the memories, and you will learn how to stop them from intruding."

Serious regression and life-endangering consequences can follow unplanned flashbacks, particularly when they have not been properly handled in the therapeutic setting. When dissociated feelings are re-exposed without preparation, healing and after-care, the client would be better off not accessing the flashback material. Pulling unconscious, dissociated memories into the client's awareness lies at the heart of therapy for dissociators. This is therapeutically unavoidable, but it needs to be done carefully. In conveying to the client that control of the intrusive memories can be learned, and by planning for the therapeutic restoration of the damage, the stage can be set for systematic memory work.

This is a key principle:

The wounds must be thoroughly exposed, under the proper therapeutic conditions, so that the client can receive healing.

The two objectives that will bring the most healing, or "decontamination," as a result of planned memory work are the *resolution* of the traumas, and the *integration* of the dissociated memories into the client's conscious life. Dr. David Spiegel listed eight Cs to think of when doing memory work with trauma survivors, which sum things up nicely:

1. *Confront* the trauma. Make certain therapy gets directed toward working through the traumatic events.

2. Find a *condensation* of the experience, and re-work the memory, including what the client was doing to try to protect himself or herself. While the events are being slowly and carefully remembered, point out to the survivor that he did not want this to happen. Too often, the perpetrator has convinced the survivor that he chose to participate, but that is a lie. When a condensed memory has received healing, the similar memories are healed as well so that reworking will not be necessary for every trauma.

3. Allow for *confession* so the client can express any feelings of guilt about whatever happened.

4. Provide *consolation*. They need to hear things like, "I'm deeply sorry to hear about the things that happened to you," because they believe the therapist will be repulsed by the material that emerges.

5. Bring all of the experience into *conscious* memory. What was previously dissociated now needs to be completely remembered—the mind's memory, the body's memory and the emotional memory of the events. The components of the dissociated event need to be attached to each other in order to reach resolution. The client is then free to attribute new understanding to the events.

6. Encourage *concentration* in the memory work on the specific task at hand. The client may be afraid she will never be able to get through the flashback. She may believe she is falling into a bottomless pit, but you can reassure her that she will be successful. Encourage her to set aside times of the day for grieving and for self-imaging.

7. Give the client *control*. The sense that the memories are controlling her is false. No matter what happened, the client has the potential to establish control over the memories.

8. *Congruence* (integration) is a major goal. Get all the alters to work together. "Whatever happened to you isn't so bad that you can't be you, and that you can't be protected." Have the alters meet each other, and get familiar with the memories. This allows for the new meaning ("I really was doing my best to spoil it for the perpetrator, so I'm not guilty after all") to be IN-TEGRATED into the client's conscious life.[3]

No alter should be stuck with the task of working through a memory alone. The therapist should set things up to get the whole system involved with the memory work, so congruence can be accomplished. Get some comforting adult alters to be present with the traumatized alter during the imagery, and allow as many alters as possible to learn about what happened. Set up protector alters to shield the child alters in a sealed-off area—

they can learn about the events later, but for now they need to be protected.

If the whole system starts breaking down, that means the memory work is going too rapidly. It is generally accepted that this kind of work needs to be done thoroughly, so please resist the client's urge to get through it speedily. "Pacing is a key word. When good preparation has taken place, when the parts of the memory have been brought together and resolved, when the traumatic episodes have been given new meaning, and when the events have been incorporated into the client's life, the memories will no longer intrude. Despite the client's fear that these intrusive memories are uncontrollable, the positive approach in treatment maintains that, no matter what happened, *the client has the inner resources necessary to control the memories.*

HELP ALTERS WITH SPECIAL NEEDS

Not all people have the stamina to work through their memories without either breaking down in their daily routines or becoming suicidal. Do whatever you can to help them slow down the memory work, but sometimes clients will not be able to maintain steady inner control.

When clients show signs of breakdown or suicidality, it may be necessary to set up a consultation with a psychiatrist, preferably one who has had some experience with multiplicity, to find an appropriate medication. Antidepressants can become a therapeutic aid in helping maintain daily routines like staying on the job or keeping children on their school schedules. It is important to keep the client in regular contact with a consulting psychiatrist because multiples do not react in predictible ways to medications. Because of their very high threshold of drug responsiveness, some clients need remarkably high levels of medication in order to get any help.[4]

Another reason for regular psychiatric consultations is that individual alters within the system have different levels of medical responsiveness. Although this seems difficult for people like me to understand, it is undeniable! Some alters get drunk on a little alcohol, but others can drink practically anyone else under the table. Some alters fall asleep on small doses of medication, but others could stay up all night on large doses. Even over-the-counter pain medication helps some alters but not others within the same person!

There is a lot to take into account in setting the appropriate level of medication for any particular MPD client, so make certain the client has frequent opportunities to talk with a psychiatrist about how various alters are doing with the medications.

Due to the fact that practically all MPD clients have periods of suicidality, it may be necessary to protect the life of the client with brief hospitalization, but it should be seen only as a last-resort intervention. Many people are practically precluded from being hospitalized because they need to stay on the job, because they cannot afford it, or because of traumatizing experiences they have already been through in hospitals. Increasing the frequency of outpatient visits and finding the right medication can often get the clients through periods of suicidality, but when even daily contact does not seem enough, hospitalization may be required.

Here are two cautions about selecting the right hospital: One is to beware of hospital settings where the MPD diagnosis may set the client up to be a circus side show. Some staff members get so intrigued with aspects of the multiplicity like "alters" and "switching" that the feelings of the client can get minimized.

The other caution is that if the client's system is not in equilibrium, the in-patient experience will not seem safe to most of the alters. Frightened alters may be accessed for the first time, and the disorientation will be upsetting not only to them but also to any other alters who may experience newly-discovered memories from these alters. Amnesic spells and disequilibrium need to be worked with very carefully when hospitalization becomes necessary. It is vital to work closely with the staff, or even to do some in-service training with the hospital staff about MPD treatment. The most desirable hospital placement is on an MPD ward, where the doctors and the whole staff specialize in dissociative disorders.

During times of upset it is crucial to work with the alters who are in the most pain at the moment. These are often recently accessed alters, who have surfaced after quite a long period of dormancy. An alter that only comes out for a *negative cue* in a particular situation usually only deals with a small portion of its own life experience. There is a well-ingrained pattern where the alter expects that only bad things will happen whenever it is called out. These "special needs" alters are not accustomed to being listened to.

When out on a *positive cue*, they usually will enjoy the chance to talk openly about new material. The amount of progress gained by an alter during a particular therapy session will be proportional to the amount of new material uncovered.

Perhaps the most difficult special-needs alter to help is a persecutor alter. That one can keep the whole system off balance when it does its job—persecuting other alters for making mistakes. It is often busy berating and verbally intimidating the child alters. The persecutor alters are often replicas of violent, rejecting parents or of some other unpredictably vicious perpetrator. They fill a defensive slot in the system—they keep everybody in line to avoid punishment.

Carla's system had closed down for a while and during one session I found out why. Fear of a persecutor alter, Tiger, became apparent in a child alter while I was talking to her. She said she couldn't tell me her secrets because Tiger wouldn't let her. When I asked her about Tiger, the child said "Tiger is a demon, and must be obeyed no matter what. You know what a demon can do to you!"

The child could hardly believe me when I said I wanted to become friends with Tiger. "I told you Tiger is a *demon*, and they don't have any friends."

I offered that maybe Tiger was misled and is not a demon after all. At that point Tiger switched in, and in a low, huffy voice, told me to quit talking to this child. "I'm in charge here, and I am a demon."

My immediate sense was that this could not be a demon. Demons flit in with evil threats and then leave without giving me a sense that they will relate to me. I asked what evidence there was that she was truly a demon.

"I swoop down and hurt people. They have to do what I say or I will send them to hell! I just come and go, and nobody knows when I'm coming."

I asked how she could tell the difference between a demon and a personality. That stopped the angry tone of voice. Tiger calmed down and engaged in a reasonable conversation. I told her about the people she shares a body with, and about many of her experiences which could be part of the MPD picture. She learned that she had served the system well, doing a good job of keeping the children out of trouble. After she learned about amnesia, she no longer considered herself to be a demon. "The blank spots," I told her, "are really not blank at all. Other people are out front, and you are waiting in the back until you are needed."

Over the next few months, Tiger became established as one of the most influential alters in the system. Her power and eagerness to protect helped her to distance the whole system from the SRA perpetrators, who had raised her to believe she was a demon. Her knowledge of the child alters, especially the SRA child alters, contributed greatly to understanding and unifying the system.

It is particularly difficult to befriend an angry, special-needs alter. On one occasion I met Slugger, a male alter in a female's body, who could be called on to fight. He was also a baseball player and was known to be quite a good batter.

It was scary for me to invite this dangerous member of the system to talk with me. For starters, Slugger stood up and stared at me, and told me that he could "tear this room up in a minute" if he chose to. Then he sat on the arm of the sofa and did not look at me while talking for the next thirty minutes. After his threatening and fuming, I asked him if he would please tell me what it is like to have a fight, since I am a non-violent person. That surprised him—he believed that every man is violent. He became quieter and began to tell me about his life.

He had lived with an uncle who had repeatedly abused him and had always humiliated him before the whole family. The hurt and anger stored up in Slugger was immense! After one particular abuse episode, Slugger was called upon by the system to get revenge against that uncle. He grabbed a poker from the fireplace, took hold of it like a baseball bat and started slugging his uncle. For an 8-year-old, he was very successful, and he hurt the uncle badly enough to make him see a doctor. As a result, Slugger and the whole system were moved out of the home.

He was a successful fighter and was called on in times of danger. Slugger did not show me any emotions except the determined kind of anger that it took to do his job. However, when he became reflective for the first time in his life, I believe he felt truly human. Before that he had been more of a functionary, robot-like creature. Now he was getting in touch with feelings.

PLAN INTERVENTIONS
TO ERODE THE AMNESIA

I asked Slugger if he knew about the people who shared his body. He didn't. Then I asked him if he could hear the voices in his head.

"Sometimes, but they seem like they are a long ways off, sort of like they are at the other end of a tunnel."

I told him the names of two powerful alters and that they would be trying to develop coconsciousness with him, which means they would try to be with him whenever he was out. He was not very comfortable with what I was saying, and he started to switch out.

"Please, Slugger, stay here for a few more minutes. In order for you to do a better job of protecting everybody, it will help you to become coconscious with as many inside people as possible. That way you will know when you are needed."

That was appealing to him. We talked at length about the dynamics of MPD, and I gave him some ideas about working together with the others. I showed him some diagrams and charts about how he fit into the system of alters, and by the end of the hour he was looking at me without anger in his eyes. He had literally changed. It was a great feeling for us both, and I'm sure he picked up a sense of what a friend is like. He had learned that not all men are violent, and his amnesia had been eroded a little. He had gotten relevant information about MPD and had come in contact with some of the other alters. Those experiences were really helpful. The amnesia was eroding, which made it possible for him to cooperate with the other alters and take a voluntary role as part of the system. From now on, he would decide when to come out instead of just being cued in some unknown way. There would be no more negative hooks after the amnesia eroded.

Here are some interventions that seem to work well in eroding the amnesia.

(1) *Get a lot of accurate information into the system* about how MPD works. Talk with alters about how dissociation takes place, and how they fit into the system. Talk about roles, components of dissociation, flashbacks and the varieties of symptomatology, and maybe even show them where they fit on the Figure 5 matrix. Get them to do as much reading as they are ready for, including some first-hand accounts by therapists and clients.[5] Keep talking about safety and about using their support system.

Whenever they bring up questions about the integration and fusion of alters (discussed more fully in the next section), keep things matter-of-fact. When unity is achieved, people find that life becomes easier. Take care not to force fusion, because some of the alters have no wish to give up their separateness, even for the good of the whole system. Just talk to the alters in terms of goals and objectives. "For now, let's just think about getting the whole orchestra to follow the conductor! The Inner Self-Helper can direct, and the others can learn to take their cues from her. When alters are each playing their own songs, it gets chaotic. Your immediate concern should just be to make good music together."

(2) *Encourage coconsciousness and group efforts.* One thing that helps with work on painful memories is to get a comforter alter to be coconscious with the alter who has to work through the memory. Try to get other alters to be present with someone going through a flashback because it can get overwhelming for an alter who is alone at a time like that. Usually the injured ones are child alters, so to have a caring adult around can be helpful. When the system learns to become fluid enough to use this approach, the memory work becomes a lot easier.

Journaling and Artwork

(3)*Journaling is a good assignment* to get the alters to learn about each other. Particularly for some clients, the journal they carry around everywhere becomes a reference point for all the alters. Each has a distinctive handwriting style, and most of them take advantage of every chance they get to work out their feelings about a therapy session that just took place, or to get their memories out on paper. There is usually a map of the alters attached to the journal, and each alter knows his or her position on the map, and uses it to learn about the others. The journal becomes a great starting point for the next session. If some alters are reluctant about coming to therapy, they can at least write to the therapist, and maybe at some later date they will be trusting enough to rotate out and speak in therapy.

(4) *Artwork is a good way* for some of the alters to show their dreams to the others, and to the therapists. It is also a good way for the child alters to display what really happened during their traumatizing episodes. Blood, candles, upside-down crosses, five-pointed stars standing on one of the points, and/or a circle of people in robes are highly indicative of SRA memories.

Imagery

(5) When there is difficulty getting in touch with an amnesic alter, *imagery can facilitate the contact.* When dissociative ability is very high, imagery will likely be an effective tool for piercing the amnesia. Four types of imagery seem effective. The first involves creating a safe place where the hurting alters can go for recovery. It is important to establish this scene before any others, because if an injured alter is found, it will need such a place. One that works well is a safe meadow, with all the appropriate sights, sounds and smells. A gently flowing brook and a warm breeze set the stage for recovery. For Christians, it is good to have Jesus waiting there to help in any way He sees fit.

Before I had done any imagery with Tricia, I asked her if she had ever imagined a safe place where she could just go whenever she needed. She had been using just such a place since age 4! I asked her to close her eyes, imagine it again, and describe it to me. After she did, I asked her if she could see Jesus coming to that meadow to provide healing for any alter who needed to be with Him. It took a minute or two, but she was able to see Him there. We were now ready for the next scene.

The **second** type of imagery helps in getting to know more about the system. "This is a house, with a room for each of your alters, and a conference room right by the front door. I want you to imagine us standing outside, and when you are ready, go on in. I'll follow you, and close the door behind me. Let me know when we're inside."

Tricia was really surprised at how effective this was at learning about the alters in her system. A number of them were already in the conference room, and seemed to know each other pretty well. There was a door on the right which led down to a basement, and she went over to it and put a lock on it.

"We will never go down there. That door will stay locked up forever."

Although I knew we would eventually have to take a look down there, this was not the time to tell her. I asked her to take me on a trip through as much of the house as she could, just to get to know where everybody's room was. We didn't get through much of the house that session because some of the alters in the conference room were dead set against exploring the house. It turned out that there were three alters who had the job of denying that anything was wrong. We would have to spend a few weeks befriending them before we could expect to get much farther in our exploration of the house.

The **third** kind of imagery is intended to recover the awful memories in as soft a way as possible. It is the "screening room" imagery, in which I talk about how the two of us can go into a theater by ourselves, and watch pictures that tell the person's life story.

I cautioned Tricia to keep the pictures on the screen, and to not let the feelings get connected to them. I also gave her a remote control device so she could turn off the picture if she wanted. We started out by showing the meadow to test the camera. It worked fine. Jesus was in the meadow, and a few of the child alters were with Him.

With her eyes closed she saw the next scene—it was when she was 4 years old, at night in her room. She started to tense up. She did not believe what she saw and said she surely must be making this up, and opened her eyes. She did not want to go back in there if that is what she is going to have to watch. I told her that after the 4-year-old shows what happened to her, it will be helpful to take her to the meadow so that, no matter what happened, she could recover. For the sake of the little girl, Tricia went ahead with the imagery. That was her first recollection of her father's molestation.

"I must be making this up, right?"

"I'm not certain, but we need to get to know the little one better, and let her tell us what she knows."

That imagery got us into the memory work. I knew there was a lot of difficult therapy ahead when SRA scenes began playing on the screen. None of this seemed real, but through coconsciousness, watching a video with her husband about SRA, journaling and mapping, the amnesia continued to erode. The imagery itself was essential, but that was not enough. However, it gave us the right material to work on, and without it, the SRA memories may have remained buried for a lot longer.

The **fourth** kind of imagery helps the whole system deal with dissociated traumatic memories—(inner) group memory work. When preparing for this kind of memory work, the alters' roles and functions need to be well understood. A house with a conference room, a recovery room, and a sound-proof chamber facilitates this kind of memory work. Getting quite a few alters involved in the imagery is the goal, so secluding the child alters in the chamber with some comforting adults is a good way to start the imagery. Then inviting the supportive adult alters to the conference room will make the victim feel more certain there will be help available. Get as many involved as possible—the more the better. Guards can be stationed at the conference room doors, Observers, Writers, and Inner Self-Helpers need to be present, and anyone who is safely ready to hear the traumatic memories. Take steps to keep them all involved as the victim remembers the event for everyone, and take steps to keep the victim at least partially in the present while the details of the event are being recounted. After the victim recalls everything, all the way to the end of the "flashback," the recovery room will be needed for the victim. The other alters will also need to be allowed to talk about how they feel and what they think about the material shared. The amount of amnesia eroded will be proportional to the number of alters who can be involved.

Do not feel limited to these types of imagery. Let the client develop her or his own imagery as much as possible. This not only gives an outlet for the creative display of the system, but it also allows the client to take a more active role in therapy. The more initiative the client takes in solving inner turmoil, the sweeter the successes will be. "Your alters did a great job!" means "Congratulations!" and not, "You did a good job of following my lead."[6]

PROMOTE INTEGRATION AND FUSION

Integration is the process of bringing the separated alters together. All the interventions mentioned in this chapter are integrative in nature. When erosion of amnesic barriers is promoted through coconsciousness, cooperation and group efforts, integration is under way. Maps, journaling and artwork contribute to the breakdown of amnesia so thoughts, feelings, body memories and the will (intentions) can be shared. (*Merging* is a good synonym for integrating.)

Fusion is the point at which two or more alters actually become one. Fusions can occur spontaneously in places other than therapy, but it seems safer and more predictable if they are accomplished during the therapy session. The use of imagery facilitates the process nicely. Imagery is the tool, but the alters need to be willing to make it happen. (*Joining* is a good synonym.)

There are many scenes in imagery that can facilitate fusion, and it is best to let the person choose the scene that fits him or her best. Beth did her fusions in a garden. There was a stone wall around the garden, and each alter had its own section. When the alters decided to become fused, Beth would imagine taking the stones from the wall between the two alters' plots and using the stones to strengthen the garden's outside walls. She would see the alters then become one, sort of like having a set of X rays superimposed on each other, and the newly-formed person would contain every part of each alter's components. It is a remarkable thing: The parts that make up the two alters become unified, and what emerges is the total of the two alters. For example, if one is a rather quiet alter and one is an angry alter, you will find that after they are fused they will go through an adjustment period, getting used to each other's habits. The new, unified core will be able to go back and forth between the different habits without dissociating.

Martha's fusions always took place in the "rainbow room" in her alters' house. It was a special place used only for that purpose. When the alters had been properly prepared and de-contaminated, she put her hand over her face, let her head bow a little, and watched the alters go over to the rainbow room. The fusion took place, and a smile appeared on her face. "I've got my cloud around me!" The fusion was successful, and no unexpected painful memories came to mind as a result of it.

Tricia's fusions took place in the meadow she had been using for safety since childhood. The alters who were ready to go ahead with the fusion would come there and kneel in front of Jesus. He blessed them and had them line up, facing him. Then they would unite, one at a time, if they had no drawbacks.

Some people need privacy in order to let the fusion set fully in place, but some do better talking about the new memories that come in shortly after the fusion has happened. Tricia preferred writing an account of the fusions. Beth would lay on the sofa with her eyes closed and tell me the things that the newly-fused alters had gone through.

Here is an instance of a fusion that illustrates the wonderful interconnectedness between the imagery and the memories. Beth had a difficult time seeing the alters in their human form, because they could not easily approach Jesus in her garden. There was so much physical abuse in her background that she sometimes could not get Jesus out of the perpetrator image. It worked better for her to see Him as the good shepherd, with His staff and His shepherd's robe. She would see her alters as sheep, let Jesus hand them to her, and, to complete the fusion, she would "pull" them into herself by hugging them. That happened at a rate of three or four per week for about a month.

Near the end of that period, she saw a little sheep with a black face in her garden. That was quite unusual because the others had all been without any distinctive markings—they were just white all over. This one didn't answer when asked its name, but we decided to let it be fused. After she "pulled it inside," she gained the memories of the little black-faced sheep. It was very young, probably preverbal, and there were no words to go with the memories.

As Beth lay there quietly after the fusion, she saw herself at her grandmother's house. To her shock, the grandmother had beaten her badly a few times, and now she had those memories. About the third memory that came from the newly fused, black-faced sheep's memory bank was when her grandmother had punished her for getting into the shoe polish box. The grand-mother's idea of punishment was to smear black shoe polish all over her face! It was no coincidence that this sheep had a black face—it could not talk about the experience, but it could show its bodily memory, using the visual memory of that incident. It probably would have been an easier fusion for Beth if we had let this little one work through her memories first, but with prever-bal alters, decontamination work is not as easy.

Integration is a process that leads to fusion, and then it also continues for weeks or months after fusion while the fused alters' components and memories are being lined up and combined. The memories from both alters seek each other out and negotiate with each other for a while before things are finished. For ex-ample, a child alter has a notion that dad is a very big person, and when the child is fused with the adult core, it takes time for the perceptions to be put into chronological sequence and the notions adjusted.

At the moment of fusion, the barriers between the alters come down, and everything gets combined. Once, just after a child joined the core, Beth had to leave my office right away, and her driving skills were disrupted to the point that she dented another car in our parking lot. It would have been better for her to wait until the fusion became more settled. She was forced to drive before her child-level coordination had been properly fused with her adult driving skills!

There are certain things that can occur after a fusion which help to confirm that it actually has taken place. The most common experience after a fusion is exhaustion. It is helpful to have the client's daily schedule arranged to allow for extra rest after fusions.

Another post-fusion change is that the room can seem a little brighter or darker, or colored in a slightly different hue when the client's eyes are first opened. For example, one alter brought in a green color overlay for the visual field, and others have seen things in slightly different shades or different levels of brightness. The handwriting of the new core personality contains elements of the formerly separate alters but does not quite resemble either of them. Some alters need glasses and some don't, but after the fusion process is complete it is sometimes necessary to get a brand new prescription!

Often a warm friendship develops in a system, which is understandable because the alters really did rely on one another all along, usually without knowing it. When the alters consider fusion, some expect that they will be losing friends in the process. Even if things are explained intellectually, there is an emotional reality that the alters experience—there will be a loss when all are united. Preparing for fusion should take this into account.

The alters who are getting ready for the fusion should be encouraged to go ahead despite their misgivings. Nothing will be lost. Every alter will contribute feelings and memories. Coping power will increase. Amnesia will no longer be necessary. The skills and mannerisms of each fused alter will show up from time to time, which will help with the feelings of loneliness. The feelings that go along with losing a friend are bound to pop up, but there are abundant benefits that make fusion desirable. For many of the alters who have been properly prepared, the fusion point itself is much like getting together with an old friend—that joyful mood has been called "post-integration elation." This helps compensate for the fatigue and disorientation which may develop within a few hours—the "post-fusion confusion!"

Help the client to build a core personality leading to the fusion of all the alters and fragmented part-alters. Some alters have reasons to want to remain separate, but it is generally accepted among MPD therapists that the best clinical outcome is complete unity.

At the beginning of the core-building process, it is advisible to make an agreement with the client to try to avoid creating new personalities. This may be difficult, since usually no other coping methods are available. Therefore, along with the fusion process, new methods for stress menagement need to be developed to take the place of dissociation.

When I first introduced the idea of complete fusion to one MPD client, she was rather quiet. We had come into contact with more than sixty "characters" in her system already, and she had difficulty knowing what kind of a person might result from combining them all. At our next meeting she told me that a number of the characters were against it. "They don't want to be part of that. It would be like a big pot of split-pea soup!" As her therapy progressed, she began to view fusion positively because she was seeing the ways it could help. By the time they began fusion, most of her characters were eager to "join the core personality." After her level 1 alters had joined together, she said that her mind was clearer than ever, things around the house were accomplished more easily. She was particularly glad to report that "integration" did not mean "death."

There are two tracks to unity.

(1) *If there is a lot of fragmentation, or if there is no Inner Self-Helper, or if the level 1 alters have become too contaminated, it is preferable to work through the pain before fusion.* On this track, fusion is not expected early in therapy. A much larger emphasis is placed on group decisions, group efforts and peacemaking between alters. Building a core personality is considered later.

In cases of extreme fragmentation, as is found with some SRA survivors, it is helpful to fuse the part-alters who are similar to one another, into mini-units apart from the core. This can help them do their job better. It can be a step up in general functioning for the whole system, as each sub-part gains more coping power and more information to work from. The combinations of the part-alters can be a stabilizing and morale-building influence for the whole system. Some of the personalities are quite invested in their separateness and may sabotage therapy if they are not helped to gradually accept the importance of unity. The development of this process is described nicely in *Suffer the Child.*[7]

(2) *If the most active level 1 alters are rather uncontaminated, it is preferable to take the track aimed at early fusion.* If there is an Inner Self-Helper who has a good working knowledge of the system, early fusion is possible. Identifying the Inner Self-Helper is usually fairly easy. It is often weak at the early stages of treatment and not given to social exchanges, but it is a wise observer. The Inner Self-Helper is the one who probably knows more about the client's whole life than any other alter. Befriending such a wise personality and helping him (or her) to accept the job of coordinating information can help him to gain strength within the system.[8]

If the alters are encouraged to operate separately longer than necessary, they seem to become more invested in their separateness than if they take the second track to unity. The feelings of loss are not as intense with early fusion.

However, another consideration is the degree of decontamination. If the memories have not been decontaminated prior to fusion, the upsetting feelings will be "brought into the core," and life will become more difficult. The core can get contaminated and healing is much more difficult than it would have been for the single alter simply because of the complexity. When fusion is attempted prematurely, the newly-fused alter can split off again. Sometimes it is better to let this happen so the healing process can be completed, but it can be discouraging to the client.

Unanticipated developments can take place along this track, and they need to be understood in terms of how the fusing alters' characteristics work together with each successive fusion. For Tricia, as some of the functional, non-contaminated alters were uniting, her family life became disrupted. For example, after the Good Mother alter was fused, we expected that the core Tricia would now take over the child care duties at home. Over the course of the next week, we found that child care was more taxing than ever, and she hated it!

Looking at her map, we found that Dutiful Mother had been left in charge of the children as a result of the most recent fusion, but she did not like the job of being a mother. The core Tricia was not yet ready to take over the mothering job. "I resent the kids, and I just want to stay in bed all day!"

I suggested to Dutiful Mother that she could get some help with her child care duties if she chose to fuse with the inner core, "Tricia," as Good Mother had. She agreed to give it a try, and the fusion process in her meadow went smoothly. I encouraged "Tricia" to go ahead and get involved with the "everyday parenting routine."

"If somebody else gets hooked, someone who is not ready for parenting," I said, "things could get a lot worse." The core Tricia saw the importance of being in charge of the children and decided she would get involved. That turned out to be a successful intervention, and her children were in better hands.

At this point along the second track to fusion, we need to review and look a little more closely at level 1 and level 2 alters, particularly their relationship to the fusing process.

For most higher-functioning clients, level 1 alters are not usually as contaminated as the others. They do their jobs but are protected from knowing how painful life has been for the level 2 alters. Most of the level 2 alters are separated by amnesia from the first level because they are the ones who have been traumatized. They may be completely amnesic to everyone else, which makes them think they are the only person when they come into executive control of the body. They know about their own painful life episodes, but become disoriented when they appear in the therapist's office. They have been used to getting a "hook" for a particular kind of experience, which is when they do their job. That is all they know. It is important to emphasize that these will not show up in therapy unless things are safe and unless they are encouraged to make an appearance.

A male level 2 alter showed up in my office one day—right in the middle of a session with Beth—and he could not make sense of things. Many of the other level 2 alters already had been befriended, but neither the client nor I had previously known about Frank. He was a 12-year-old boy in the body of a 30-year-old woman. He had been waiting for eighteen years to get a cue, and when it came he expected to be in the principal's office.

"Are you the principal? Am I in trouble again?"

"No. Everything is fine. You can just take your time and we can get to know each other for a little while."

He looked at his arms and then at his body, and then at his dress, and got somewhat upset. "Who are you, and what is going on here?"

I asked if he knew what year it was, and he said it was 1970. The story unfolded that Frank had gotten in trouble at school all the time. He was rebellious, which was an appropriate 12-year-old's response to the confusion of his amnesia-riddled school life. He spent lots of time in the principal's office and no time in the classroom. About that time, another boy took over his slot by taking a scientific, non-emotional approach to things, like Mr. Spock on *Star Trek*. That kept him out of trouble better than being rebellious. Frank had not been needed in all that time, and was totally disoriented now. After a few minutes of letting him tell me about himself, I asked him if his body was as he remembered.

Frank was working very hard to understand the entirely alien experience taking place. "What is this, some kind of trick or something?"

I casually mentioned that it was 1988, and he needed to know about a few things. I asked if he could hear any inside voices, maybe the voice of the core personality. He did, and that laid the way for me to explain about MPD, and about amnesia. I got out a blank sheet of paper, made a few diagrams about how systems operate, and Frank was welcomed up to level 1. It took a few meetings before he got things worked out with the other alters in level 1, but he turned out to be a good team player. He was able to accept things according to the explanations of the other alters. They had already learned a lot about MPD, and about working together as a system.

Most of the multiples I have seen need about five to ten level 1 alters, who help get each other through the day. There is a host, an Observer, an Inner Self-Helper, and some who are needed for parts of the regular routines of life. These can switch back and forth as necessary, and there is no reason for them to expect that there is anything other than level 1. MPD is virtually undiagnosable when level 1 alters are filling their slots appropriately.

When stress forces one of the level 2 alters into action, diagnosis is easier. The routine is broken, some amnesia appears and some disorientation sets in until a new slot can be established for the person, who is then incorporated into the level 1 routines. If this cannot happen, the recently accessed alter recedes back to level 2, and the slot is not opened up. About ten seems to be the ceiling for the number of level 1 slots that can be opened up for effective living.

If therapy uncovers too many active alters from level 2, there will not be enough slots to go around, and functioning can break down. The level 1 alters will not be able to set up the sequence for the day and maintain it because there are just too many personalities on the scene. Pandemonium is produced, and things resemble more of a brawl than equilibrium. This is why it is important to go slowly. If there is a big system, equilibrium is maintained only when things go slowly.

Knowing about the two levels and the limited number of slots, we can begin building the core personality. For the second track, it is best to get the uncontaminated level 1 alters to fuse fairly early. That produces a core personality which has a good understanding of daily routines. It is to be expected that after fusion occurs a slot will open up, and another alter from level 2 will soon fill it. This will be upsetting because new traumatic memories will likely surface with the level 2 alter, and those will be difficult for the core to accept. The memories are truly unknown to the core, and the core often objects, saying that the new "memories" cannot be true! "There must be some other way to explain things, because those awful things could not have happened to me!"

At that point, the client usually feels it would be easier to stop therapy than to deal with the guilt-producing memories borne by the level 2 alters. That is why it is good to build strength by fusing the level 1 alters prior to level 2 work. Each alter has a certain amount of coping power, and after they are fused they possess the total of their combined power. They will likely need all the coping power they can get when they are in the middle of level 2 memories.

Work closely with the Inner Self-Helper to plan the fusions. Take into account the degree of contamination of each alter, and the degree of similarity between those to be fused. Many times there are male-female pairs with quite similar jobs, which makes it easier for them to fuse into the core at the same time.

In many cases the Victim alters have one or more Protectors. Do not fuse a Protector before the Victim has been helped and fused. The Protector alters should be among the final ones to join the core.

It is a good idea to keep the Inner Self-Helpers and Observers in their slots, so that they can keep giving updates about how the system is reacting to all the changes.

There is a sense of accomplishment whenever a fusion takes place. The hard work that has been undertaken to prepare for it and its actually happening are cause for celebration. However, it is easy to load the integration/fusion process with too much importance. The heart of therapy is the decontamination process. These people have to do serious psychotherapy with many of their alters—there is no short-cut. Noxious feelings and post-traumatic symptoms have to be worked through. Unity is the goal, but it is a long way off, especially for the alters who have suffered so much.

In order to keep equilibrium intact as much as possible while the level 2 alters are getting help, it is important to use the amnesia to protect the host from getting overwhelmed.

If possible, get the decontamination process under way during the therapy session without the host knowing the particulars. The host will need to go to work after the session, and therefore needs some protection from too many negative feelings. If the host realizes the need for this kind of protection, it can be agreed that it is okay if he or she doesn't know everything that has been going on for the last hour. "Please let me spend some more time with the level 2 alter I just talked to before I tell you his story. You don't want to share his feelings yet. Let me work with him on his feelings first so you can keep up your concentration while you are at work."

It is almost with pride that the host acknowledges there is decontamination going on which he knows nothing about. With a smile, he may say, "I know it is better for the comforter alters to work with level 2. I need to keep the money coming in. Everybody depends on me to pay the bills, so I'd better not know too much about level 2."

If all the memories and feelings were to rush into the core being developed, the host could disappear. When that happens, clients tend to lose their jobs, get hospitalized, or stay in bed for days on end. Don't overwhelm the host.

It has been said by some that after unity has been achieved, the result is single personality disorder instead of multiple personality disorder. That may be what is found by researchers who work with MPD clients with low DAs, but my observations have been different.

It appears to me that after unity is achieved, including careful work in decontamination, the person will be functioning at the level of the most healthy alter. In other words, if the person has a good DA and has a healthy group of personalities on level 1, the level 2 personalities will tend to rise and function about as high as the level 1 alters. So if a person's position on the Figure 5 matrix is at 2, therapy may not need to continue very long after unity has been achieved.

On the other hand, if the client's position is at 6, there may be a single personality disorder after unity is achieved. However, it remains a personality disorder after fusion because there was a low level of mental health among the level 1 alters in the first place, and not because the final whole person is the sum total of its unhealthy parts. My observation is that the person's adaptability and capacity for intimacy are dependent on how well the level 1 alters have been functioning, and how successful the decontamination process has been.

ACCEPT DISTORTION

Although, as is indicated on Figure 5, dissociation can protect some alters from distortion, this is not necessarily true of level 2 alters. Many of them contain substantial amounts of distortion. In general, integration and decontamination tend to clear up distortion, particularly if there are healthy alters prepared to be coconscious with the distortion-overlaid alters.

The most blatant examples of distortion that I am aware of involve SRA perpetrators. The cult members do things to child alters that play havoc with their sense of reality, intentionally producing a lot of distortion. Two SRA adult survivors gave me similar accounts about their "resurrection" during the same week. They were given sleeping pills just before they were placed in a coffin and lowered into a grave. They lost consciousness while hearing shovelfulls of dirt landing on the lid. When they woke up the next day, all cleaned up at home, they were told that Satan had chosen them, and had raised them up from the dead— and that they owed the rest of their lives to him.

As cult children, they had observed other children being offered to Satan as sacrifices. They were then given a choice of being sacrificed or of signing their name with their own blood in the big black book, which would guarantee them a place in hell that was not as hot as most places. It was not hard to decide. They signed.

That is a gross distortion.

They still believed—as adults—that they had sealed their fate when they were only children, and that they were therefore hopelessly on the road to hell.

Other distortions SRA victims are subjected to involve going through rituals where they get married to demons or to Satan, and those are also used to convince children that their fate is sealed. Such distortion produces hopelessness and despair, and it must be broken during therapy. Distortion-ridden child alters need to be informed about reality by the level 1 personalities so they can gradually come to understand that the cult people play dirty tricks on kids.

Other kinds of distortions occur in unpremeditated ways. They involve manipulation and deceitful behavior patterns developed by the victim for stress management, on the basis of distorted perceptions. Usually these patterns show up in the child alters or in the more poorly protected adult alters, and they decrease substantially after unity is achieved. They get combined with better reality assessment from the other alters, which promotes the post-fusion part of the integration process. Clearing up distortion is one of the ways in which the injured alters gain health, and because it is facilitated through fusion/integration, the unified individual is healthier than the pre-fused alters.

In general, it is probably not a good idea to try to talk an alter out of a distortion. Keep the positive, supportive posture going. If reality is revisited, and if healthier alters can be called upon to help assess the reality, the solution will come from within the individual's system.

TREATMENT FOR
OTHER KINDS OF DISSOCIATION

Non-Amnesic Dissociation (NAD)

Diagnostic and Statistical Manual of Mental Disorders (third edition, revised),[9] the most recent standard for psychological diagnoses, does not specify that amnesia must be present in the diagnosis of MPD. NAD clients need a treatment approach that is different from the approach for those with amnesia. After we became familiar with multiplicity, the minimal progress over a long period of time in a few very difficult cases at our clinic began to make sense to me. These clients had distinctive "characters," or "ego states," and they showed clear signs of the mesa response, but they indicated no evidence of amnesia.

After we found no guidelines for working with "non-amnesic multiples," we decided to try using the same interventions that we were were using with the amnesic multiples. Here is a brief, preliminary overview of what seems to be successful and what seems to fail in working with NAD clients.

The goal is to get their characters to communicate with each other about feelings. Since they already know about their life history—they have not dissociated the "mind component"—it is usually not difficult to help them remember the traumatic events in their life. Neither is it difficult to trace the experiences of each character.

The tough thing is to get the characters to share their feelings with each other without switching—the feelings tend to stay in their separate compartments, the characters. Most of the characters can express their feelings but they have little capacity to empathize with each other. The degree of improvement for these clients seems directly proportional to the amount of empathy the characters achieve with one another. Developing a cast of characters and a map and doing some role playing and journaling for each character seem to be effective in promoting intra-system empathy, particularly for clients with a high DA.

The most common therapeutic obstacle we have encountered at our clinic with lower-functioning NADs is that they have a very strong protective character, usually a Critical Parent. NAD clients do not appear to have an Observer character in the system. If there were amnesia present, an observer alter would need to be developed to try to keep track of things. The absence of such an alter means that when it comes to particular issues, there is not much of a "reality check" on the feelings of the characters.

The stubbornness can get very strong when the Critical Parent character gets engaged. This character can make attacking remarks about the other characters in the system and can be highly critical of the work the therapist is doing! The Critical Parent has a lot to protect as the system is exposed to close scrutiny—the other characters would like to take away that one's power. That is a big problem—the others are tired of the perfectionism the Critical Parent has utilized in running the system, and a power struggle within the system often develops around whether it is acceptable to make mistakes! The Critical Parent can start complaining about the cost of therapy or find a weakness in the therapist, and it may even use its power to drop out of therapy if its empathy for the other characters does not develop.

It appears that this character's intensity often makes the therapist feel like moving *back* from the client while it is doing its best to carry out its role in its angry way. At that point, I believe it is helpful to move my chair *toward* the client and relate to the perspective being shared, even if the perspective is that I am being an insensitive therapist.

"I know how disgusting it feels to have things happen like that. Doctors disappoint me too. You pay them all that money, and what do you get? Now I'm not saying I'm a lousy doctor, and you should dump me, but I do know how it is when people disappoint me."

I try to get the Critical Parent to talk with the other characters in a role-playing exercise. During the time it is showing intense anger directed at the others, help it "hook up" the "body awareness" dissociation component with the feelings. This begins to erode that amnesia that the characters have for each other's feelings. As long as the feeling component remains dissociated between this character and the others, the attacks on them will continue. However, some physical contact with the NADs while they are in their critical state tends to break through the emotional dissociation that is blocking the internal empathy.

Here is how that works. If the therapist or a significant other person can hold the NAD's hand or put an arm around her (or him) while she is angry, it tends to put her in contact with feelings other than anger. This is not a particularly revolutionary intervention, but it shows how the components of dissociations tend to split into layers and therefore need to be re-attached. This intervention has been effective in our clinic, so it looks like the dissociation model has led to the development of better treatment for NAD clients. (This conceptual advance for treatment with NADs appears to help also in treatment with borderline personality clients, as will be discussed later in this section.)

When NAD clients have a very high DA, it can be difficult for them to stay in therapy very long, because their NAD method of coping works well enough to limp along in life without having a major breakdown. If it is strictly up to their Critical Parent, therapy is usually abandoned before major progress is achieved. NAD clients tend to dodge their negative feelings rather than go through the painful work of facing them. They appear to rely on the dissociation of feelings as their only coping method. When strong negative feelings surface (the feelings that initiated the dissociative process in the first place), it seems that their plane is going down in flames and they have no choice but to bail out. For clients with high DAs, the NAD response is almost like a knee-jerk—they do not know how to react any other way. Their motivation to stay in therapy will need to be very high in order to go through the painful process of sharing negative feelings throughout the whole system.

NAD clients tend to mistrust their therapist. The Critical Parent keeps deep feelings from emerging, which usually stops the therapist from bonding with the wounded characters. The NAD system wants to function as it always has, under the direction of the Critical Parent who works very hard to maintain control. Be careful not to push for quick change.

There should be no mention of frightening terms, like "partial amnesia," or "NAD." It is *not* necessary to have these people accept the diagnosis, as that almost always upsets the Critical Parent too much, and the therapist is even more mistrusted. It is preferable to carry out therapy without telling the client about the dissociative framework. Be honest with the alters about their divideness, and be genuine in carrying out the interventions that seem to help promote empathy between the characters, but do not talk about multiplicity. Without flashbacks or unusual perceptual experiences, the dynamics are very different from totally amnesic experiences.

Therapy does not need to take an "informational" approach, as is the case with total amnesia. Life is not fraught with as many surprises for NADs as it is with MPDs, so the information which helps assure the MPD that she is not crazy after all is not necessary for the NAD. It is more important for the client with NAD to maintain that she is not really very different from an average person.

Non-Confrontation

Non-confrontation and the rest of the positive approach interventions are necessary because NAD clients are really much more fragile than they appear. As is the case for dissociators who have amnesia, they profit most when the therapist goes slowly and makes good connections with many of their characters.

Some of our clients who were initially diagnosed as NADs were later found to have a few fully-amnesic alters. The level 1 (NAD) characters were quite unaware of the abuse that had been hidden, and the dissociative processes were not uncovered very early. There were no headaches or dizziness, or any of the other symptoms that signal the presence of amnesia. Only after some therapeutic progress was made among the level 1 characters were the dissociated alters discovered.

As was mentioned in chapter 5, the varieties of dissociative symptoms are almost endless. MPD is a disorder based on creative ability, so a system can develop to fit practically any circumstance. As one of my colleagues puts it, "MPD is a 'create-your-own-disorder disorder'!" When the DA is very high and the client has a safe living environment, the client's system can remain in a stable equilibrium over a wide range of life's circumstances as we have seen by the dissociative arrangements depicted on Figure 5. Level 1 may be able to handle practically any circumstance which makes the other alters miss their cues. Degrees of amnesia, partial amnesias and micro-dissociations, produce many kinds of dissociating systems.

It seems that a key to unlocking the diagnostic mystery in any particular case is to utilize the client's DA in treatment. When the person uses art therapy, or engages in making a map for the characters, or utilizes some imagery during therapy, what usually results is that the little-known characters show up and express their opinions and get their feelings considered—to the surprise of the more active alters. This brings internal conflicts into focus for the whole system, and the well-functioning equilibrium is challanged. When an NAD client's very high DA becomes evident, it is more likely that a fully amnesic alter will be uncovered at some point during treatment.

Traumatic Dissociation (TD)

The TD alters are created if the first trauma/dissociation episode occurred after about age 6. For example, when a client's family member dies, a character can be created to contain the loss feelings, and can be fully dissociated or partially dissociated even if other coping methods have already been established. When other coping methods are available to the child, the level of trauma necessary to produce a dissociation is higher, but even then a violent enough trauma or a serious enough tragedy can produce some kind of dissociation.

From the observations we on the MPD team have made, it appears that traumatic dissociators do not usually have as high a DA as NADs, and the NADs do not usually have DAs as high as the MPDs do. In different ways for each diagnosis, when the feelings are shared across the system, progress will occur. The TD alters need a lot of decontamination (ventilation and validation) and help with the feelings produced by their traumas to prevent them from interfering with the client's daily routines. Some flashbacks and headaches/dizziness may occur when the TD alters are uncovered, so some explanations about partial dissociations or even about traumatic dissociations may help the client to understand these unusual experiences.

There can be many combinations of traumatically dissociated alters, non-amnesic alters, part-alters (alter fragments), and fully-dissociated alters within a system, so the therapist should keep conclusions tentative, when examining NAD or TD systems. Fully-dissociated episodes can appear in NAD and TD systems, as therapy runs its course.

When the client has serious doubts as to the accurateness of the memories, care should be given to keep her (or him) informed about how dissociation works, and how some dissociated characters get distortions in their memories. The assurance should be given that it is inevitable for dissociated memories to feel "like they didn't happen to me." The memories should get more realistic and more distortion-free as therapy progresses.

Even though despair can be strong at some points in therapy, the outcome is expected to be positive. The dissociation framework provides an effective direction for therapy, but the therapeutic work itself remains difficult for client and therapist alike. There is no substitute for patient, thorough therapy to deal with the after-effects of serious traumatization. The investment is great, but so is the reward.

Borderline Personality (BP)

BP is a diagnostic category that has always been controversial. Colin Ross has provided a good discussion of the history and features of BP, which concludes that it is best understood as a kind of dissociative disorder.[10] The most convincing point I find in his discussion is that what BP theorists have called "splitting," is virtually identical to what MPD theorists call "dissociating."

As is illustrated on Figure 5, I believe that when a traumatized person is not very adept at using dissociation and can barely manage to split life's experiences into two categories, good and bad, the person develops BP. If they were better dissociators, they would have coped better; they would have had more categories for their experiences and may have been able to protect a healthy group of level 1 alters. It makes sense to understand BP as a primitive kind of partial dissociation. Serious abuse is not effectively dealt with by using partial dissociation or other less effective coping methods. The way I see it, if a person can use dissociation only a little bit, that will not be enough to deal with chronic, family-related abuse. Other kinds of coping methods, which are often used by BP clients, will be added, like repression, manipulation of others and the histrionic acting out of feelings.

Although Dr. Ross has provided the conceptual framework to understand BP as a dissociative disorder, his book does not provide guidelines for treating the BP or the other types of dissociative disorders. BP therapists' customary expectation is that a BP client will need many years of therapy, three to five times weekly, and that even then the recovery rate is not high. They fail to make progress for years!

For MPDs, an early study found that clients averaged almost seven years in therapy, with very little progress before they received the correct diagnosis. The inference was that until they were treated for their dissociative disorder, they made practically no progress in therapy.

I wonder if BP clients wouldn't respond to treatment better if they were treated according to therapeutic principles for dissociating clients. It appears that when BP clients receive the kind of interventions described above for NAD clients, developing empathy between the "good" and the "bad" characters, they tend to improve. The therapist tends to receive a high level of hostility from the bad character who does not want to be empathic, but progress nonetheless seems to take place.

It will be important to discover whether these trends can be verified. If BP clients fail to make much progress until they are treated for their dissociation, therapists need to know that. More important, since the clients' welfare is at stake, therapists need to determine whether dissociative therapy helps BP clients better than traditional, confrontive approaches.

CONTINUE THERAPY
BEYOND THE FINAL FUSION

After Beth had completed her therapy, she evaluated it with me. She helped me to understand something I had read about and that I was observing in other MPD clients. Level 2 alters can be so well hidden that they may not be found until after the "last ones" had fused. An empty slot in the almost-empty system and a stressor that resembles the cue for the hidden alter will very likely bring another alter out. Headaches, time loss or mesa-like feelings indicate that there is another one to meet. It is extremely disappointing, maybe even one of the lowest points in treatment, to achieve what seems to be the final fusion, and then later find that there is at least one more hidden alter left to bring into the system.

"I thought I was finished! Then when the new alters appeared, I didn't want to tell you. I pretended as long as I could, until I just had to deal with them. I don't know how many there are—will this go on forever?"

Beth first found a cluster of teenage alters and a cluster of preschool alters, and then one or two more would show up every month or so until the end. We started off by fusing the original eighteen and thought she had completed things. We began to talk about discontinuing therapy, and a rejection-laden alter with enormous amounts of sadness made her presence known.

Then it was nearly a year and a half later before the final alter, Windy, made her appearance. Windy told us that she had been waiting for the rest of the alters to unite and get healthy before she was ready to show herself. She had a great personality and a great self-image, and we had to promise her three pairs of new shoes before she could be persuaded to fuse with Beth. She had been observing me during therapy for quite a while and had come to trust me enough to follow my advice to join with the others.

It had gotten to the point where Beth and I both began to wonder how many more alters there could be hidden in level 2. After Windy's fusion no others appeared, and Beth's sessions were thinned out to one each month for about six months. By that time she had been through some heavy stress, had made fine progress in a new career, and was a very healthy person. There were no more alters to be encountered. She was happy, healthy and whole! What a tremendous accomplishment. As had been the case with Chris Sizemore, Beth had reached her potential, which revealed that she is a splendid individual.

It seems that nearly everyone who reaches the "end" of the fusion process finds there are some alters who have remained well hidden, so the best guarantee that the integrative work is complete is to remain in therapy. The despair-causing thing about these later alters, is that they are usually more seriously injured and therefore more plagued with negative feelings than the previously met alters. The thicker the amnesia is, the more difficult the material tends to be. Beth found that the final alters turned out to have the most powerful feelings, and she needed good coping skills to even stay in therapy. What a paradox! She had made all that progress, and felt worse than ever until each one was decontaminated and fused.

Beth had been developing coping skills other than dissociation during the course of her therapy. Group therapy turned out to be a good arena for developing her self-confidence, and that helped greatly in her new career.

She had also worked through a treatment trap—rejection. Beth had learned in her family of origin to pair good feelings about people with impending rejection. Things had always fallen apart on her when she got close to people, with the exception of her husband, and when she talked through the rejection feelings, she was headed toward more fulfilling relationships. She found herself getting closer to healthier people, and she enjoyed the out-going side of her personality quite a lot. She also learned to accept compliments and to compliment herself. When the most difficult alters were encountered, she did not need to switch out of her core alter, because she had learned more effective ways of coping.

Learning to live with ambivalence was another accomplishment for Beth—one that must be achieved along the road to fusion. Alters usually have one feeling, and *only* one feeling. That is how they always operated, and that is all they needed. Whenever another feeling was called for, the alter who dealt with that feeling switched in. Alters know their particular feeling, and they know when it is needed, so the appropriate alter is usually engaged. A tough problem that is encountered as the core personality is consolidated is to learn how to deal with more than one feeling.

The definition of *ambivalence* is understood by looking at the two parts of the word. *Valence* is a force, or a power exerting an influence, like gravity, for example. *Ambi* is more than one. *Ambivalence* is the presence of more than one feeling—more than one incompatible feeling—exerting an influence. People who are not dissociators are used to that—that is the way they have always lived.

However, to the multiple, ambivalence is hardly a "pay-off" for a good job done in therapy! It is difficult for these people to tolerate the presence of more than one feeling, but when they do develop that skill, it helps a lot. At first, ambivalence is not a pay-off because it is so uncomfortable, but after the core has gotten quite a few feelings brought in, the new feelings do not stick out as conspicuously as they would if there were only one or two other feelings in the core.

A major goal of post-fusion therapy is to help the client establish a history of success as a unified person. While the person had been divided, projects were almost never carried out to completion, and fulfilling relationships were rare. After the unity is achieved, a strategic problem is faced: The individual alters had few experiences of success, and now that they have pooled their experiences, the problem emerges that nobody brought self-confidence into the unified core. It is helpful to point out experiences of success and to make the development of self-confidence a stated goal while the former multiple is trying out new skills.

SCIENCE AND CHRISTIANITY

When I was studying psychology at the master's level, one of the professors and I had a discussion about the history of psychology, and I mentioned that I am a Christian. He asked if I came from a Christian home, and when I said yes, he said he is convinced that some people believe in God because they were taught that as children. He went on to say that he believes someday everyone will be won over to the scientific point of view. I was in no position to debate with him, so I just left the subject alone with him after that. He is among those popular science proponents who have placed their faith strictly in science.

Contrary to the popular scientific position, though, I do not believe science is opposed to religion. The scientific method is simply a way of gathering data and reaching conclusions, a way to make sense out of what we see and hear. The problem I see with some scientists is that they have incorrectly placed themselves in the atheistic category. That is incorrect, because they do believe in science. It is their religion. They have used the theories of evolution and the "big bang" to make sense out of history, and out of their experience. "Survival of the fittest," "selective breeding" and "the expanding universe" have been adopted as their guidelines to give life meaning. Also, people who have made science their religion take the stance that there can be no such thing as a spirit because it isn't "scientific."

To take a "science as religion" approach, is to say that things are not always as they appear, and need to be understood in ways that fit into particular laws of science. In other words, a "science as religion" person rejects whatever cannot be fit into his or her framework. However, a pure scientist is open to whatever is true, even if it doesn't fit a framework. The true scientist is eager to expand horizons. Here is the point:

The existence of the human spirit and of a creator-spirit does not deny the validity of scientific method.

It is possible to gather data about the spirit world and about God without abandoning our hope of making sense out of things. Scientific method does not automatically deny that there is a spirit world.

If I want to believe in God and believe in things that cannot be seen, that doesn't automatically make me anti-scientific. It is possible to be faithful in gathering data and still to believe in God. A true scientist does not have to hold on to science as a religion, because the scientific method does not automatically block out belief in God.

I take a "pure" scientific approach—I want to be open to all the data, without fitting them into a narrow framework. When it comes to religion, I am open about what I believe. I believe that God made everything, and that ever since the fall of man, He has been in the process of reclaiming this planet. I believe that He has called people to join His Kingdom and to participate in reclaiming it. Part of reclaiming it is to carry out spiritual warfare against Satan and his servants. There is abundant meaning to life—to love God and to be loved by God, and to be part of His Kingdom, which means spreading goodness each day and taking a stand against evil. It is an exceedingly wonderful feeling to see God at work, using the citizens in His Kingdom to defeat evil, while reclaiming the earth.

PART THREE:
SPIRITUAL RESTORATION

7

GOD'S PERSPECTIVE

UNCOVERING THE CLUES

WHEN MY CLIENT'S boyfriend called me at two o'clock in the morning and said, "My girlfriend has just been levitated onto the bed from the floor; she's in some kind of bizarre trance, and I'm scared to death!" should I have believed him?

Child Abuse

A few decades ago no one would have believed anything like that. In fact, practically no psychologist even believed that child abuse, something we are quite familiar with today, would happen to more than one child in a thousand. When children were brought into hospitals with multiple bone fractures, the doctors and nurses believed the parents—just a slight fall produced the serious injury! Some doctors came up with theories that there must be some form of genetic bone deficiency to account for the fractures, but hardly anyone believed that they were looking at child abuse. Denial of the obvious was taking place. We would have had to conclude that craziness or evil abounded in our society in order to face the fact that child abuse could be so widespread.

So the denial was maintained. People did not have to change their ways of thinking. The belief was held that most families are like those portrayed on television. *Leave It to Beaver* and *My Three Sons* were thought to typify the American way of life. It was a breach of public trust to talk about child abuse. "That is not nice, and it surely does not happen around here!" People who brought child abuse up in therapy were not believed. Society had a lot to lose if child abuse became a topic of open discussion. Why, that would challenge our cultural identity, so the clues about its incidence remained uninvestigated.

But therapists began discovering the truth. Child abuse turned out to be much more rampant than anybody had thought. Clues were brought together, studies were made and society's consciousness was raised. The cultural illusion about family safety was dispelled, and the first part of the roller-coaster ride had been completed—child abuse victims were finally believed, and protection measures appeared.

In the 1960s many states passed laws which made it mandatory for therapists to report any instances of suspected child abuse to the police. Within a few years so much of it was reported, that the nature of the mental health profession was irreversibly changed. Child abuse prevention programs were developed, abusing parents got into treatment, and therapists either reported child abuse or faced the loss of their clinical license. The mental health organizations had become instruments of change for society.

Incest

In the 1970s incest came into focus. Even in the '60s, when child abuse was finally talked about, almost nobody was talking about incest. One of my adult clients told me she had been sexually abused by her parent as a preteenager during the '70s. Her behavior had become unruly at the time so she was taken to a psychologist to see what the problem might be. When she told the therapist about the incest, she was rudely asked why she was making up such a terrible lie!

That was the mood of the times. We could then admit to a high incidence of child abuse, but incest was too awful to think about.

Thankfully, that attitude changed, too, and over a period of time programs were developed to help adult survivors of incest—those who before had kept quiet about their horrible childhood traumas. The consciousness of our culture had been raised another notch. We could now talk about incest, and society was becoming more compassionate. As a result of the consciousness raising, it is now more accurately estimated that approximately 25 to 35 percent of women were sexually abused as children! It is about time women are believed when they describe what happened to them in their early years.

MPD

During the 1980s our awareness about the effects of physical and sexual abuses continued to grow and another notch was reached. From the offices of well-respected therapists and researchers came stories that are still doubted by some. These were stories of extreme abuse, but many of them were not verifiable because they came from very early in childhood. They were the kind of stories that used to be dismissed as demented fantasy. Now they began to have a ring of truth to them because they fit into a specific syndrome. When adult survivors of extreme childhood abuse got deeper into therapy, increasing numbers of therapists found that the syndrome known as multiple personality disorder (MPD) was much more widespread than anyone had thought possible. A group of survivors of sexual abuse has helped us see that MPD is a distinctly identifiable pattern, and thousands of therapists are now being trained in its diagnosis and treatment. It is wonderful to know that some of those who have fallen prey to such serious abuse are now able to find help for their suffering.

SRA

As psychology becomes increasingly willing to accept the emerging data about MPD, it is getting ready for the next phase of the roller-coaster ride. Some therapists are talking now about the potential for evil that exists in human beings. We are facing the fact that genocide and holocausts happen, not only to people in some long-ago century or some far-away country, but also over all time and across the whole world because people are capable of perpetrating evil. Mass murders, random crimes, unexplained disappearances and worldwide terrorism are harder to ignore. Millions have suffered and even perished from violence in China, Cambodia, the Middle East and parts of Africa, to name only a few.

Those acts were carried out by human beings against other human beings, and we have recently discovered that human beings in contemporary North America also are carrying out cruel, evil acts. More people have died in Los Angeles as the result of gang violence than have died in Northern Ireland's years of civil war! More than a hundred preschools in California have been reported to the police on charges of grotesque abuse, and that represents only the tip of the iceberg of evil allegedly perpetrated against young children. Adult survivors have told therapists of identical abuse practices in more than forty of the United States and across Canada!

We are not talking about spanking the children too hard, or about the use of excessive forms of punishment. We are talking about children reporting that they were drugged, terrorized and subjected to horrifying abuse, and that they witnessed the murder of animals and of other children during ceremonies of Satan worship. They have reported satanic ritual abuse (SRA). Psychology needs to help society come to grips with the denial of the frightening fact that human beings are capable of such acts. Of course they are. Look at history, and look at the news today. Events described by international news media and events described in offices of prominent therapists are leading us further along. We are facing human evil, and we are finding it darker and more widespread than we want to believe.

Even though our awareness continues to lead psychology into deeper levels of discovery, therapists still find only a few places to talk about SRA. In the 1990s, we therapists are becoming more candid about the SRA events uncovered in our offices, and we hope to help society focus on this issue. Society improved when it came to grips with the truth about child abuse. It improved when it came to grips with the truth about incest. For those with MPD, society is a better place because it is now generally okay to talk about multiplicity.

However, it is not yet evident that people are ready to face the heinous human evil being uncovered in clients' SRA memories. Some believe it to be dangerous for therapists to expose it, and sometimes it appears to be dangerous for clients who tell about their experiences, because of the potential for retaliation from the alleged perpetrators. Despite these dangers, a growing number of therapists are talking about SRA as openly as they can. The truth is becoming harder for society to ignore. The roller-coaster ride is getting more scary, but we are not about to get off!

Here is why I believe SRA will be the next level in society's consciousness-raising journey: Studies indicate that approximately 25 percent of those with MPD in North America have been subjected to SRA, and SRA is why they developed MPD in the first place. The dissociation of MPD is the best way children have of dealing with the trauma. In my discussions with Southern California MPD therapists, I have found a consensus that 25 percent is a low estimate. Many of us believe the percentage is much higher, at least in our own region. I have heard estimates as high as 50 to 60 percent! It is hard to believe, but there may be 100,000 people or more in the United States who were subjected to SRA as children! That is extremely disconcerting.

Therapists are learning to treat SRA survivors, but not from books or articles. For some reason—I think it is fear—most therapists do not want to become known as experts in helping SRA survivors, so they do not write about their experiences. In fact, it is amazing to me that even the most prominent therapists in the MPD field are devoting almost no articles or books to SRA. About the only place SRA education takes place is in seminars, newsletters, and conferences, where people are finally getting brave enough to talk about it. It looks like SRA is an important issue for the 1990s, and therapists who devote themselves to writing about it will help all of us face the enormity of the issue.

SPIRITUAL INTERVENTIONS

Maybe I am getting too far ahead of society's journey for people to believe me. Maybe I am too far out on a limb for people to take me seriously. Nonetheless, it looks to me like the next issue which will come out of Pandora's box, right into the middle of the field of psychology, will be "spiritual interventions." As MPD therapists have come to a fuller understanding of how incredibly complex the human mind is, we are finding that the realm of the spirit is an important part of healing.

It appears to me that after MPD is believed, and after SRA is understood, psychology will have to take into account that demonic appearances, levitations and some other pretty non-scientific-sounding things have been observed in the context of worshiping Satan. Clients will have to be believed when they speak of the satanic forces they have observed in SRA rituals.

Just two weeks ago a memory came to a client during her therapy in my office which fits this pattern. She remembered lying flat on a table, surrounded by hooded cultists, being dedicated to Satan. She could scarcely believe what her mind was telling her. She later described to me how the high priest was repeating some chant in another language when a demon materialized. It came out of the priest, dove into her, and her whole body flinched as it entered her. She was then told she would never be able to escape the demon's control, and it would make certain that she would be a cult member for her whole life.

She had so much trouble accepting the accuracy of the memory when it came to her that she did not risk telling me at that time. When she mustered up enough courage to tell me all about it at the next session, she initially believed I would doubt the story, and she was relieved to find out I did not. Between those sessions, she had been obsessed with the message that she constantly heard in her head, that nobody would believe what she had remembered. She took the risk of telling me only because she feared she was going crazy.

Imagine what happens to people like her when they open up and then their therapist says there must be some other explanation! My hope is that that kind of response will be eliminated, because too many similar stories are being told to discount them all.

Evident Need

It is becoming more and more evident that SRA survivors need their therapy to include spiritual as well as psychological interventions. Many survivors know that they have been dedicated to Satan, and part of their therapy must involve spiritual restoration. The clinical results look promising at present, so I hope the journey will be continued and spiritual restoration will become accepted as a valid part of the therapeutic process. This may not happen until the 21st century, but I hope that therapists in the meantime will keep their eyes open and try not to be dominated by a purely "scientific" mindset.

Let's keep gathering the scattered clues that will help clinical psychology continue its transformation. People need to know about child abuse, incest, MPD and SRA so the survivors can be helped. People need to know they will be believed when they call their therapist at two o'clock in the morning to say their girlfriend was just levitated onto the bed from the floor, is in some kind of bizarre trance, and they are scared to death. When scientifically unexplainable things like that occur, psychology needs to broaden its boundaries, and let the journey continue.

Psychology has a lot of hard work ahead. It must sharpen its focus to bring more effective healing to people who have survived grotesque childhood traumas, and it must delve more deeply into the riches of the human psyche and spirit.

Clues to Psychological/Spiritual Restoration

In the remainder of this book I hope to bring some of the clues together that will shed light on the interconnectedness between psychological and spiritual restoration. I trust that it will be a contribution to society's on-going transformation. We have not yet finished the roller-coaster ride, and we must be determined to stay on board. In order to do that, therapists will have to follow courageously wherever the truth leads.

THE BATTLE IS THE LORD'S

The ancient land of Israel did not always flourish as the "Promised Land," flowing with milk and honey, that the Lord had given to His people. Some years after Moses led the exodus out of Egypt, before Israel became the earth's most powerful nation under king David's leadership, the Israelites "did evil in the eyes of the Lord, and for seven years He gave them into the hands of the Midianites." These Midianites invaded the Promised Land, ransacked it, and destroyed the Israelites' crops and animals.[1] They "came up with their livestock and their tents like swarms of locusts. It was impossible to count the men and their camels; they invaded the land to ravage it." The Israelites were driven from their homes, and survived by fleeing to the mountains, where they stayed in shelters and caves. Not only did the Midianites severely oppress God's people, but they served an idol named Baal, whose worship involved infant sacrifice.

The Baal worshipers' sacrifice of their children was a terrible offense to the God of Israel, and He promised to bring punishment on them:

> This is what the LORD Almighty, the God of Israel,
> says: Listen! I am going to bring a disaster on this
> place that will make the ears of everyone who hears
> of it tingle. For they have forsaken me and made this
> a place of foreign gods; they have burned sacrifices in
> it to gods that neither they nor their fathers nor the
> kings of Judah ever knew, and they have filled this
> place with the blood of the innocent. They have built
> the high places of Baal to burn their sons in the fire
> as offerings to Baal (Jeremiah 19:3-5).

Gideon's Call

The word of the Lord came down to a young man named Gideon, the youngest son of an insignificant farmer: "Go in the strength you have and save Israel out of Midian's hand."

"But Lord," Gideon asked, "how can I save Israel? My clan is the weakest in Manasseh, and I am the least in my family."

The Lord made him a promise: "I will be with you, and you will strike down all the Midianites together."

Willing to follow the Lord's command, Gideon soon pulled down the local altar to Baal, and built a proper altar to the Lord Almighty in its place. This was a challenge to the Midianites, under whose reign of terror the Israelites had been forbidden to worship the true God. Gideon's fellow Israelites decided that he should be killed to appease the Midianites for pulling down Baal's altar, but Gideon's father spoke up in his defense:

> Are you going to plead Baal's cause? Are you trying to
> save him? Whoever fights for him shall be put to death
> by morning! If Baal really is a god, he can defend himself
> when someone breaks down his altar (Judges 6:31).

Gideon's courage to stand up to Baal and to the Midianites inspired courage among his peers. Then "the Spirit of the Lord came upon Gideon," and he sent out a call for the Israelites to get ready to fight. Under his leadership thirty-two thousand men gathered at Mount Gilead. The Lord said to Gideon,

> You have too many men for me to deliver Midian into their hands. In order that Israel may not boast against me that her own strength has saved her, announce now to the people, "Anyone who trembles with fear may turn back and leave Mount Gilead" (Judges 7:2,3).

Twenty-two thousand men left, but the Lord said to Gideon, "There are still too many men. Take them down to the water, and I will sift them for you there."

When Gideon had taken the remaining men down to the water, the Lord told him to separate those who kneel down to drink in a defenseless position, from those who scoop up the water with their hands, and remain alert fighters while drinking. Only three hundred men lapped water from their hands, and the others all got down on their knees.

Victory

The Lord said to Gideon, "With the three hundred men that lapped I will save you and give the Midianites into your hands. Let all the other men go, each to his own place." Although Gideon had only a few men against countless hordes, the Lord made good on His promise. The battle was the Lord's. As Gideon obeyed, the enemy was delivered into his hands.

Gideon divided his men up into three groups, and gave each man a trumpet, a torch, and a jar big enough to fit over the torch. The groups reached the edge of the enemy camp in the middle of the night, just when the guards were changing shifts. Gideon's men were holding their burning torches covered by the jars with one hand and their trumpets with the other hand. At Gideon's command, the three companies smashed their jars, raised their torches and shouted, "A sword for the Lord and for Gideon!" While each man held his position around the camp, the Midianites rushed around in terror, only half awake. Then Gideon's men sounded the three hundred trumpets, and the Lord caused the men throughout the Midianite camp to turn on each other with their swords. The surviving Midianites fled and were followed by increasing numbers of Israelite volunteers, who drove them away and reclaimed the Promised Land.

Gideon had been led by the Lord each step of the way, and was acclaimed by the people as a great hero. When the Israelite leaders offered to make him king, Gideon demonstrated that he knew where his power had come from, and he knew who should rightly rule the land. He replied to them, "I will not rule over you, nor will my son rule over you. The LORD will rule over you." During the remaining forty years of Gideon's lifetime he directed the people to continue to follow the Lord, and they enjoyed peace. The land flowed once again with milk and honey.

GOD'S PEOPLE SPREAD HIS KINGDOM

God works today in the same way He did then—He works in and through His people to overcome evil with good. Jesus' teaching strongly asserts that God wants His people to keep carrying out His work in the world.

On the final day of a great feast, with practically the whole countryside celebrating together in Jerusalem, Jesus stood up in the court of the Temple and proclaimed:

> If anyone is thirsty, let him come to me and drink.
> Whoever believes in me, as the Scripture has said,
> streams of living water will flow from within him
> (John 7:37,38).

Jesus was challenging the people to draw their power from Him as they proclaimed His kindgom to the farthest reaches of the earth. That power is still available and is continually defeating Satan.

It is particularly uplifting to see God's power free cult victims from their bondage. No matter what offense has been committed, people are free to turn to God for restoration. The cult experience is designed to brainwash its followers into believing that they are not free to join God's kingdom. The victims may have signed Satan's book with their own blood; they may have married Satan, or they may have become involved in infant sacrifice. Cultists have put them through all these steps because they want the victims to believe they have no alternative but to remain cult members. The greatest honor is to give themselves or their infants as sacrifices to Satan. He promises that they will rule in hell with him as a reward for that act of obedience. The cult victims have had their free will destroyed, and cannot imagine there could be a way out.[2]

Jesus' parable about the "lost son" provides restoration for this kind of cult brainwashing:

> There was a man who had two sons. The younger one said to his father, "Father, give me my share of the estate." So he divided his property between them.
>
> Not long after that, the younger son got together all he had, set off for a distant country and there squandered his wealth in wild living. After he had spent everything, there was a severe famine in that whole country, and he began to be in need. So he went and hired himself out to a citizen of that country, who sent him to his fields to feed pigs. He longed to fill his stomach with the pods that the pigs were eating, but no one gave him anything.
>
> When he came to his senses, he said, "How many of my father's hired men have food to spare, and here I am starving to death! I will set out and go back to my father and say to him: Father, I have sinned against heaven and against you. I am no longer worthy to be called your son; make me like one of your hired men." So he got up and went to his father.
>
> But while he was still a long way off, his father saw him and was filled with compassion for him; he ran to his son, threw his arms around him and kissed him.
>
> The son said to him, "Father, I have sinned against heaven and against you. I am no longer worthy to be called your son."
>
> But the father said to his servants, "Quick! Bring the best robe and put it on him. Put a ring on his finger and sandals on his feet. Bring the fattened calf and kill it. Let's have a feast and celebrate. For this son of mine was dead and is alive again; he was lost and is found." So they began to celebrate (Luke 15:11-22).

No other story anywhere else contains a plot like this one. It is unthinkable to imagine that a son would demand his rightful inheritance while his father is still alive. No father would comply.

What father would shame himself in front of his friends by acceding to such a request? To make the parable even more unthinkable, the son dared to shame his father again by coming back! Who would think that any father would bless his son when he came back in rags? The father would hear things from his friends like, "I told you your son was a loser, and now so are you! He gave your fortune away, so you are the fool! Your place in our village is dead."

The Love That Is Great Enough

Jesus told parables that got to the heart of things. Here was a son, as ungrateful as a son can get, who had hit bottom, and his father did not give him a shame-based response when he returned. This father took the shame of the son's return upon himself—he offered his life and his reputation to restore his son! He bore the cost of his son's disgraceful behavior, which was the price necessary for the son's restoration. He said to all his friends, "Let's celebrate! There is no shame in welcoming a son home, no matter what the circumstances. Nothing my son could do would cause me to disown him."

That father's love was greater than the love of any father in any story ever told. That love is great enough to break through mind-control barriers. It pictures the love of the heavenly Father which comes to cult victims with freedom—freedom from guilt, freedom from despair, and freedom from self-hate.

That is the way love is to be practiced by those who are in God's kingdom. His people follow His example. The Father is the most accepting person imaginable, and in God's kingdom people go out of their way to welcome those in distress. Jesus proclaims Himself to be the Good Shepherd who goes after one lost sheep until He finds it, and He carries it on His shoulders back to the safety of the fold.

It takes a lot of commitment to put that teaching into practice. When cult-injured people want to leave their covens, God's people need to be willing to stand against cultists, to protect cult defectors. The survivors do not need to remain helpless, which is what they were brainwashed to believe. Although they have accepted that they are no match for their perpetrators, nor for the demons who have pestered them with confusion and fear, the Good News comes to them. God and His people will be the instruments of their freedom. His people are ready to bear the cost of the cult survivors' restoration—their love provides the power to overcome evil with good.

The Power That Is Strong Enough

As God's kingdom grows, His followers will claim the land while the enemy is being routed. Those who worship false gods and those who sacrifice humans to Satan are no match for those empowered by God. Under the leadership of the Lord Almighty, His people will reclaim the land and live in peace. Their land will once again flow with milk and honey.

Some people have considered Christians to be helpless, so to invite people into God's kingdom would only bring on more helplessness—caught up in the throes of the struggle between God and Satan. That is 180 degrees from the truth! People who follow the Lord are not powerless, or merely sitting ducks waiting to be picked off by cultists or evil perpetrators. God's people are not just ping pong balls being bounced back and forth between the forces of good and evil. We know that the battle is the Lord's, and His plan is to put us in a "mop-up" operation, restoring the land God has given us.[3]

God's power is in us. It is important to state boldly to those who falsely believe Christians are mere victims in the middle of a titanic struggle between God and Satan that we are secure. That is the foundation of the positive approach in therapy. God's power comes to those who call on Him, and He offers them citizenship in His kingdom. The Promised Land will be theirs. Victory is at hand.

"Spiritual restoration" is to be understood in the context of using the power of God to spread His kingdom. The power is generated from God, so spiritual restoration is more than just saying the right thing to a client. It is based on healing methods that are declared by the Bible, and it is supported by thousands of years of practice. Those who have faith in Him are carrying out battles against a weaker enemy who is already in flight. Spiritual restoration is not to be attempted outside a day-by-day walk with the Lord. It is to be carried out only from a base of operations within His kingdom, through the power of prayer.

As I found out in college, the world of the demonic is not to be taken lightly. Using the name of the Lord Almighty against spiritual forces is only to be done by those who know Him well enough to follow His leading.[4]

THE VOICE OF THE LORD
AND OTHER VOICES

For those who routinely hear voices in their heads, it is confusing to think about hearing the voice of the Lord. It is hard enough for those of us without alternate personalities to be able to discern when the Lord is imparting a message to us. There are competing voices. Those who try to follow the voice of the Lord find themselves with calls from other voices. *Which shall I follow? Is that my own "inner child" calling out for the approval of my Christian friends, or is God telling me to help those who are homeless?* A simple answer would be misleading. On the one hand, it seems easy enough to advocate that listening to God's voice is something that can be learned. However, that is not always simple. When inner voices are in disagreement and the roar of discontent drowns out the voice of God, it is difficult to recognize the voice of the Good Shepherd.[5]

Jesus' words from the Gospel of John, chapter 10:

> I tell you the truth, the man who does not enter the sheep pen by the gate, but climbs in by some other way, is a thief and a robber. The man who enters by the gate is the shepherd of his sheep. The watchman opens the gate for him, and the sheep listen to his voice. He calls his own sheep by name and leads them out. When he has brought out all his own, he goes on ahead of them, and his sheep follow him because they know his voice. But they will never follow a stranger; in fact, they will run away from him because they do not recognize a stranger's voice. . . . I tell you the truth, I am the gate for the sheep. All who ever came before me were thieves and robbers, but the sheep did not listen to them. I am the gate; whoever enters through me will be saved. He will come in and go out, and find pasture. The thief comes only to steal and

kill and destroy; I have come that they may have life, and
have it to the full. I am the good shepherd. The good
shepherd lays down his life for the sheep. The hired hand
is not the shepherd who owns the sheep. So when he sees
the wolf coming, he abandons the sheep and runs away.
Then the wolf attacks the flock and scatters it. The man
runs away because he is a hired hand and cares nothing
for the sheep. I am the good shepherd; I know my sheep
and my sheep know me—just as the Father knows me
and I know the Father—and I lay down my life for the
sheep. I have other sheep that are not of this sheep pen. I
must bring them also. They too will listen to my voice,
and there shall be one flock and one shepherd."

Two of the things that leap out of this text at me seem
important enough to highlight. A *lamb* does not hear its shepherd's voice. It hears its mother's voice. It takes gentle training
and it takes time for a lamb to become attuned to the distinctive
voice of the shepherd. While the lambs are young, they need to
receive lots of protection, because they could be fatally misled if
they followed the wrong voice. Jesus said that His *sheep* hear His
voice—the ones who have come to know Him, and who have
learned to live their life by following where He leads.

The other thing to be highlighted here is that life as a sheep
is dangerous! Sheep can fall as victims to thieves and robbers, or
even wolves—but the Good Shepherd is willing to do whatever
is necessary for their protection, even die for them! He says He
is also seeking to bring other sheep to join His protected flock.
They will learn to recognize His voice, and they will be under
His care. His promise is that there will be one flock and one
Shepherd. That is what I am looking forward to—the day when
all sheep will hear His voice and will follow Him.

As I was taught in college, the character of God in Christianity is distinctive. In other religions, people reach up to God—
following rules is seen as the way to reach Him. In Christianity,
God reaches down to people. There is nothing people can do to
reach high enough to "earn" God. We cannot be good enough.

However, the Good News is that in God's grace, He reaches
down to people and pulls them up, no matter how far down He
has to reach. People all over the world have found, throughout

history, that God desires to reveal Himself to us, and He will do just that if we give Him half a chance. Those who seek Him will find Him. For those who knock, the door will be opened (Matthew 7). As competing "voices" are recognized as such, His lambs mature and become His sheep, attuned to the voice that leads them into greener pastures where they will be safely guarded from thieves, robbers and wolves.

THE RESULTS ARE POSITIVE

> Do people pick grapes from thornbushes, or figs from thistles? Likewise every good tree bears good fruit, but a bad tree bears bad fruit. A good tree cannot bear bad fruit, and a bad tree cannot bear good fruit (Matthew 7:16-18).

If "spiritual restoration" is helpful, that will become evident. If it is harmful, that also will be evident. There is no study that I am aware of which demonstrates conclusively that people progress better when their therapy includes a spiritual component, but I believe that spiritual restoration helps. Of course, I recognize that I have only a limited sample of observations, and I know that someday new approaches may offer better results than anything I have seen. However, I believe that if spiritual growth promotes health, that will be an important consideration for therapists. If, on the other hand, bringing spiritual issues into therapy is a source of confusion and damage, that also will be an important consideration.

I believe there is a spiritual element which is a part of everything in our lives. Healing for the whole person must include the spiritual element or it will be incomplete. Here is how that can be conceptualized using the dissociative model: The "will" component of dissociation is spiritual in nature. When an alter chooses suicide, that is a spiritual disaster. When an alter has the will to help others, that comes from the spirit.

If healing comes to the spiritual component of the traumatic memories, the healing spreads to the other components. When the spirit is helped, so is everything else—bodily healing takes place, emotions are soothed, and distorted memories become more aligned with reality. If the spirit offers this kind of healing power, and if the spirit is interwoven with the fabric of human experience, it is logical to expect that people will get healthier when their therapy includes a spiritual dimension. I think Jesus' teaching is invariably true: You cannnot pick grapes from thorn-bushes—people get healthier when they follow the voice of the Good Shepherd.

However, there is a prevailing opinion among at least some leaders in the ISSMP&D that "Christian therapists" are turning out spoiled fruit. The following quotation is from *Dissociation*, September 1988, which is the only journal dedicated solely to advances in the treatment for MPD. Thus it is read by many therapists who work with the dissociative disorders, and these therapists probably consider the following quote to be highly credible. It comes from the article titled: "On Giving Consultations to Therapists Treating Multiple Personality Disorder: Fifteen Years' Experience," which is written by one of the foremost spokesmen for MPD treatment, Richard P. Kluft, M.D.

> I began to get a number of calls from clergymen and practitioners who added the prefix "Christian" to their profession, e.g., "Christian Psychiatrist." Such calls usually began with reference to the work of Ralph Allison ... or M. Scott Peck ... and inquired about issues that bore on exorcism. I learned of a massive subculture in which such practices were commonplace, and had occasion to take a number of failed exorcism patients into treatment for what appeared to me to be classic MPD.

Dr. Kluft's observations should be taken seriously. MPD therapists have found repeatedly that alters are never destroyed. Even though they may remain hidden for years, they cannot be erased. So, whenever an alter is accused of being a demon, that can frighten the alter seriously enough keep it "buried" for some time. However, the alter will necessarily re-emerge at some point down the line, and when that happens it will be in a lot of pain and/or confusion. No doubt, Dr. Kluft has seen MPD clients who have had alters attacked and "driven out" by well-meaning Christians, who thought they were exorcising demons.

It is very likely that the personalities themselves became convinced they were demonic as well, and they were unmercifully persecuted. They did not receive the careful treatment necessary to bring them to health. If that sort of thing has happened, as Dr. Kluft has noted, it is a great tragedy. Every person and every part of each person deserves truth and respect. To conclude that a personality is a demon is dishonest and degrading. As noted earlier, it is religious abuse.

Things get a little more complicated for a therapist who concludes there is no such thing as a demon but his client turns out to have one. It would be an error to call a demon "good," and proceed to include it in therapy. If a therapist believes that everything which shows up in therapy is a "good" part of the internal system and therefore a necessary part of recovery for the system, that can be dangerous. While I do not look for nor expect to find demons, nonetheless they sometimes make their presence known, despite my wish that it were not so.

Figure 6
Discerning Alter Personalities From Demons

Alter Personality	Demon
1. Most alters, even "Persecutor" alters, can become strong allies. There is a definite sense of relationship with them, even if it starts out negative.	1. Demons are arrogant, and there is no sense of relationship with them.
2. Alters initially seem ego-dystonic but that changes to be ego-syntonic over time.	2. Demons remain ego-alien—"outside of me."
3. Confusion and fear subside with appropriate therapy when only alters are present.	3. Confusion, fear and lust persist despite therapy when demons are present.
4. Alters tend to conform to surroundings.	4. Demons force unwanted behaviour, then blame a personality.
5. Alters have personalities with accompanying voices.	5. Demons have a negative voice which has no corresponding personality.
6. Irritation, discontent and rivalry abound among alters.	6. Hatred and bitterness are the most common feelings among demons.
7. Images of alters are human in form, and remain consistent during imagery.	7. The imagery of demons changes between human and non-human forms, with many variations.

When demons "manifest" it is different from the way an alter "takes executive control of the body." A different quality, a different image seems to emanate from demons as opposed to alters. Demons are vile. They work against the personality system. They remain external; they promote fear and confusion, and they do not form relationships with people.

Persecutor alters are not demons, even though I have met some who told me they were. I immediately feel a sense of relationship with Persecutor alters. Demons flit in, strike or accuse, and instantly vanish. They are a nuisance and a pestilence, and the fear they spread can paralyze the whole personality system.

When a raspy, low male voice takes over a petite woman's body, and foam begins to form around the edges of her mouth, and the voice says things like, "She's mine! I will not let her go!"—that is not a personality. The client's vision of the dastardly entity who has spoken confirms its demonic nature.

Figure 7 on page 241 in the next chapter is an example of an image that a demon took for one client. It does not seem possible for a personality to take on such an image. To treat such a thing as part of the personality system is to invite chaos for the forseeable future.

Figure 6, here, is an outline of the clues that have helped me determine if an entity is a personality or a demon. Some people are able to recognize the presence of a demon more accurately than I am. Discerning them directly is not something I am comfortable with yet, but these guidelines have helped me with the recognition process.

A bad tree cannot produce good fruit. The evil spirit needs to be removed in order for peace to be established in the personality system. Among the exorcisms I have seen, none has later been considered a mistake. When dissociation is properly understood, and care is taken to make certain that the demon is actually external to the personality system, I have not seen a false positive or a false negative. The properly exorcised demons do not appear later in therapy as personalities. The positive, long-term results indicate that demons were cast out. You can't argue with success. A tree is known by its fruit.

8

SPIRITUAL
WARFARE
In MPD Therapy

DR. RALPH ALLISON played an important role in shaping the MPD field. Until he made his historic contribution—*Minds in Many Pieces*[1]—there was no place for clinicians to get an understanding of MPD which combined case histories and a discussion of treatment strategies. The son of a preacher, Dr. Allison was familiar with and open to the possibility of spiritual healing as he worked among MPD patients.

It is important to note that he was truly a pioneer in his work—there were no adequate materials to guide him while he was developing treatment plans for the first few MPD clients who showed up in his caseload. *Minds in Many Pieces* is autobiographical, and as Dr. Allison reviews the development of his clinical thinking during his early MPD years, the 1970s, his account retraces the complicated clinical issues he faced.

He always clung to the guiding principle that a physician must follow: Put the health of the patient first.

> Despite my skepticism at the time [1972], I believed then and still believe that a good psychiatrist must be open to new ideas. The welfare and eventual cure of the patient must be his only consideration, and when conventional techniques fail, he must be willing to explore new options.[2]

Of course, Dr. Allison was considered by many of his fellow psychiatrists to be on shaky footing at that time just because he was working within the MPD framework, and he experienced

225

frequent opposition. The thing that put him on a direct collision course with his cronies more than anything else was his discovery that spiritual interventions can have profoundly positive effects with some MPD clients. In his book, published in 1980, he courageously illustrated a few examples of how exorcisms were carried out, including their therapeutic results.

This openness about his work put him into the category of a pure scientist—reporting treatment that worked, without prefitting his observations into a popular scientific framework.

Breaking With Tradition

Here is how he discussed his first exorcism:

> With these thoughts in mind [being open to new options], I decided to give the concept of spirit possession a try. Carrie was desperate and she wasn't responding to any of the textbook techniques I had tried. I told her I had a new idea that might help her and she agreed readily.

> Spirit possession is not part of a psychiatrist's school curriculum. When I decided to accept Bonnie [previously presumed to be one of Carrie's alters] as a spirit and perform an exorcism, I knew I was breaking with tradition. And I realized that the contemporary psychiatric literature would be useless.

> An early session with Carrie had revealed, among other things, that she had once experimented with witchcraft while in high school. She had also once had a boyfriend who was serious about "black magic." Her involvement appeared to be typical of the seemingly silly things many high school students do and it did not worry me. However, it did indicate that she believed in the concept of good and evil, of God and the devil. Thus, I felt that a religious approach such as an exorcism would appeal to her, although I had no intention of talking about Bonnie beforehand. I didn't want to place the idea in her mind, creating a problem where none existed if that proved to be the case.

> I went to the Bible and began reading about possession. The New Testament discusses Christ's casting out of demons and I chose to follow this concept. It seemed fairly simple as I interpreted it. An exorcist must call out each demon by name, then command it to leave in the name of the Holy Trinity—Christ, God the Father, and the Holy Spirit.

> It is important to remember that religion and mental health are not as contradictory as they may seem. In earlier times, the church cared for the mentally ill. The fact that doctors have taken

over this function doesn't mean that bringing religion to a treatment program is wrong. Essentially, I was bringing mental health full circle, combining the best of medicine and religion. Since my family has produced a long line of ministers, it seemed quite natural for me to mix a religious act with my psychiatry since this seemed to be in the best interest of my patient.

Dr. Allison hypnotized Carrie in the presence of another doctor, and the session was preserved by the use of a tape recorder. After the initial hypnosis was not successful in finding Bonnie present, the other doctor wrote a note suggesting that Dr. Allison go deeper than hypnosis.

I had no idea what he meant but I later learned that his suggestion resulted from a course he had taken. He was told that if hypnosis doesn't produce the desired results, the subject can be taken to a deeper level where almost anything might happen.

I literally suggested to Carrie that she enter a deeper level, which she apparently did. I don't know how she did it. I don't really know what happened. This type of situation has not come up again, and at the time I was interested in results, not reasons.

Next, I asked Carrie if someone named Bonnie was influencing her life. This time she said yes. She also became highly agitated. She told me she wanted to get rid of Bonnie and her words were an agonized plea.

My voice grew deep and authoritative. I felt that an exorcist would have to be a strong, commanding person in full charge of every situation. His booming rhetoric would act as a conduit for God's healing power, terrorizing the spirit and forcing it to leave. If that was Carrie's idea of an exorcist as well, then my approach would be perfect.

[My comment: It has proved effective for me to carry out exorcisms using a calm voice.]

"Above your head is a crystal ball," I stated in a booming voice. I was holding a crystal ball on a chain, a souvenir I had received from one of the hypnosis courses I had taken. It had no significance except a symbolic one. "I command Bonnie to leave Carrie's body and enter this crystal ball. In the name of God, the Son, and the Holy Ghost, Bonnie—leave Carrie, leave Carrie in peace! I command you, Bonnie, leave Carrie! By all that's holy, leave Carrie! Leave Carrie in peace and depart for wherever you go! Wherever spirits go, go there and leave Carrie! When the crystal ball stops swinging, then Bonnie will be gone and Carrie will be at peace."

I thought the last was a nice touch. Of course, I was holding the [chain] as still as I could so the ball couldn't move. Or could it?

I glanced at the crystal and noticed that it was moving in a circle with a centrifugal force all its own. I was surprised. I looked at my hand and it appeared to be steady, yet that ball was rotating fairly rapidly.

"All right, Carrie, as soon as Bonnie is gone from you, tell me yes by raising your right index finger." . . .

Suddenly the crystal ball began slowing. As it did, Carrie raised her "yes" finger, signaling me that Bonnie was gone. . . .

The entire exorcism took approximately two and one half minutes. Ten minutes later I talked with Carrie, who commented, "I've always thought there was something, a spirit or a vision or a shadow of something, always with me. But it's not there now. I used to hate to close my eyes because I'd see it. Just a haunting evil feeling that I'm going to die. It was separate from the feeling of wanting to die because of the hell of all this. . . . This is a different feeling than I've had for a long time. Now I feel like there is hope where I didn't feel like that before." . . . Carrie later said that while I held the ball over her head, she felt some force move up through her body and out through her head.

Considering Spiritual Elements in Treatment

After making the important point—Carrie lost her fear of impending death by choking—Dr. Allison added that this experience put him in a rather precarious position:

As far as I was concerned, if my actions helped my patient progress toward a normal, integrated personality, they were a success. However, I had no intention of embarrassing myself in front of my colleagues by admitting the experiment.

Dr. Allison's initial hesitation about sharing his findings were eventually overcome, and the book was published with the accounts of exorcisms included. However, the number of therapists who have incorporated his "psychological and spiritual" model has remained small. The majority of MPD specialists do not include Dr. Allison's work when they consider treatment strategies. His call for science to open up to spiritual dimensions, at least in an honest search for ways to improve treatment, has gone largely unheeded. Yet, to my knowledge, his conclusion that spiritual treatment components seem to have unexplored power has not been directly disputed.

As Carrie's therapy progressed, the spiritual elements in her illness had been uncovered. It became apparent that something had been disrupting her life—the fear of death by choking—and the cause seemed to have been a spirit! Her progress had ground to a halt.

I believe that her story is consistent with the model being outlined in the present book. The histories of people with spiritual oppression have a point in time in which they were apparently opened up to it, and the consequence was confusion and fear. There was already a lot of torture and pain in Carrie's childhood. She had a "mind that was in many pieces," which made her easy prey for Satan. The fear spread by her spiritual oppresser was quite clear—and it stopped after the exorcism. The confusion that was of spiritual origin was also evident—she was able to talk about the confusing spiritual influence only in retrospect, after it had been exorcised. I also have found that this kind of confusion is usually seen to be active, retrospectly, by the client after an exorcism. The final point in Carrie's experience that is shared by the people I have seen is that her therapy had been seriously stunted by the spiritual disruption.

Another Client's Experience and Treatment

Let me reinforce this model by describing the final therapeutic obstacle for Beth, whose MPD history we have looked at several times. She and I had been thinking for a few months that no other personalities remained undiscovered, and we were fairly certain that Beth had completed the integration process.

Then one Wednesday, at the beginning of a session, she shared that things were not going very well and she could not figure out why. We were unable to find exactly what was going on during that session—the usual imagery that had been successful with her was not giving us anything but fuzziness, and there was a lot of confusion in the air. We went an extra hour, but got nowhere. Beth, who had already joined about forty alters and had expelled an evil spirit, was whimpering, and was in as much agony as ever. It was a tremendous point of despair for us both. I was exasperated, and Beth was writhing in pain of an unknown origin. I did the things that usually pulled secretive or hidden alters out into the open, but it failed. We scheduled an emergency meeting for the following day, and had the same results. By the end of the Thursday session, I had come to the conclusion that there must be some inarticulate, emotionally volatile young personality who needed extra time and encouragement before we could go any further. We set aside two more hours on Friday afternoon to get to know what we believed would be a fear-ridden child personality.

Beth was in as much fear as ever when she arrived for the Friday meeting. We prayed, used imagery, introspected, and eventually went through several steps that should promote communication between the as yet unknown alter and the unified core personality.

I think, looking back, that I probably acted more out of an urgent need to find a solution than I did out of good clinical judgment on that Friday afternoon. Beth was in bad shape! I decided that in case we had a very young personality emerging, it may need to fuse with the whole personality before it could express its troubles in words. We carried out a variation of a fusion exercise but were not pleased with the results. Beth did have a vague sense that things were calming down. I had been in quite a bit of tension and was hoping that we had done the right thing, but I was not at peace about Beth's situation by the time we stopped.

I checked by phone to see how she was feeling on Monday, and she let me know that things were not as good as they usually had been after a fusion but she believed she was a little bit calmer than a week earlier. When Beth began her regularly scheduled Wednesday evening session, I had no sense that there was anything spiritual going on, but I was very intent on finding out why this particular personality was so difficult to make contact with and what the fear was all about. It was a general sort of fear, and it kept us from accomplishing any meaningful work. I felt very much as though we were back to square one, despite all the remarkable progress Beth had made. As a matter of fact, things were even worse than when she had begun therapy! We were about thirty minutes into our hour, and Beth was in anguish, trying to tell me about the many ways in which things were not making sense to her, and when she put her hand to the back of her neck with a painful expression on her face, I had a flash of an idea. I doubted it at first but was immediately led to act on it. Beth had not heard about this, but I had been talking to other therapists who had unexpectedly found spirits lodged in their clients' shoulders and necks, and the spiritual manifestation was the pain where they were located. These therapists had told me that after the spirits were expelled, the pain ceased and the surrounding confusion cleared up.

Confronting a Demon

Since exorcising spirits from body parts is so extremely unverifiable and seems on the surface to be a primitive idea, I resisted it, but at the same time I was compelled to give it a try. I changed seats at that moment, right in the middle of her sentence, and moved to the chair only three feet in front of her. Without asking her if I had her permission to make any spiritual intervention, I just said calmly, "In the name of Jesus I command you to come out of Beth and never return."

Beth looked at me in a puzzled manner. I had never done anything like that with her before. The spirit that had previously been exorcised out of her had been expelled at home with her husband by her side, so there was no precedent for what I had just done. I am still unsure what made me do it.

She didn't understand why I had done it either, but as she continued to develop her train of thought, she said that all of a sudden she was feeling better. The soreness in her neck, which she had not told me about earlier, had vanished immediately. Her fear was gone and her mind was clear again. We were both so astonished that we hardly knew what to say!

Retrospectively, we reasoned things out in this way: Some kind of spiritual foe had been uncovered in her therapy, and it tried to disguise itself as a personality. It had spread fear and confusion, so it would not be recognized as a spirit.

As had been the case with Carrie, Beth could not figure out what the problem was at the time because of the spiritual confusion. Therapy was retrogressing instead of progressing! It was wonderful to find that no upset of any kind remained as a result of the five hours of difficult therapy that we had undertaken.

Therapeutic Progress

A few sessions later, Beth's final alter, Windy, the healthy one, a distinguished personality who was waiting for Beth to get healthy before she would let herself come out in the open, emerged. This was confirmation that the spiritual warfare had been successful.

Beth has been living without any serious obstacles since that time. Fear and confusion are no longer present. Not only is her mind in one piece, but she seems also to have no remaining openings for spiritual oppression. Spiritual interventions were needed, were used and were immediately successful. There were no ill effects afterward, and that was more than two years ago.

Other Examples of Successful Exorcisms

This instance of long-lasting success is not an isolated occurrance. Here are accounts of others. Each person's case has something a little different to learn about, but God prevails, and lasting spiritual healing is accomplished.

During a two-week period while one of the other MPD therapists at our clinic was on vacation, some things happened that taught me quite a bit. Despite the fact that I had been involved in expelling spirits before that time, the nature of spiritual warfare became clearer to me because the battles going on in front of me were undeniably of a spiritual nature.

I was covering the other therapist's cases while he was away but had no appointments scheduled with any of his MPD clients. On the first Tuesday morning, one of his multiple clients, Karen, called my office for a "sort of emergency" appointment. I knew Karen pretty well from weekly contact with her in the MPD group. It is a good thing that we could work together so quickly, because what we ended up doing could have been much more difficult and could have increased her fear and confusion.

Karen came in during her lunch hour and could hardly wait to get into my office before she started telling me that although it had never seemed so before, she thought she may have an evil spirit in her. I was surprised at this because she had never talked to me about exorcism, or "deliverance" as she referred to it. She was totally in the dark as to whether I had any experience with this sort of thing but had called me because she knew I was the one to talk to while her therapist was away. The two of them had been working together for a number of years, and although she had already united many personalities into a solid inner core, there had not been any previous evidence that an evil spirit could be anywhere in the picture.

I was quite reluctant to consider that she could be right. It seemed to me that she was probably upset by the sense that she had been "deserted" by her therapist, and that would be enough to explain the out-of-control emotions she was encountering. Maybe some new personality was surfacing. I was trying not to leap to conclusions. Karen persisted in her declaration that she really had a sense there was an evil spirit. I gave in to her urging, and we decided to go through the guidelines (shown on page 222) that were developed by the MPD team to determine whether we were working with a personality or a spirit. She maintained it was a spirit that was bothering her. I was not in the frame of mind right then to begin an exorcism and just did not take the initiative to get it started. I asked if she would be open to praying about what we should do. She was very willing to pray, and so was I. During the prayer I became ready to do what she was asking—expel the spirit! A change in attitude came over me, and I became almost eager to begin the process.

As I had been taught, I told Karen ahead of time how a deliverance is usually carried out, and we began. I started by saying, if an evil spirit is present it is required, in the name of Jesus, to speak its name. From the lips of Karen came the answer, but in a very low voice: "My name is Dispersion."

"How did you gain access to Karen?"

"When Karen was 2 years of age, her mother made a deal with me."

"Tell me about the deal."

"I do not want to."

"You have no choice. You have been commanded to do so, in the name of Jesus."

"Her mother owed somebody a lot of money, and she asked me to get it paid off. I got her the money she was asking for, and she gave her daughter over to me."

"What is your function?"

"To keep her financial situation messed up."

"In the name of Jesus, you are commanded to leave. Go directly to Jesus' throne, and wait there for His orders. You must leave now and never come back. Be gone!"

Momentarily, Karen lifted her head and a smile appeared on her face. She looked exhausted, but hopeful.

"Did you hear what was going on," I asked?

"Yes, yes! That must be why I have never been able to figure out where my money was going to! I presumed an alter personality must be absconding with it. I feel like a different person!"

After closing the session in prayer, she went back to her job, and a wave of wonderful feelings came over me. It was great to think that she had been delivered of an unwanted spirit who had been keeping her off balance since age 2!

The next Tuesday morning, one of the therapist's other MPD clients, Larry, called me in the morning, urgently wanting to make an appointment. Larry had become very depressed on Monday, and he had fears flare up during the night. Since he also had been in a group I led, I knew him well, as had been the case with Karen. We spent the hour very unproductively. My sense was that I didn't know his personalities very well and that could account for the poor session.

The next day he stopped by to find out if I had a few minutes to see him. As things were developing that day, I was able to fit him in between other sessions for about fifteen minutes. Things were even worse than the previous day. He was deeper in despair than ever, quite hopeless that he would ever feel close to his wife and children. Shortly after he started, he mentioned that his mother had dropped by two nights ago. That put me on the right track. His mother probably was an active cult member, and our MPD team had known for months that she could "drop off" demons wherever she went.

I asked Larry if maybe his mother had dropped off something while she was there. He knew exactly what I was asking about. We went through the guidelines, just as Karen and I had done, and this time I was ready to go ahead with the deliverance. It really bothered me that a cult member would foist despair on her son while his therapist was away, and I wanted to deprive her of the success she had achieved in delivering the spirit to him!

"In the name of Jesus, if there is a spirit present here, you are to tell me your name."

After a little silence, Larry said "I don't hear anything."

"You have no choice. You are commanded in Jesus' name to identify yourself."

A different voice came from Larry's mouth. "Despair."

"How did you gain access to Larry?"

"You already know."

"Tell me anyway."

"His mother."

"What is your function?"

"You already know."

I was getting a little perturbed with this spirit, but kept a calm voice.

"Tell me anyway."

"To make him upset."

"In the name of Jesus, Despair, you are commanded to leave. Go directly to Jesus' throne, and wait there for His instruction."

"Larry will still have as much despair as before," the spirit retorted.

"That is not up to you or me. You are commanded in the name of Jesus to leave. So, depart."

Larry's body wrenched and then relaxed. He was quite disoriented when he "came to." He did not have any idea what had happened. After I told him about the spirit, he said that with his other therapist there was one time where quite a few spirits were expelled, and he assumed that would be the end. Now he realized that his mother could deliver new ones whenever she saw him. He knew that meant he would have to avoid her in the future, but it also became apparent to him why he had been upset after his mother's visits. He was still in some despair, but certainly not as much as he had been a few minutes earlier. His mind was clearer, so it appeared to me that some of the confusion had departed with Despair.

I wondered if Larry's mother had left some spirits in his house as well, so I instructed Larry about how to "clean them out" of each room. He thought that would be a good idea, and decided to try it, and talk it over with me the next day. His report the following day was that when he had arrived at home, he sensed a heavy oppression. He went through each room, cast out spirits in the name of Jesus, and sang a hymn in each one. The children clung to him silently during this deliverance, and the whole family's mood improved immediately.

As we continued to talk Larry showed absolutely no signs of despair, and we had a very productive session. That was our confirmation that the spiritual warfare had been successful.

Casting Out Spirits—Not Alters

There is something that must be stressed, as a final point here:

Casting out spirits successfully always leads to peace for the client, and the exorcised spirit has never yet been discovered to have been an alter personality in any case I have been associated with.

If we were to "cast out" an alter, he or she would necessarily show up later in therapy. Every personality eventually becomes involved in treatment. Dr. Allison and I, and other MPD therapists I have talked to, are certain that the demons or evil spirits that left were not alter personalities. They were not part of the person to be integrated, but were external and destabilizing. Worse than that, they were evil, and it made no sense to try to get them to cooperate with the personalities. They were expelled and their absence led to health.

This final point is supported by *Suffer the Child*,[3] the recent publication of an account of MPD/SRA therapy. It is eloquently written by an author who followed the therapy of an MPD/SRA survivor for five years. The book is sensitive and accurate, and it is a pleasure to read. In it I found great affirmation to what I have seen.

I was particularly eager to find out what, if anything, would be said about expelling demons, or if the therapists found exorcism to be a necessary part of therapy.

Throughout the book, the survivor's stories about demons were presented matter-of-factly, as something which might be nothing more than suggestions and tricks played on the survivor by the cult perpetrators, or the accounts could even have been self-delusional material. However, the writer never completely discounted that there might have been some kind of external force which needed to be expelled. With that in mind, I had been mostly disappointed that no account of exorcism was given—until page 334.

Well into therapy, with many of the four hundred personalities having already been joined, the therapists ran into a major interference. Just to show similarities with cases listed in this chapter, let me add that Jenny, the survivor, had been raised as a child who was chosen to be a high priestess for a cult group. She was often the person whose body was the medium, used to conjure up spirits during the satanic rituals. When therapy got to the stage where healing for those memories was necessary, an entity was encountered who at first appeared to be an alter personality, but there were some indications that it was Satan himself, or at least he claimed to be. He went by the name "The Father," and he struggled with the therapists—he wanted to control the personalities.

Rachel, one of the therapists, encouraged Jenny to "stand against him," and told her that she could think of it as divorcing Satan. After Jenny asked how that would work, Karl, the other therapist, gave the answer.

> I don't know that much about it, only what I've read. From what I understand, you need only to say, "In the name of the Father, the Son, and the Holy Spirit, Satan, be gone."...
>
> Selena [an alter personality] surfaced to tell what she had seen and heard [while The Father was being cast out]. The words had been screamed inside by everybody [all the personalities] together. Things had seemed dark, hazy and confused for a time,

but now the room seemed light and very real. Selena was more peaceful than Karl and Rachel had ever known her to be.

The same sense of peace was evident in Jenny when she surfaced. . . . She described essentially the same experience as had Selena. Jenny had taken a stand. The Father would not return.

Peace had been established as never before. The exorcism worked.

SEQUESTERED SPIRITS

Spiritual warfare is not as simple as it may seem. There is a lot more to it than killing the enemy and claiming victory! Even veteran battlers are continually surprised at the stealth and the flanking maneuvers of the enemy. I feel compelled to make it very clear that I am not an expert in this area, but I have had enough experience to discover that one of the most successful spiritual ambushes seems to involve sequestered spirits.

Here is how I have seen that concept at work in MPD clients. In order for people to be free of oppression, they must have faith and trust in God, and they must be willing to turn over every part of their lives to Him. That would seem a straightforward experience for most people. A simple prayer and a heartfelt desire to be His follower in every aspect of life is all it takes. But when many personalities share the same body, things are quite a bit more complicated—turning over every part of the life is impossible because the different parts don't know each other!

Even if many alters have joined into a unified inner core personality, if there has been psychological and spiritual healing, and if evil spirits have been cast out, that still may not be enough to ward off attacks from sequestered spirits. Particularly in cases where the client was raised in the occult, there can be alter personalities who are loyal to Satan, or there may be victimized alters who have been occultly oppressed but are amnesic to most of the other alters. There can be disagreement between the personalities about loyalties, or worse yet, the host alter can be loyal to God, but there are other alters, amnesic from the host, who are loyal to Satan! The host can be going to church regularly, doing the things that seem right, but there can be an occult life being lived by the same body. The host may have no suspicion that some of the personalities have every intent to serve Satan.

I know of three cases in which children were married to Satan during cult rituals, with their parents present. As is the case with other cult rituals, marriage is carried out in ways that mock a Christian ceremony, including sacrifices, orgies and terror. The alter who experiences those rituals can develop into a personality who is either loyal to Satan and/or maximally intimidated by the experiences. In either case, a batch of demons is always called up through an incantation and delivered during the ritual in a most terrifying fashion to the child.

Can you imagine what would be going through the mind of that child? She has full knowledge at that moment of the reality of demons, and she has been duped into believing that she has actually married Satan, shortly after helping carry out a human sacrifice! That kind of an experience would have to be walled off from the rest of her awareness through amnesia, or the sense of impending disaster would be too great to tolerate. Therefore, an alternate personality develops to contain these memories and protect the rest of the personalities from them. The loyal/victimized alter then becomes a satanic stronghold where the demons have been attached, and the stronghold is unknown by the other personalities. From this stealth-protected base, the evil spirits can spread fear, confusion and hate in subtle ways to keep the other personalities off balance.

Level 3 Warfare

This is where level 3 warfare, spoken of in the first chapter of this book, comes into play. The personality now has become totally loyal to Satan and has carried out sacrifices as proof. Level 3 people are possessed by powerful spirits. Their suffering is great by the time of exorcism, and their lives have been in danger. The flanking maneuvers and spiritual ambushes carried out from this stronghold have been destroying relationships and keeping the person isolated from those who could help the most!

One person's therapy portrays how the sequestering was uncovered. Martha had been in MPD therapy for a long time before she started making the kind of progress expected. Her therapy was interrupted frequently by unexplained absences, and by many "trust" issues with me. She would be angry with me over things I knew nothing about! It was baffling. Eventually, she read some of the articles I had written and said she was pretty sure she had some demons in her.

By that time, her host alter had gotten very close to God, and the heat of spiritual battle was difficult to miss! During a prayer she said she had a revelation about the origins of five evil spirits. When she told me about the spirits, there was a struggle going on in her just to reveal them to me. I called out each one, learned about their points of entry and found out their functions, and they were expelled. Martha reveled in a peace she had never known! Her body felt warm all over, whereas, she had often brought sweaters to therapy even on warm days. Those evil spirits had entered while she was experimenting with three other religions during her teenage years. She had been chanting, or worshiping, in their "churches," and the demons entered. They created fear, confusion, lust and hate. It was wonderful to see how her relationships with her friends softened after those spirits were expelled.

A few months later, when we were able to contact alter personalities who knew about her family life as a child, we ran into some more spiritual interference. This cluster of memories had to do with the long history of her family as Gypsies and occultists. Eight more spirits, which would fit into the category of "family spirits," were expelled. These had been given to Martha at birth, or at the death of relatives who had the spirits. They were passed on to her by direct family transmission. She had no choice but to accept them! They were finally located and discharged when she had reached age 40, after much of her life had been overlaid with fear, confusion, lust and hate.

Things improved a great deal in her life, and her therapy showed good progress, as it had after the earlier cluster of spirits had been taken care of. However, when we got to memories of cult rituals, we found another cluster of sequestered spirits.

These were the most devious and vicious spirits we had met. They would harass her alters, pick on the weak ones, and try to keep her from coming to therapy. They were the ones that were attached to satanic strongholds, one of which was a young alter, Ursela, who had been married to Satan. It was extremely dangerous for Martha as we worked with these demons, because

Figure 7

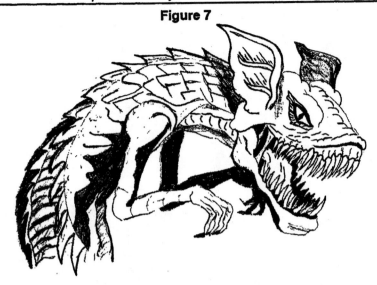

A Demon Drawn by One of Martha's Child Alters

they had always promoted hate and destruction. She became highly suicidal, and it was a miracle that she survived. The demons knew Martha's weaknesses and made their best efforts to destroy her. One of Martha's alters drew a picture of a demon that was terrorizing her, which is shown here in Figure 7. The frail alter believed her life easily could be ended by the demon. Thank God, she had quite a few people praying for her during the most difficult period.

It was not until the personality named Ursela turned her life over to God that we were able to exorcise the demons from this stronghold. The final exorcism was not difficult because Ursela had already seen how wonderful it had been for Martha's other alters to turn their lives over to God, and she was ready to follow their example. Looking back, it seemed to us both that whenever she would get close to people something would go wrong, and it was the demonic activity that was at fault. Following the final exorcism, Martha's life improved, and she became able to develop the kind of friendships that were more satisfying.

What Dr. Allison said about client progress is important—the well-being of the client must be my primary concern. If my clients suffer from spiritual oppression, they need deliverance.

9

EXORCISM

DISCERNMENT-EXORCISM AS A GIFT

AFTER I HAD BECOME involved in the MPD team at the Christian counseling center where I work, I received an invitation to attend a conference on the psychological and spiritual dimensions of evil. That was a necessary part of my training. Three presenters there made important contributions to my understanding of spiritual warfare. One was Tom White, a counselor who had extensive experience with exorcism in a relatively small counseling center.[1] Another was Ed Murphy, the leader of a worldwide missionary organization, who had carried out exorcisms in many countries, including America.[2] The third was M. Scott Peck, who gave a detailed account of the exorcisms mentioned in his book, *People of the Lie.*[3] These people helped me to proceed boldly with the work ahead. Not only did they give me specific training in how to carry out exorcisms, but they also gave me the confidence that it can be done, and that at times it is a part of therapy that *must* be done if certain clients are to be fully healed.

Two Cautions

We will discuss carrying out exorcisms more extensively a little later, but a few points need to be highlighted here.

The **first** is that *the exorcist must have a solid spiritual foundation.* There is great danger if one enters into an exorcism without the proper armor—a here-and-now relationship with God, a clear idea about His role in the exorcism, and a life that is free of openings for spiritual harassment. It is not the exorcist who has the power, but it is the exorcist who targets God's power, and in order to do that, he must be a clean conductor of the power. God

243

uses people to carry out His work. He relies on us to carry out the warfare, even though it is He who supplies the firepower. This is a crucial part of training in spirutual warfare—the exorcist claims no credit for the victory. The victory belongs to God. Ring up another victory for Him, and thank Him for using us as warriors in His battle. If we allow egoistic satisfaction to lure us into thinking we deserve the credit that belongs to Him, we will soon find ourselves embattled and defeated.

Second, *don't get into exorcism because it seems interesting or because you want a taste of power over evil.* Get into exorcism because God has put you in the position to direct His power in that way and has adequately prepared you for the battle. You will need to be trained and supervised by someone who has experience with exorcism, or you may face any number of counterattacks.

One of my friends put it this way: "I keep telling God that I want to fight His war on a different front, but He hasn't given me transfer papers!" That expresses my position very well. I don't seek to be an exorcist, but when it appears to me that God has brought a person to me with an evil spirit, I thank Him that He has prepared me for the battle, and I am willing to direct His firepower. After all is considered, I believe I am within the mainstream of Christianity—Jesus said that His followers would "cast out devils" (Mark 16:17). At one point He even sent out some of His disciples, and among the things they were prepared to do was to cast out spirits (Matthew 10:1). I am not implying that every follower of Christ is supposed to cast out spirits, but I accept the teaching of the apostle Paul that some Christians have received the gift of discernment-exorcism of spirits (1 Corinthians 12:10). It appears that God has given me that gift.[4] I do not want to suggest that every Christian should seek to become an exorcist, but merely that my gift of exorcism has a place in the Christian framework.

While I was listening to the presentations at the conference on the psychological and spiritual dimensions of evil, it occurred to me, because of my earlier experience with breaking up seances, that I did have the gift of exorcism. Only a few months later, people began to show up in my office asking me to help them get rid of spirits. I have not sought spirits to cast out, but people have sought me out to have me practice the gift of exorcism God seems to have given me. It is only within this framework that I would even consider performing an exorcism, but it gives me a lot of confidence to know that as long as I work within this framework, God will keep using my gift for His glory.

LEVELS OF DEMONIC INFLUENCE

Alters Versus Demons

Whenever I teach classes, though, or consult with other therapists, or talk to my clients, I make it clear that "spiritual warfare" is not something people should get fascinated with. Deliverance or exorcism may occasionally be called for, but it is foolish to go looking for it. As Dr. John White recently put it, there is a danger that Christians can get caught up in "shadow boxing" with demons who may not even be there. I have heard accounts of Christian groups who sense a spirit of some general quality hovering among them, and after emotions have risen and fallen, the people are relieved and exhilarated upon becoming convinced that demons had been cast out. Such occurrences could be instances of shadow boxing, but I cannot tell for certain.

Unfortunately, personalities also could get cast out in those kinds of situations. The person who is the object of such an "exorcism" could end up in Dr. Kluft's office as an example of the damage that occurs when dissociation is not understood by the exorcist.

Dr. White's approach seems sensible to me. He advises that it is enough to deal with the demon when it "manifests." The therapist's concentration should be on the person at hand, and on Christ—not on the demon. "As we come to persons with love and with compassion, the demons leave." In Dr. White's experiences, and he evidently has seen quite a few cases of demonic involvement, the demons have scrammed quickly when they were uncovered in the presence of the love of Christ. I believe that is the most common way in which evil is overcome by good.

There is a long history of dealing with spirits when they "manifest." A major problem for the MPD therapist is the many similarities between the bodily signs that indicate a dissociation (of a personality) and those that indicate a manifestation (of a demon)—the two could be confused easily. Rolling eyes, voice changes, twitches, or marked shifts in facial expression could indicate either. Exorcists likely have not known enough about MPD to tell the difference. It is time for responsible friends, clergymen and Christian therapists to become informed. When I have presented my ideas about how to understand alters versus demons, Christians who have had years of experience in deliverance work say they knew all along that certain entities seemed like demons initially but didn't respond to exorcism like demons do. Characteristically, these Christian practitioners appreciate the instruction they receive about dissociation and seem to use it well. They often let me know at some later time that they found a therapist to take over the majority of the psychological work, while they continue as a spiritual guide.

I always hope that any particular person I am working with will be free of demonic oppression, but that hope is sometimes dashed. In those cases, I am calmed because I have learned how to deal with the demonic. As was mentioned in chapter 1, it is useful to think about demonization in terms of different degrees of entanglement. Although any demonization can be dangerous, even life-threatening, there seem to be preferred ways of dealing with them at their different levels.

Dealing With Level 1—Flirtation

We are all subject to this kind of demonization. It is a flirtation to think that life would be wonderful if we could be more powerful, even godlike. This level is experienced by those who go to card readers or who have seances. It starts out as a tease or a childlike impulse, but it grows. There might be some kind of magic or demonic power which would provide an escape from a serious disease or offer some sense of mastery in an otherwise unfulfilling life.[6]

Temptation

Not only does this kind of power draw people like nails to a magnet, but just a taste of power also calls for more power, and so on. It becomes a habit that needs increasingly higher levels to keep it satisfied. For people who are practically powerless, or for young people who have dreams of "becoming somebody" (who is powerful), it is a highly alluring temptation to go to a card reader or to a seance or to do something to establish contact with the "other side." The fantasy is that life could be wonderful if only they could take people right out of their path. The temptation to flirt with this power holds the promise of making a person feel special and powerful.

One thing that tempts me is to become rich and famous. Here is how I flirted with that briefly—but I avoided a romance with it. Not too long ago I received a call from an investigative reporter who was doing a TV piece on satanic ritual abuse. When I discovered he was working for a big talk-show host who was putting together a special, I began to get a taste of excitement. Then he told me this host wanted to come to my house and interview me on tape because they were interested in the "spiritual warfare" aspect of my therapy with SRA survivors. The allure began to grow. I was told that this host really wanted to include my material on the special. It didn't take long for me to be drawn by the prospect of national level attention.

I began to ask myself, *Wouldn't it be pleasing to God for me to become a spokesman for those who are trying to tell the truth about SRA? Wouldn't it be wonderful to become known for exorcising demons from survivors of SRA? The fame would take me to circulate among entertainers, authors and celebrities. Wouldn't it be nice to cash in—and get rich—with this chance to break into the public light? I would hardly be able to go to the store because everybody would know my face! Fame and fortune! Don't I deserve it?*

This started out at a low level of temptation, but it gained momentum over a period of about four days. I mentioned the talk-show host's offer to the members of the MPD team at the clinic. "Are you out of your mind?" they asked. "This business is not meant to be just treated like some spectacular topic that is here today and gone tomorrow. You would not get a chance to say what you really want to say, and the tape would get edited anyway. You would lose control of your material."

But the temptation was strong. My career could take off. Everybody would worship me. I would become a nationally known figure, championing truth and justice.

My wife wanted nothing to do with the talk-show special either. The temptation did not hit her the same way it had hit me. She was free and clear of any sort of outside influence from it. None of those I trusted thought it was anything to get involved with. I was amazed! *How come all these "friends" of mine want to deny me a chance like this?*

It started to gnaw at my inner parts. Feelings of jealousy, pride, and resentment began to couple with fantasies of fame and fortune. It was driving a wedge between myself and my friends. I was beginning to move away from my base of support, and I even found myself thinking, *I won't need them when I'm famous. I'll have other, more important friends anyway.* It is hard for me to admit, right now, how strong the pull was. It was the American dream. I'd be somebody. It would be the jackpot. I could get a house in the country, buy a few horses . . .

The tension within me continued to mount until Saturday night at 11:00, when I came to the point where I finally prayed about it. Isn't that odd? Here was a major decision, and I realized I hadn't even prayed about it yet! Upon opening up to God about the decision, a great peace came pouring over me, and I let go of the flirtation. It was obvious to me then that accepting the offer was not the proper path to take. I hurried to my wife in the next room, exuberant about the victory God had just given me, and I told her, "God let me know that He will give me other arenas to talk about SRA and spiritual warfare. I won't be going on TV."

Looking back on that moment I can see the power that prayer played in exposing the work of Satan. He was serving up a delectable dish prepared especially for my appetite. I will never know for certain, but I believe that my efforts to be a serious clinician would have been destroyed by an appearance on TV at that point. It could have been disasterous. What I do know is that three or four days later I received an invitation to speak at an international convention of Christian psychologists—and that was the arena to share my views in. God produced what He had promised—He gave me the proper arena to talk about all of this. From that point forward, He has continued to lead me to arenas where I am free to talk openly. I continue to notice temptations now and then which offer fame and fortune, but I laugh at them and remind myself of how tersely Jesus put it:

> Seek first [God's] kingdom and his righteousness,
> and all these things [food, clothing, and shelter] will be
> given to you as well. Therefore do not worry about tomor-
> row, for tomorrow will worry about itself. Each day has
> enough trouble of its own (Matthew 6:33,34).

When I remind myself to attend to the daily tasks that God gives me, the temptation disappears, and the rift between me and my community disappears as well.

Restoration from this level of demonization is no more complicated than choosing to follow the Lord. Living a life of faith in Christ causes the demonic nature of temptations to be exposed. However, the difficulties of avoiding flirtations with the devil are not obvious much of the time. Satan is known as "the deceiver," and his forays into peoples' lives are not easy to detect in their early stages. Yet, as the saying goes, "If you give the devil an inch, he'll take a mile." When a person's flirtation has gotten serious, and the devil has taken his mile, its demonic nature becomes harder to miss.

Demonic Lures

Here is how that can develop: In the beginning stages of family therapy with the Joneses, I scheduled a session with their teenage son Tommy and one of his friends, John, who was temporarily living in the Jones household. We had established good rapport, and some family conflicts started coming into the open after a few sessions. Tommy and his friend liked certain types of drugs and alcohol, and played their "death rock" music loudly enough to make life in their house calamitous. The friends they were finding through drugs and music were infectiously evil. The boys told me one Monday evening that they had spent the better part of the preceding night with a new acquaintance, Randy, who was "into backward masking." He had records which contained hidden satanic chants in them, discernable only when the record was played backward. He would chant satanic phrases, and constantly listen to music that I would call "evil-prone." Tommy and John could hardly believe their own story as they told it to me. This "Randy" had distinctively emotionless eyes, and they never saw him sleep despite having been with him for 72 hours straight. He did not talk about where he came from nor about working or going to school. He was vacant. He gave them drugs, and he had vast knowledge about "death rock." He would sit endlessly listening to the music and chanting along with the backward masking on the records, and he would spin yarns about the attractiveness of "sex, drugs and rock-and-roll."

That night, at the stroke of midnight, the two boys said they simultaneously saw his facial features change to become devilish, and at that point they told him he had to leave. Tommy had been raised with the knowledge of God, but had not yet had this kind of a direct flirtation with the demonic. Both of the boys were spooked. I told them, without even thinking through what I was saying, "The devil is trying to kill you." That is not the kind of thing I am likely to say, but it came out, nonetheless, and they didn't miss what I was getting at. They were on the precipice of serious danger if they kept their new friends and new habits.

Six nights later, I got a call from Tommy's father. Tommy and his friend needed me to talk with the juvenile authorities so that the two of them could be placed back in the Joneses' home. Since I was their psychologist, I was asked to assure the authorities that I would be working with the boys. The call was coming from the hospital where the social worker needed to decide whether to send them to juvenile hall or back home. I said, yes, I would be continuing to see them as part of family therapy. I wanted to know what had happened to the boys. Why did the authorities need to confirm that the boys were already in therapy? I heard the whole story at our therapy session the next evening, which was exactly one week after my warning about the devil.

Tommy and John had gone to the beach with a few of their new friends, had taken drugs while still on their way, and then they drank a lot of hard alcohol at the beach. Tommy suddenly had stopped breathing, and the lifeguard was called to sustain his life until an ambulance could get there. The ambulance people helped Tommy with his breathing, and John climbed into the ambulance with him, despite the protests of the medical personnel. On the way to the hospital, John's breathing stopped too! They both almost died! That is what can happen when people flirt with temptation. In the pursuit of a demonic lure, in this case drugs, Tommy and John could have been killed. They urged me to tell every teenager I meet about the dangers of sex, drugs and rock-and-roll. They were convinced that those three things are what the devil uses to destroy kids, and many lives get wasted.

I am not certain just what stopped these boys from breathing. I assume it was an interaction of ingested drugs. It seems more than just coincidental, though, that it happened so shortly after a demonic contact.

Tommy and John, your message is well taken. Not only can kids' lives get seriously impaired from those things, but your story brings out another important message—when you start chanting and inviting Satan to show you his power, you have edged toward a deeper level of demonic entanglement.

Dealing With Level 2—Invitation

Tommy and John did not need any help to get rid of the demonic influence. They rejected the use of demonic enticements and drew closer to God without the specific need for deliverance. They needed only to make the conscious decision to give their lives to God for His protection and guidance. If they had gotten into ritual chanting or had invited Satan into their lives, their spiritual struggle would have been more difficult, as was the case for Darla.

Darla had been in individual therapy with Stan, who is a therapist at the clinic where I work. She had spent 17 years worshiping in an organization which claimed to worship God in the spirit but was actually counterfeit. Darla has had a difficult life, but I found no signs of psychotic thinking or of dissociation as I talked with her. Thus, her story seemed believable. She would not get her personality parts confused with demons or experience hallucinations. I asked to meet with her a few times, so that I could document her experiences on tape for this book. She stressed to me that she did not want to glamorize the demonic things she had been through. She just wanted to get to the truth as much as possible and spread the word that there is danger in religious experiences which run parallel to Christianity but do not center around the true God. Here are a few excerpts from our conversations.

Jim: "During your first therapy session with Stan you suddenly became aware of evil spirits, and four of them were expelled. However, on your way home you became aware that not all had been sent out. What happened after that?"

Darla: "When I got home, I started praying. I just said, 'Lord, I know You are the author of the universe. Nothing is impossible for You, and I know that You can deliver whatever (evil spirit) is left from me, and I ask You to do it.' And then in a more aggressive tack, I bound those spirits and commanded them to leave. I told them that there was no place for them in me, and that Jesus was my Lord and Savior, and that His Holy Spirit was the only spirit that was to be in me."

Jim: "Can you help me understand a little bit better how you knew that there was a residual spirit—that there was still something left?"

Darla: "That's hard. It's so hard to explain. It has to do with discernment. Stan asked me that. 'How do you know when they are all out?' That's a question I've always had. 'Hey, how do you know there's not something lurking in there?' There is a sense that there is still something else in there. I felt it when I left Stan's office.

"I had a different experience earlier. That was at an annual renewal conference—Christians of all denominations. I subsequently read about [this kind of deliverance], but up until that time, as far as I knew, I thought it was unique to me.

"I felt talons digging into my shoulders and into my hips, in a very, very painful way, while I was wanting to go up front for prayer. The more intense the desire within me to go up front became, the more strongly those talons dug themselves in. This was the 'head honcho.' I had seen him, several weeks earlier, when he had appeared to me."

Jim: "You could see him outside of yourself?"

Darla: "Yes. I was with the Lord, and then it changed, and it was a traumatic experience for me."

Jim: "You thought you were seeing the Lord, and then all of a sudden it became something else?"

Darla: "That's right. I could never accept, because of my nature and who I am, that Satan is really a dirty rat, and that he would use whatever means necessary to deceive and to destroy. I just didn't think there could be anything so vile."

Spontaneous Deliverance

"After leaving Stan's I was saying those prayers (to be completely freed from whatever was left in me), and the following morning I had an experience that I had never had before in my life. My whole body went cold and prickly. I can only describe it as very unpleasant. The whole time I had this sensation washing over me. I found myself running to the toilet and wretching—just wretching—and as I was wretching I was spontaneously praying prayers of gratitude to the Lord that these things were being delivered. I had never heard of that before. No one had ever said to me that you could have a 'spontaneous deliverance' by praying, but it was very clear to me. That is what it was. Then I had that feeling of being clean—everything at that point was out.

"As a result of those deliverances I was once again able to be in the Word [the Bible]. It had been hard for me to be in the Word. My prayers were sort of hitting the ceiling. When I opened up the Word it would be flat instead of alive, and I just couldn't connect with the Lord. After the deliverance, that changed. Going to the Word has been a pleasure. My prayers became more spontaneous—I felt I was in the Lord again."

Jim: "You said you had been involved in an organization some time earlier. One of the questions I am trying to learn more about is the connection between, for lack of a better term, 'bogus' religions and the entrance of evil spirits. What kind of a chance do you think there was that these spirits, which were expelled at different times, had entered while you were part of that other religious-type organization?"

Darla: "The ones that were delivered before [I began therapy with Stan], and the one at home, definitely [came from that organization]! There is a direct relationship. I had experienced them in another form in my worship, with the other organization. I was familiar with them from the other organization, which worships 'God in the spirit,' but it wasn't God."

Jim: "You said that since the recent deliverances, there has been a major shift in your ability to worship God, and to be vitalized by His Spirit, and through the Scriptures. Have some other areas of your life shown changes as well?"

Darla: "Well, I believe that God's the bottom line, so any time fundamental change takes place, everything changes."

Jim: "Anxiety and depression?"

Darla: "Those are my enemies. That's Satan's ploy with me. If he's going to attack me, that's where he'll do it. I've had to really pray through it, stand against it, stay in the Word—it's a battle! If there is one thing that proves things are clean, it is the sense of renewal—of really being in the Lord, and being strengthened by the Lord, and being strengthened by the Word.

"Nothing else worked to change my life. My life has fundamentally changed since I came back to the Lord, and continues to be changed. I am becoming new each day. I am becoming more the person God created me to be, and it is something tangible. Whereas before, whether I went to a workshop or saw a counselor or worshiped [in the other group] or took antidepressant medications, or whatever I did, it looked like changes took place on the outside, but inside I knew I was the same. When I came to the Lord, I was not looking for this [kind of a complete change]. The Lord called me back so strongly that when I accepted Him as my Lord and Savior, the changes were a by-product. I know that is what He promises and that is what He delivers, but it was not why I came back, or what I was looking for. For me, it's my confirmation that whatever the Word says about the Lord is true.

"Intellectually, I struggle with the fact that the road is narrow. I want it to be so wide that everyone is saved. I struggle with the fact that there are people who are good, who want the truth, who do want to worship God, but who are on the wrong path. I struggle with God, but I am willing to accept the narrow way for myself because of my reality. The truth is that the Lord is changing me and continues to change me. Sometimes Satan steps in and says, 'That's not true.'

"My husband left the family seven years ago, and I took the children with me and went back to the university. I got a degree, and everyone said, 'You are remarkable! Look at the changes, look at how you've grown.' I couldn't convince them that nothing had changed. I looked great, but I knew that inside I was the same person. The same patterns re-established themselves, and the depression reached the point where I was seriously suicidal. That's what Satan wanted! I am convinced suicidal tendencies are directly from the pit of hell. He wants to turn you from the path that God is taking you.

"God had been pulling me away from this organization for years, to come back to Christ, and I didn't because in this organization we believed we were worshiping in the spirit. People were supposed to stay in their present religion, because it was the exterior—the ritual. I was led to a certain church where my faith in Christ was strengthened, and my struggle intensified to the point where I wondered if it was all a trick. It was all like a monstrous trick to me. *That organization was a trick, so why isn't this church a trick too?*

"I believe that the truth is who I am—what the Lord has done inside me. All my efforts, all my prayers [in that other organization], those things never changed me. After three years I came back to the Lord, and in the last two and a half years, just wonderful things have happened to me."

No Magic Cure

Darla's on-going effort to become the person God meant her to be is encouraging and realistic, but don't look for it to point the way to a magic cure. I try to be as honest as I can about the nature of deliverance. I always tell people that to expel spirits is not the hard part. The power of God is sufficient to deliver people from spirits without much of a struggle at this level of demonization. The hard part is growing in the Lord and establishing a maturing life among His people. Darla's deliverances were an essential part of her growth. She ordered the demons to leave her, and they did. They lost the power she had granted them during her participation in the other organization, and as she continued to mature in the Lord, their power continued to diminish. However, her life did not become a merry-go-'round experience. The demonic oppression continued to come at her from the flirtation level. She moved from the *invitation* level of demonization to the level we are all on—the *flirtation* level—by an act of her will. She was following the instruction found in James 4:7,8: "Submit yourselves, then, to God. Resist the devil, and he will flee from you. Come near to God and he will come near to you."

For the rest of her life she will be subjected to oppression and temptation from the devil, just like the rest of us, but she will not be tormented on the inside. The demons which had entered by her invitation no longer have a place in her. She is becoming renewed daily as she builds her life.

Dealing With Level 3—Spiritual "Union" With Satan

People cannot sell their souls to the devil. People cannot become married to Satan. No contract, whether or not it is written in blood, is valid if it is made with a liar. Satan is the king of liars, and any contract or agreement with him is a sham. People can reject Satan's claim on their soul. However, when the person believes he or she is in a spiritual union with Satan, or when a demonic stronghold has been built within, exorcism is often necessary.

Ritual Marriage

There are many convincing yet deceitful tricks that cultists use to exert mind control. Here is just one: A child is elaborately prepared for a ritual marriage and given some drugs that mar her perceptive abilities. Then she "marries" someone dressed up to play the part of Satan and is later told, "Now that you have married Satan you will obey the orders that come from him." Whether the orders are to obtain a baby for a ritual, or to kill the baby during a ritual, or whatever they are, the child has been programmed to obey. The idea becomes fixed in that child's mind that life from now on will be lived as a bride of Satan. The thoughts keep being replayed in the child's mind according to the programming of the cultists: "A bride of Satan must do whatever is requested by the cult priest. Anything. I will always be a bride of Satan, and cannot escape. I will continue to be subject to the wishes of the cult leaders for the rest of my life. I have no life of my own. I belong to Satan."

For children who have signed "the book" in their own blood on their fourth birthday, or for children who have become married to someone who looks like Satan, the programming runs very deep. Hopelessness prevails, at least in the personality that remembers the ceremony.

Adults and children who have participated in such rituals develop an identity as a "bad person"—a person in union with Satan. It may have started out with flirtation and invitation, but when demonic involvement exists at this level, the person's identity becomes aligned with evil. To have participated in the murderous sacrifice of other humans in honor of Satan has to have a profound effect on one's identity. "I'm bad. That's it."

Family Spirits

Another kind of experience with a profound effect on a child's identity is the entrance of a "family spirit." I have been told by adult survivors from cult families that when they were young they were called to the deathbeds of their grandparents or other relatives and were given spirits from the dying relative. Those are known as "family" or "familiar" spirits and are passed down as part of the child's heritage. That child, or at least one alter of that child, receives the demon and gives it a place to attach. The child believes that the continuing presence of the demon proves he or she will always belong to the demon, or to Satan. "You are in the line of Satan's followers. It is in your blood."

This kind of attachment can be called a "demonic stronghold." The person's own strong belief that he or she is in union with the demon combines with the demonic strength and presents a powerful entanglement. The demonic voice rings out like a bell in the victim's head: "You belong to Satan. You will always belong to Satan. You will do as you are told." The inner fear and confusion that result keep the person constantly off balance, and the demonic possession deepens. The person gets weaker and the evil spirit gets stronger.

I do not believe we are talking about the power of suggestion here, although a person's high suggestibility makes the attachment seem even stronger. The ferocity of the demonic activity to retain "rights" on the individual's soul demonstrates more than suggestibility. If not bound in the name of Jesus, either the person or the exorcist can be hurt during the expulsion. Hissing, foaming and growling are not uncommon during exorcisms at this level of demonization.

STEPS OF EXORCISM— SEEKING AN UNDIVIDED HEART

In the account of the prophet Ezekiel, the story is told of how God's people Israel were once again scattered after they had fallen to powerful enemies. Through Ezekiel, God promised them He would restore them to their place as His people in the land of Israel. As part of this restoration, He promised in chapter 11 to "give them an undivided heart and put a new spirit in them." He went on to say:

> I will remove from them their heart of stone and give them a heart of flesh. Then they will follow my decrees and be careful to keep my laws. They will be my people, and I will be their God. But as for those whose hearts are devoted to their vile images and detestable idols, I will bring down on their own heads what they have done, declares the Sovereign LORD (Ezekiel 11:19-21).

An undivided heart. That is what it takes to live life to the fullest. When the heart is divided, chaos prevails. Progress is impossible. In the context of driving out demons, Jesus said that a house divided against itself cannot stand (Matthew 12:25). Successful living and successful therapy will be stalled while the heart remains divided.

A "Divided" Heart

It appears to me that the will component of dissociation is the first one to become divided. The mildest dissociative experience is when a person wants to do two things: A young man's responsible character wants to marry the object of his affection, but a younger, more impetuous character wants to whistle at every beautiful girl around.

"Why do I do that, Dr. Friesen?"

"A divided heart is not going to have any peace."

"You're right! I've got to get rid of that lustful part of my heart."

"Not so fast. Every part of you has good in it. You are made in the image of God, right?"

"But what about my lustful urges?"

"Temptation is one thing, but your characters need to work together better. If you 'cast one out,' your heart will still be divided, because you cannot just erase yourself. The adult-you and the lusty-you need to work together, and stop their quarreling with each other."

That is the way therapy usually goes. A person can stave off temptation without any major difficulty, and the process of unifying the heart is self-directed. However, when the personalities do not know each other, a heart remains divided. Until the alter personalities become unified, or at least until they pool all their information, a divided heart is inevitable. MPD therapy is pointed toward overcoming the divisions of a person's heart. When those divisions contain some parts that follow the true God, some parts that follow Satan, and many non-aligned parts, the spiritual struggle can disrupt life continuously. Every alter that lines up with God, and every alter that matures in the Lord, adds to the health of the whole system.

In Tricia's therapy, Jesus had always been in the middle of her restoration. Her therapy had progressed to the point where all of her level 1 alters had successfully merged, and we had come against demons in that process. They were of the "invitation" variety, and she dispelled them without much difficulty.

Unifying the Heart

But before she was ready for the difficult work with the SRA-survivor alters (who were cut off by a thick blanket of amnesia), her heart needed to become more unified.

Her core personality, which had by this time grown to include about fifteen personalities, had a strong faith. Tricia believed that God's hand had brought about the progress she had attained, and that God's presence would be necessary to bring healing to the SRA-survivor alters as they started to surface. The divided heart difficulty became evident when a strong alter surfaced—Defender. This alter had been doing an important job all along. She had been doing her work behind the scenes without ever taking executive control and actually talking. Now that the level 1 alters had become fused, she could no longer work behind the scenes, and she found herself in an open slot. She was "out," and she hesitatingly continued to do her job up front instead of behind the scenes. We talked—it was mostly me doing the talking—and she let me know she intended to keep on doing her job of keeping the SRA-survivor alters walled off from memory. Too many disruptive feelings would emerge. She believed the whole system would fall apart if she didn't do her job.

It was important to take a few weeks and build a relationship with her, and to get her to recognize that (1) she was not working together with Tricia, and that (2) Jesus' healing had been an important part of therapy. She had seen the healing that came from Jesus, but she still remained at odds with Tricia. Defender had enough power to keep doing her job, and she continued to block the work in therapy. I had no sense that she was demonized. We were talking about how important her job was, but now she needed to change her job description. My challenge to her was that she needed to let these SRA-survivor alters come out in therapy for healing. She had been protecting them, but now I asked her to carefully let them out to receive the restoration that they had been awaiting all these years.

Silence.

I then suggested that, since she knew of other alters who had used imagery well already, we could do the same with these hurting child alters.

Defender began to shake. She could not speak.

I asked her if she was ready to follow Jesus. The bodily shaking temporarily got worse, and then stopped. Without looking at me, she nodded her head. She was ready to turn her heart over to God. We prayed together, and she was freed from her burden. Jesus would help her with her job.

Tricia's system was now unified enough to delve into the SRA memories. The division of her heart no longer kept her from getting on with the necessary therapeutic work.

The process of turning over each part of one's heart to God is the preferred therapeutic pathway. As new alters are uncovered, they are introduced to Jesus. Many of the younger ones have never heard of Him so the faith of the adult alters is important. When the Christian alters are able to share their life-giving Christian experiences with the other alters, the system becomes progressively more unified. The more spiritual maturity there is in the core personality or in the level 1 alters, the less difficulty there will be in subduing spiritual dividedness. For Tricia, that included exorcising demons who were attached to the SRA-survivor alters. The exorcism proceeded well, in large part because her heart was becoming unified.

The Path of Spiritual Growth

The other therapeutic pathway for exorcism is not quite as straightforward. There are times when the Host alter, or some other powerful alters, are not in alignment with the will of some alters who want to unify the heart. When the demonic ferocity is strong enough, and/or when the alter(s) are not able to follow Jesus, the system's equilibrium can stay out of balance. The dividedness can influence the will of some alters about turning their heart over to God. The dividedness of the heart can be serious enough to make self-deliverance ineffective. There may not be enough of a spiritual concensus to cast out the demons.

Jesus warned about this kind of a situation in Matthew, 12:43-45. The way I understand it, that teaching was directed to the unbelieving people who were all around Him. He was saying that, even if an evil spirit were to come out of one of them, unless the one who had just been delivered would turn his heart over to God, the spirit would return with "seven other spirits more wicked than itself . . . and the final condition of that man [would be] worse than the first." That is particularly instructive to an exorcist. It is not hard to direct the power of God to cast out a demon. The hard part is turning over every part of the heart to God and keeping on track with discipleship. If that doesn't happen, the spiritual warfare that is stirred up can be quite violent. This caution seems warranted on the basis of Jesus' teaching: Don't start casting out demons until the person is ready to turn his (or her) heart over to God as much as possible.

The second exorcism pathway is designed to follow this teaching. In cases where demons get cast out by some alters but are allowed to re-enter by others, it is vital to have a network of Christian friends around who will be able to gently lead in the process of discipleship. The daily walk with God is a necessary step as the alters learn how to turn away from temptation and stop inviting demons in. It is helpful to have the oppressed individual bind evil spirits in the name of Jesus at the beginning of each day and continue to bind them whenever they are noticed so that the process of discipleship can be effectively pursued.

Under these conditions, the friends and/or therapist can exorcise the demons in behalf of the person because the person's heart remains divided. Continuing care and attention to the oppressed person's well-being by the whole network of people is an important part of restoration. The community is to be involved, praying for and supporting the survivor. Then as new satanic strongholds are discovered, they can be dealt with.

Satanic Strongholds

A few difficult cases indicate that there is danger when some people in the survivor's support network pay too much attention to demonic issues and not enough to growth and discipleship. As a result, the psychological issues tend to go nowhere, and the support network gets "burned out." When the support team works with the oppressed person from a continuing basis of assaulting demonic entities in the absence of patient psychological and discipleship care, discouragement results instead of progress.

Here is the way an exorcism session proceeded in Rosie's MPD/SRA therapy. We were doing some "house" imagery, and the new alter that we had met in the conference room was in a lot of torment. Although Rosie had evil spirits delivered from her at different times previously, this alter turned out to be a demonic point of attachment that had resisted previous expulsions—a satanic stronghold. The demons were able to use the divisions of her heart, including the parts that were occluded by amnesia, to maintain their attachment. They could keep hiding from the "Christian" alters, and thereby avoid being directly exorcised. Now that the demonized alter had been uncovered, we were able to go ahead with the exorcism.

Eight Steps of Exorcism

Step 1 had already been accomplished. Rosie really wanted to turn herself over to God as much as she could. Her faith in God, and her reliance on Him to guide her through treatment had already been established. Nonetheless, I asked the host if she was ready to cast out the unwanted intruder. She said she certainly was, and we were ready to get on to the the next step.

Step 2 is to bind the spirits so that they can do no damage during the exorcism.

"In the name of Jesus, all spirits are bound, mute and immobile. You cannot influence Rosie in any way. You cannot hurt her on the way out, and you will be able to respond only if spoken to in the name of Jesus."

Step 3 is to get the spirit's name. This is not always success-ful because some of them continue to resist. They can even try to sidetrack the exorcist.

"In the name of Jesus, you are to speak your name."

"Fracture."

Step 4 is to find out how it gained entry to the client, which can help defend against future assaults.

"In the name of Jesus, tell us how you got into this person."

There was no answer to this question, so we left it un-answered. It seemed the spirit was trying to get us off track.

Step 5 is to find the task or function of the spirit.

"In the name of Jesus, what is your job?"

"Function to fracture." [This spirit impelled an SRA-sur-vivor alter to partake in violent acts during rituals.] It was now becoming apparent that the spirit had been given access to the child alter during a ritual.

Step 6 is to send the spirit out.

"In the name of Jesus, you must leave." (This is said matter-of-factly, in a direct fashion. It is not necessary to use strong, emotionally charged voice inflection.)

"That was easy. It left right away."

Step 7 is to find if other spirits have been exposed which can now be exorcised.

"We need to find out if there are any more demons lurking around this child alter."

Rosie was almost surprised by my comment. "I think that was all."

I continued, "In the name of Jesus, if there is another spirit present, you are commanded to state your name."

The next one was the powerful one. It is not uncommon for the strong demons to try to quietly stay around, while a weaker one is expelled. Rosie was shocked at the scarey, intimidating image that was presented to her.

"It has six rows of teeth, and looks like it would kill me if it could, but it is quietly standing there."

It was a good thing that we had bound it ahead of time, so it would cause no damage during the exorcism. After that one was expelled I told all remaining demons to quietly line up.

"There is an infinite line of them!" she said.

Rosie was not particularly upset, because the demons she was seeing were not able to intimidate her. She had seen the power of God. They were looking like they were already defeated, and they knew their destiny. Rosie saw a whirlwind take them all away. A peace set in that was better than ever.

"Are there any others? In the name of Jesus you must also appear."

With her eyes closed again, Rosie said that she was seeing little stragglers, like roaches from the back end of the room in which the imagery had been taking place. They were cast out, and no others appeared after that.

Step 8 is to seal the work with prayer.

"Dear Lord, thank You for the freedom You have given Rosie! May Your name be praised, and may You receive honor from those who hear of the mighty works You have accomplished today. May Your kingdom come, may Your will be done among us, and may everything that has happened here today advance Your kingdom. Please send Your Holy Spirit to fill all the empty places that have been created by the departing demons, and let Your love permeate Rosie's whole system. And now let Your protecting angels hover around her and continue to protect her from any attacks that would prevent her from enjoying what You have done today. In Jesus' name, amen."

NON-MPD VICTIMS

I have gone through periods in which I seriously doubted the validity of this work—integrating alter personalities and casting out evil spirits—because of the remarkable similarity between alters and spirits. Both usually have names, points of origin and a specific function, and they are identifiable mainly through the client's introspection. It would be short-sighted of me to ignore these similarities. I would reject my conclusions if it were not for the strong evidence that evil spirits can and do also bother non-multiples where there is no possibility of confusing them with alternate personalities, as was the case with Darla. Let me describe two of these non-MPD cases.

Mr. and Mrs. Neal had seen me for marriage therapy a few years ago, and their difficulties were worked out nicely. I got a call recently from Mr. Neal; he asked if he could bring his wife in to talk about something that unexpectedly had come up. I agreed to see them, and they came in a few days later. It was good to see them again, and they had been doing well in every area of their lives until two weeks earlier. They had taken a vacation and visited his mother in another state. Things had not been the same since they got back. He described high anxiety that would grip him daily, and I had no idea how to explain that. He had no anxiety in his history, and there was no evident cause for it.

From my point of view, the most likely cause was the vacation to his mother's house, which must have connected to family dynamics in some way. I started with that premise and set out to find what had happened on the trip.

He detailed things for me, and I found nothing connecting the visit and his anxiety. He had a fairly unremarkable relationship with his mother, so that was not bothering him. When he started talking about her new husband, though, it soon became evident what was going on. His mother's husband had a whole library full of books on astrology and had gone through some of them with Mr. Neal to try to show him how he "wins people to Christ through astrology."

In the Library

While I listened to this story, I kept a poker face. They told me how they couldn't sleep restfully in the astrology library where the guest bed was located. Mr. and Mrs. Neal were dedicated Christians, and they did not entertain the possibility that Christ and astrology would be connected, but they had both tried to see the man's point of view. I asked them if they thought an evil spirit could have been picked up in the library, and they both immediately knew that had happened. The sleepless nights followed them home, and anxiety developed. Spiritual warfare was being waged, and the effects were fear and confusion. They cast out the evil spirits right then and there, and that was my only session with them.

I telephoned Mr. Neal at work the next week, and he said everything was okay. There was no more anxiety, and neither he nor his wife had any lingering sense that something might be wrong. As far as he was concerned, it was an open and shut case—they had expelled the evil spirit! About a week later I received a letter from Mrs. Neal. She wrote about how their life had shifted back onto its proper course after the deliverance. She said she usually had no trouble getting a good night's sleep and would wake up fresh each morning, ready for the day. Since the vacation she had seemed to wake up tired, and her sleep was not deep at all. The letter said she was certain it had been a case of spiritual oppression. She said that after the deliverance, she woke up fresh the next morning just like before, and their family life was great again. That was the shortest therapy possible—one visit. The panic attacks were gone, and their family life was back on track.

There is a pattern here often found in spiritual warfare. A person involved with a bogus approach to religion spreads spirits which perpetrate fear and confusion wherever they can find an opening. When the Neals tried to connect astrology and Christianity, they were attacked. That was the opening. When the attack ended, so did the fear and confusion. The opening had been identified and was now closed.

Uninvited Hate and Lust

A second case of non-MPD spiritual oppression that I found was through Don, one of the interns I supervise. Don told me he thought one of his new clients, Perry, might have an evil spirit. I had never talked with Don about spirits before, and I said to him that, from what he told me, there was nothing in particular that seemed to indicate spiritual oppression so we should probably not bring it up with Perry. Of course, we would not ask him if he thought he might have an evil spirit without being fairly certain that was the case. That could provoke a lot of fear. Don and I decided to let that idea wait until other information about Perry's life became available. Week after week, Don and I tried to figure out how to help Perry in his marriage and in the struggles of his life. He was not getting better, and we could not put his therapy on a steady course. Things kept changing from week to week, and I was stumped.

Then Don told me about an event that Perry had described to him, which bothered him very much. One Sunday morning, during the pastor's prayer, a bunch of vile words came lurching through his mind, and he had no idea where they were coming from. He was thinking filthy swear words; he had a surge of hatred toward the pastor, which had never happened before. Then he looked around the audience, and started to imagine he was having sex with the pretty women during the prayer. It all seemed so wierd to Perry that he had to talk about it with Don.

I knew that uninvited hate and lust often accompany spiritual oppression, so I asked if Don thought Perry might allow me to sit in on a session. Perry accepted my offer to sit in because he was eager to make some progress, but Don said nothing to him about our spiritual oppression concerns.

When I entered their session, I came in about five minutes after the start, and Perry made a sarcastic statement about my presence despite his stated wish to have me join them. I sensed "bad vibrations" in the room but still did not think any spiritual warfare was afoot. I let Don carry the session for about thirty minutes, and then gradually began to ask some questions without being sure where they might lead. I doubted that any spirits were interfering until about ten minutes before the session was scheduled to end, when I asked if he had ever become involved with other religions.

"Yes," he said. Ten years in a new religion and two years in an ancient religion. I knew that both religions he named could be practiced in ways which allowed the entry of evil spirits. Something within me clicked, and I intuited that we needed to begin to fight spiritually.

He told about the chanting in the ancient religion, and about literally inviting in "helpful" spirits in the new religion, and we got a clearer idea about the spiritual influences that had been working against him. Don, Perry and I had a short time of prayer in which spirits were bound, and we asked God to guide us in dealing with them.

Deliverance

"Perry, are you willing to turn over as much of your life to God as you can?" I asked. "The only way that deliverance can be successful is if you are fully in agreement with us that the evil spirits must be expelled." At first, Perry had a hard time with that question. He was definitely experiencing conflict about his willingness to turn everything over to God.

Then his face lit up and he started speaking with confidence. "Yes. I want to clean up my life. Let's get on with the deliverance."

His decision to let God work in all of his life turned things around. We found eight spirits, each of which had a name and a function, and each was expelled. It was satisfying to watch Perry gain strength as we continued to find the evil spirits. I called upon the power of God to cast out the first six as they were named, and Perry himself cast out the last two. He did so with much authority and felt good about the deliverances. I did not see him for about two weeks, and when I did, he reported that he was doing great. His life had changed completely. Before, he had masturbated every day since he was 14 years old, but the exorcism ended that! His relationship with his wife was improving, and he was just so very happy that he could hardly restrain his glee. It was a miracle, and I could not see any way it could have happened without God's power.

10

RESTORATION THAT ENDURES

PRAYER FOR THE HEALING OF MEMORIES

THE POWER OF PRAYER, unspoken or audible, is one of those elusive issues that has been controversial throughout history. My comments here will certainly not end the controversy. However, if sharing my experiences can promote healing in a few individuals, it is worth the risk of stirring up controversy.

The activity of God in peoples' lives is an experience that changes them forever. People have told me it is as if their life were at a crossroad, and when God intervened in their behalf they found themselves on a new path, never to look back. The faith created by God starts out like a tiny seed, but it grows and grows until it becomes the most stalwart plant in the garden. Whether the work of God can be factually documented or not, or whether it takes place alone or in a group, those who have seen the power of prayer attest that they will never be the same.

People should not get into deliverance or exorcism procedures without the presence of experienced, mature Christians. Although I have outlined steps that can be used, there is one thing I cannot prescribe—the work of the Holy Spirit in the middle of things. Spiritual interventions at the second and third levels of demonic entanglement necessitate a team of people who have had some prior experience in this area, among whom the work of the Holy Spirit is well known. Those who are interested in getting help for afflicted people need to seek out these groups.

A few of us therapists have set aside two hours each week to bring in clients who are in need of prayer. For people who are survivors of severe child abuse, this time of prayer has been an important part of their therapy[1]. In fact, I would say that practically every one of the prayer sessions has concluded with a tremendous sense that God has delivered the healing we asked Him for. Sometimes the client brings in a spouse, a friend or a pastor, but whoever joins in the prayer time seems to experience the power of God in a fresh and exciting way. It is good to share the experience as part of God's family, and it is good to be involved together in the struggle against evil. No doubt, God could work as well through a small number of people in prayer, but he seems to use each person there to minister to the afflicted person. Here is a summary of a recent session, which is typical of the way God works through each of us.

Help for Sally

There were four of us who came to pray with Sally. We had prayed with her on two other occasions, so it helped that we already felt comfortable together. Her MPD therapy was at the point where she was meeting SRA-survivor child alters, and her progress was getting blocked. We were able to talk with her easily during the prayer session, using "MPD language." Her therapy had progressed to the point where she could usually switch between alters whenever she tried. Sally already knew that, since some of the alters do not want to take executive control of the body, especially those who fear further hurt, we could use imagery profitably to get to know them.

We opened the prayer time, as we always do, by asking the Lord to take over, and to help us put our own agenda aside.

"We don't know Sally as well as You do, Lord, but we pray You will guide our focus to things that will help her the most. Please keep us from getting off on a sidetrack. Please direct the work we do with Sally during this session so it will result in the healing You want to accomplish for her today. Please reach deep down into her mind and help her to find just the memory that needs Your touch today. May Your kingdom be honored right now, and may Your name receive praise for the healing which You want to bring about in Sally."

Sally was brave but frightened. She had received a few pictures from Hazel, the SRA-survivor child alter, and already knew about some of the things she had gone through. The pictures were of being in a grave for a very long time, of going through terror and horror, and of performing awful tasks that were required of her. The other alters wanted nothing to do with this child. She was considered evil, in union with Satan. She was covered with filth and contaminated with guilt and shame. None of the other child alters who had been brought into the imagery could stand to be with Hazel, considering the things she had been through. That was the therapeutic impasse she had been stuck in for about two weeks.

One of us asked if Sally could bring Jesus into the picture, as the imagery developed. She did.

"Let Jesus attend to the needs of Hazel. He knows what will help her the most."

We continued to pray in silence for a few minutes. My inner prayer included the picture of Jesus picking Hazel up and hugging her but saying nothing—her filth disappeared and her guilt dissipated. My prayers continued, and so did the prayers of the others. As I looked on, Sally's eyelids showed movement from side to side, and various expressions scurried across her face. I knew that the Lord was working.

When she opened her eyes, she said that Jesus not only had restored Hazel to look as perky as the other child alters, but He had directed them to accept her as one of them. In her imagery, one of the child alters became Hazel's special friend and took her by the hand to the recovery tent. The therapists did not direct any of the crucial parts of the imagery. It was a matter between her and God. All of us thanked God together, rejoicing for the healing which had been accomplished in our midst. The joy generating from each of us was infectious. We had witnessed God's answer to our prayers: Sally had gotten the things that would help her most—healing for Hazel, and agreement among the children in her system to treat Hazel more kindly. Her therapy sped ahead to the next obstacle. It was a miracle!

Spirit "Friends"

It can be a big letdown to have such a great sense of progress only to crash into another wall a few days later, but that is often the way MPD therapy goes. It seems each alter has its own decontamination to go through, and then another alter shows up with a new set of problems. Soon after the prayer session, Sally discovered another SRA-child alter, Violet. This one had been given three spirit "friends" to "be with her for the rest of her life." They were telling her to destroy Sally. Sally scheduled an extra session with me to work things out.

"Hurt her." They would insist. "She is evil. Hurt her. She is so evil, you must destroy her. Hurt her."

"Just a minute, Violet," I said. "Please tell me who is telling you to hurt her."

"My friends."

"If they are really your friends, you will be able to find that they have personalities to go along with their voices. However, be careful, because if they are only voices without personalities, that means they are demons. Demons lie, and if they are telling you to hurt her, you'd better do just the opposite."

There was a thoughtful silence.

"They are just voices, but they are saying they are my friends."

"I believe if they really are your friends, they will be alters."

"I can't find any alters. They are just the voices of my friends."

"I am going to help you discover whether they are friends or not." Then I spoke to the "friends." "If you 'voices' are really personalities, please talk to me, but if you are demons, in the name of Jesus you are bound and will not be able to speak at all."

After a moment of silence I asked if Violet could hear anything.

"They're gone. But they can come back. They always do."

I was not about to let this chance get away. "If they are your friends they should be able to stick with you. Ask them if they are demons or friends."

She looked up at the ceiling for a pause, and then looked soberly at me. "I can't hear anything, and I can't see anything."

"That is the way demons are. You were told that they would be with you for the rest of your life, but where did they go? The prince of lies is the devil, and his demons are full of deceit. You just can't trust them. Stay away from them, and do the opposite of what they say."

Jesus' Faithfulness

So I taught her how to cast them away in case they should ever return. The power of the name of Jesus had been demonstrated to her, and now she was prepared to use it to ward off the urgings of the demons who had been given to her years ago. A satanic stronghold had been broken, and Sally had pushed through another therapeutic impasse.

It seems to me that unless such demonic voices are silenced, people like Sally could get seriously stuck in therapy and might never fully recover. I have been present when Jesus was in the imagery of at least twenty-five people, and it is always the same. I don't put words in His mouth, and I don't suggest what He should do to care for the client. He does the things in the imagery that He would do if He were present in bodily form. Sometimes He talks to them and sometimes He just holds them. Sometimes the healing is dramatic and sometimes the healing is subtle, but it is always the result of the power of God through prayer. I pray that He will be present and that He will bring healing in the way that only He can. I am initially surprised when "miracles" happen, but when I think back and remember how many other times He has done just what I asked Him to do, the surprise turns to the awesome recognition that He has acted decisively. My faith grows a little each time because He has acted decisively again.

WALKING BY FAITH AMONG GOD'S PEOPLE

Perhaps one of the biggest problems experienced by astronauts on future journeys to distant planets will be loneliness.

Human life is meant to be lived in community. Isolation is torture. In the absence of human contact, people lose touch with reality. Within us all lies a deep need to be in close contact with other people, and that means more than just one person. We need to be connected with a group of people on whom we can depend for frequent doses of pleasure and nurture. Without that we will surely wither.

Cult members know about this human need, and they exploit it in shaping the lives of their victims. By isolating them from family or friends through intimidation and fear, and by artificially meeting their community needs through sinister rituals, cult members can maintain an incredible hold on their victims.

I know of a case where an MPD/SRA survivor's therapy was running into snag after snag. Whatever would work at one meeting would be ineffective at the next. The cult high priest had formed an exclusive relationship with a lonely child alter in her system. She was his "special friend." He gave her cute little gifts and phoned her every day. Her part of the relationship was to phone him after each session with the therapist, and after each meeting with her pastor. The cult leader thanked her for being his special girl, and her loneliness diminished for another day. However, because this girl was not in community, she was totally dependent on the high priest to meet those daily needs. She gave him information about what the therapist and the pastor had talked about, and he gave her human contact. The cult priest was using this child alter to keep up with exactly what was being said in therapy to each alter, and later he would influence them by directing the strong cult alters. Therapy was being seriously sabotaged.

A Sense of Community

When that lonely alter finally was converted from the cult, she needed daily contact with people who would make her feel special. Fortunately, she was developing a sense of community with the church she had joined, and people reached out to her. Her therapy began to move along without so many snags when this lonely alter's needs were provided for in a community instead of her being exploited by one person.

God's people are to provide safety, encouragement, nurture and friendship as part of living life to the fullest.[2] We have found an unbelievable number of children in our society who have been abused, and it is important to provide safe families for them. It is also vital that when these children grow up they find a safe, reliable family. The alternative for them is to live a lonely life. The Christian community is to provide a healthy extended family life. If Christians fail to deliver a proper community experience to these abused children and adults, many of them will be left out in a dangerous world. Their lonely quest to find community will continue, and their need can be exploited by self-centered people. If the cultists are willing to extend themselves to the daily routine of looking after lonely people's needs, shouldn't the people of God be willing to do an even better job? [3]

Jesus said it best:

> Love the Lord your God with all your heart and with all your soul and with all your mind and with all your strength...and love your neighbor as yourself. There is no commandment greater than these (Mark 12:30,31).

Those who love God find that the love they have for Him extends to others, and they wish to live in community together. Christians are willing to go to great lengths to extend their community to those people who are suffering from loneliness and whose wounds need the healing that only God can give. That is the way the Christian life is designed. When it helps restore victims, it is operating as it should.

THE TIDE IS TURNING

I have heard rumors and incidental accounts of seditious plans of cult members. The accounts suggest that some cultists have taken leadership positions in dynamic, growing churches. The undercover cult leaders are said to have sabotaged the spiritual life and programs of those vital churches. Names of particular pastors and religious leaders have come up in the investigations of cult activities.

Of course, it would be ridiculous to bring charges against church leaders with nothing more than the testimony of dissociating people, who could have been tricked into perceiving who the perpetrators were when it was actually imposters disguised to look like the church leaders! The court testimony would end quickly when the witness's MPD and SRA are described; the witness/cult survivor would be subjected to alienation, and people involved would be seriously damaged.

The pathway to the successful prosecution of these criminals is full of potholes, to be sure. It is hard to believe that such a charge could stand up to the rigors of current court procedures. However, do not rush to the conclusion that such a case will not come up in court, because the evidence can be strong. Because cultists want to maintain highly respected positions (physicians, attorneys, child care specialists and church leaders) to keep themselves above suspicion, we know where to look for them—in highly respected positions!

In fact, some in those positions are known SRA perpetrators. Their "cover" as respected leaders will not last as the information about SRA activities becomes more widely accepted as accurate. I have heard too many memories—and so have other therapists—of things which take place in churches to believe that churches can continue to be the arenas of cult rituals. The truth will be known.

A Revealing Report

In recent years, cult leaders have been carrying out aggressive plans. They are apparently opening up and/or taking over existing preschools and setting out to recruit helpless children to become future cult members. Los Angeles is one of the areas targeted for this kind of recruitment. Quite a few L.A. therapists have been identifying the child survivors, though, and have been educating the public about SRA, and the cult plan is being weakened because of increasing public awareness. Therapists, pediatricians and adult survivors of SRA are having press conferences, writing reports about SRA, representing public hearings about SRA, and generally saying as loudly as they can, "Save the children."

The report of the L.A. County Task Force on Ritual Abuse has been a wonderful addition to SRA literature.[4] It is hoped that the Task Force's report will promote prevention and healing and will help therapists all over the world to believe their clients when SRA stories start to emerge in therapy. As more survivors are coming out of hiding to tell their stories, more people are believing that the awful things described actually could be happening. The events recounted by SRA survivors are gaining credibility.

An Alarming Development

According to therapists who work with SRA survivors, unverifiable but important messages have been delivered. A word of warning seems in order: As part of their aggressive plan to take over the world by the turn of the century, the cult groups have been infiltrating churches with a more sinister objective than merely disrupting church programs. They have decided to "let go of" unimportant cult members by programming them to commit suicide at the churches. Not only would that discredit the counseling ministry of otherwise dynamic churches, but it also could challenge the churches legally. The publicity would be awful, and attendence would fall.

One church found that they had become the target of such a plan. Here is their story: A cult member was sent to them during the spring of the year with orders from the local coven leader to get into counseling with the senior pastor. She was supposed to drain him of his energy and his time in difficult counseling and then commit suicide in his office! That would deflate a growing church and would seriously undermine the confidence of a fine young pastor.

Counterattack!

However, the cult people did not know that the pastor had been trained to recognize MPD, and he got that woman into therapy with a therapist who uncovered the sinister plan. She had been programmed to hang herself in his office but the plan did not quite work—the pastor felt a need to take a final check of his office before going home after one Wednesday night meeting, and he found her—choking, but alive!

The cult people continued to stay in contact with some of her SRA-survivor personalities, and programmed them to do the same thing, with the same results. She did not stab herself duringthe morning worship service, and did not slit her wrists in the middle of communion. Naturally, the head of the cult group was not happy, as he had met his match.

The pastor and the therapist helped this woman grow spiritually and psychologically, and she got farther and farther away from the cult leader's control. Nonetheless, he orchestrated a barrage of intimidation to try to coerce the now-unwilling cultist to leave that church. It was to no avail. By Christmas, she was devoted to following the Lord God with every part of her life, and she renounced her membership in the coven. She was welcomed into the church and has withstood the harassment of the cult leaders as they have continued to intimidate her. The church as opened itself up to protect her, and there are a number of people in that church on whom she can call at any time, day or night, for support and protection.

That is the way it should be. Church leaders should be able to spot the enemy's agents when they infiltrate, and provide them a way of escape from their tormentors.

Information Getting Out

The tide is turning. The word is spreading. It is getting harder for cultists to successfully cover up their rituals. Therapists are working hard to learn about treatment for MPD and SRA. Churches are becoming involved in helping unwilling cult survivors escape from their covens. An underground network is developing in which former cult members who want to escape can assume a new identity and start over in a new place. For cult members who want to escape yet cannot leave the area, friends are forming networks using beeper systems to keep track of them in case they get abducted by other cult members.

Because I have been speaking at national level conferences, each week a call or two reaches me from therapists who have discovered they are working with an MPD/SRA client. Many are having a difficult time—they have never had so much trouble knowing what to do. Of course, this is quite a different sort of therapy from what they were prepared for in school, and it requires a new therapeutic framework. They are usually looking for consultation, just as I was when I first learned about MPD.

Most of these calls come from people who are looking for other MPD therapists to network with. They are taking their work very seriously, and they are doing a commendable job.

A Dissolved Coven

Reports are surfacing also of instances in which cult members have left and their covens have dissolved. Last summer a different kind of phone call came to my office. A pastor called and said he was not asking for advice but was calling to say "thank you" and to promote change on a national level. He gave me permission to share his story here. His church had helped a cult member break with a coven, and the church's spiritual assault had completely broken up the coven. In that case, MPD/SRA therapy for one person was not enough. Extensive prayer by the entire Christian community was needed to protect the survivor, and it developed into a campaign that turned the tide against the local coven and defeated it.

Shortly after the Reverend Mr. Moses took his position as a pastoral counselor in his church, he started working with a woman who turned out to be a cult survivor with MPD. As he began to search for some readings to prepare for this therapy, he was given a paper that I had presented at a conference, with the title, "Treatment for Multiple Personality Disorder: Integrating Alter Personalities and Casting Out Evil Spirits." He called to thank me for helping him conceptualize his work with Kay, who was the MPD/SRA survivor, and he told me how he learned to "fight back."

The level of cruelty, terror, and humiliation that Kay suffered at the hands of the coven had become so intense that she reached a point of no return. She determined she would rather die than ever be abused again. Instead of allowing herself to be taken to the ritual site for the winter solstice ceremony, she checked herself into a hotel and swallowed enough pills to render herself unconscious for the weekend. Ten days later, two cult members followed her into a post office parking lot and abducted her into a van. She was brutally punished for not obeying their commands to take part in their rituals. It was made very clear to her what the consequences would be if she disobeyed again.

Kay had lost all hope of escape through any other means but death, when an acquaintance and member of the church noticed her depressed state and suggested that she see pastor Moses. With nothing to lose, she kept her appointment.

Pastor Moses tried to treat her depression and get her into medical care. Her suicidal desires and unusual fears of pastors, doctors and police confused him at first, but her positive response to the Christian message of hope and healing was encouraging. In his fourth session with her, he met the first alter, who gave her history of SRA, which had begun at birth. The cultists found out and feared their identities could become public, so they began their intimidation. By the time of the next satanic high holiday, the cult was threatening her life. Her apartment was watched constantly. Threatening notes, messages on her phone recorder, and dead animals on her car became an ever-present reminder of her life-threatening predicament. She wanted to give up and be dead rather than endanger the lives of the church people who were attempting to protect her.

Pastor Moses responded by organizing a group of thirty mature Christians to pray for her daily and to escort her whenever she left home. As the coven became more concerned about losing her and of the possibility that their identities might be revealed, they became more determined to apprehend her. Pastor Moses responded by mobilizing the entire congregation to pray for her protection and for the demise of these cultists. Other churches joined the battle, and on the next ritual date as many as 1,000 believers were in prayer at the exact time the rituals were to occur.

After the ritual date had passed, the church office began receiving threatening phone calls which convinced the pastor that the prayer had worked. Soon, one of the cult members, afraid for his life and needing help to escape, contacted him. He had seen one of the cult leaders die of a heart attack during a ritual, and at the black mass the high priest had "gone crazy," falling to the ground, babbling incoherently. This all happened in rituals targeted by the massive prayer campaign!

The coven members became suspicious of one another, and accused this member of leaking information to the church. The ritual became hysterical. In the confusion, and realizing his life was at stake, he gathered a young lady and her baby, who were intended victims of that night's ritual, and fled. He quickly made contact with Kay's church. Pastor Moses helped him relocate in another town, where he has been working ever since, attending church and putting his life back together. He has remained in contact with Pastor Moses and has given him eye witness reports on the effects of the churches' prayers.

The girl had been a runaway, whom the coven had held captive in a basement for almost two years to provide babies for their sacrifices. She is now being restored at another location.

Kay is no longer in any danger from the cult and is well on her way toward healing, but the memories and nightmares still linger. At times, both Pastor Moses and Kay wondered how the church people would accept her, but they have responded to her with lots of love and understanding.

The church has come to be a place of healing, protection and safety for Kay. It has also grown as a result of this work. They have seen this case, where the survivor felt hopelessly trapped by cultists, turn around into a smashing victory. Their only weapons were prayer and the courage to tell the cult leaders that the church was praying for them. Their faith in prayer has mushroomed, and a network of home prayer cells that were formed during the months of struggle still meet monthly to pray for their church and city. As a further blessing, Pastor Moses is confident that no cultist could successfully infiltrate the church as long as Kay is there. Her sensitivity would be an early warning system to prevent such a scheme.

Sharing the Need

While communicating with me about telling his story, Pastor Moses wrote something that should be shared: "We need churches to get into the fight and pastors need to know that there would be great benefits for them, as well as the victim, if their church were to help. It is unfortunate that many pastors are afraid of these victims—and this fear only plays into the hands of the coven leaders."

The tide is turning, and Pastor Moses told me he is looking for a chance to help churches across this country learn how to do the same thing for other trapped cult members. He wants churches to become equipped to help survivors and to network with other churches so that SRA survivors can escape from their covens. These escapes require team efforts involving Christian therapists and local churches that can become safe families for the survivors.

The time has come for cultists to face the fact that the tide has turned. The mood has been changing at recent conferences I have attended. The therapists and friends of cult survivors have seen enough successes that the aroma of victory is in the air. Only a few years ago the mood was shock and head-shaking disbelief. Now, seminar presenters are getting standing ovations when they speak of hope and faith—recovery is attainable, despite its difficulties. It is no longer safe for covens to carry out their unspeakable acts. It is no longer safe for cultists to infiltrate churches. It will not be safe for them to face God when they die. God is in charge, but their "master" is the prince of lies. If they repent, it is not too late. If they don't, their fate is sealed. They will not be awarded a cooler place in hell, as has been promised to them, for their obedience to Satan. That is just another lie from the prince of lies. They will be held accountable for their behavior. If they follow Satan, they can expect misery for the rest of their lives, and for a long time after that. If they repent, there is still time to find peace in this life and in the life to come.

CONCLUDING
THOUGHTS

THERE SEEM TO BE two kinds of reactions to the material in this book which thwart healing.

The **first** is *when therapists let their previous training stop them from taking the dissociation phenomena seriously.* Many times I have presented material about MPD to therapists who have argued about my observations, even though they have not seen my clients. A few times I have conducted diagnostic interviews with clients of other therapists who have asked me to help them determine if they may be working with dissociating clients.

When I found that the clues, particularly those listed in Figure 6, point to the high probability of dissociation, these therapists, who have no idea what dissociation even looks like, often try to interpret the dissociation-related symptoms in other ways. When they think about how a very bright client can remember nothing from the previous session, when they hear the description from their client about what it is like to come out of an amnesic episode, or when they hear an account of completely losing a car at the mall, it is beyond my imagination how they could interpret this kind of a pattern in any other way than dissociation. The only answer I can come up with is that they must be self-protective. If they were to admit they have missed a diagnosis, it would make them look bad. It might even make their career training suspect.

Yet therapists are mandated by laws and by ethical codes to keep up with developments in the mental health field. Our growing understanding of the way dissociation works is a development therapists need to catch up with if they do not yet know about it.

In a few cases, therapists who were initially suspicious of the MPD diagnosis I came up with for their clients came to see the importance of working with them from a dissociation-based framework. When they came back to me for further consultation, they admitted that they had been somewhat self-protective, and therefore, they had misdiagnosed the dissociative symptoms they could have been seeing in their clients.

In other cases, friends or relatives have just yanked the clients out of therapy when they heard that they had received the MPD diagnosis. People are really heavily steeped in the belief that "multiple personality disorder" is synonomous with "circus freak." They are insulted that such a diagnosis would be given to their loved one! These well-meaning people have the preconception that multiplicity would be an obvious disorder. They will not take the time or effort to learn enough about dissociation to be able to see what the phenomena look like. Unfortunately, when therapy is not directed toward overcoming the dividedness, the dissociator will continue to suffer.

The **second** anti-therapeutic reaction to the material in this book is *when the sufferer concludes that the only problem is demons.* When people come to their therapist saying they are suffering from "demon possession," that is a highly suspect claim. Only a careless clinician would accept such a claim without careful scrutiny. I have found that where too much hope is placed in a quick spiritual solution, serious disappointment usually follows. It is widely known that dissociation results from early, serious damage, and in the absence of psychological healing, symptoms will certainly re-emerge. Serious damage has to receive more than a deliverance and more than only a prayer for healing. While on the one hand I would argue that it is important to include spiritual healing in the treatment of serious childhood traumas, I need to emphasize that on the other hand it has proved to be a serious problem for the sufferer when only spiritual healing has been provided.

Therapists and clergy need to be psychologically and spiritually sophisticated and committed for the long-term restoration of those who are suffering from early childhood traumas.

Finally, I need to include here one thing an MPD patient told me to say when I asked her what I should emphasize in an

MPD treatment seminar I was preparing. She said, "The therapy is very difficult; don't let them forget that."

If you, reader, can try to imagine what it is like to discover that your brain has been fooling you practically all your life, and that you cannot even be certain what things your body has done, that is a good place to start in knowing what life is like as a multiple. Then if you can imagine that there are irreconcilable differences between what your brain tells you to do from one minute to another, you will be even closer. And when you can sense what it is like to discover and experience terrorizing feelings that result from previously unknown childhood traumas, you will know why treatment is so difficult. Don't forget that.

Many times dissociators have become conditioned to expect that therapy equals torture. Precisely because of the difficulty of the treatment, it is incumbent upon the therapist to find ways to make therapy a place where creative approaches are taken. If treatment becomes drudgery, it will not likely continue. There is a better chance to reach the pot of gold at the end of the rainbow if treatment can remain positive. Even though some people may warn that to use the "positive approach" can minimize people's feelings, my sense is that it is far better to believe that the pot of gold will be reached. That is not minimization of feelings; it is the seed of hope from which traumatized people can derive enough strength to overcome the effects of evil.

REFERENCE NOTES

Foreword

1. Kevin Marron, *Ritual Abuse: Canada's Most Infamous Trial on Child Abuse* (Toronto: McClelland—Bantam Books, Inc., Seal Books, n.d.).

Preface

1. M. Scott Peck, *People of the Lie: The Hope for Healing Human Evil* (New York: Simon & Schuster, Inc., 1983).

Chapter 1 Spiritual Warfare: Three Levels

1. Mark 1:23-28; Matthew 8:28-34; Luke 11:14-26; Matthew 15:22-28; 17:14-20.
2. Harry E. Wedeck, *A Treasury of Witchcraft* (Secaucus, NJ: Citadel Press, 1961), p. 94.
3. Ibid, p. 102.
4. Ibid, p. 157.
5. Kurt Koch, *Christian Counseling and Occultism* (Grand Rapids, MI: Kregel Publication, 1972).
6. M. Scott Peck, *People of the Lie: The Hope for Healing Human Evil* (New York: Simon & Schuster, Inc., 1983).

Chapter 2 Multiple Personality Disorder (MPD)

1. *The Diagnostic and Statistical Manual of Mental Disorders (Third Edition)* (DSM-III) (American Psychiatric Association, 1980).
2. Bennett G. Braun, *Treatment for Multiple Personality Disorder* (Washington, D.C.: American Psychiatric Press, Inc., 1986). A collection of chapters written by prominent researchers and clinicians in the field of MPD.
3. Richard P. Kluft, *Childhood Antecedents of Multiple Personality* (Washington, D.C.: American Psychiatric Press, Inc., 1985). A collection of chapters written by MPD experts.

Chapter 3 Satanic Ritual Abuse (SRA)

1. The Los Angeles County Commission for Women set up a Ritual Abuse Task Force comprised of therapists, SRA survivors and concerned citizens. The Task Force has produced a report which compiles what is known by the members, and is *must* reading for therapists and survivors and for their friends. For those who question the occurrence of SRA, that report is required reading. (Write to Los Angeles County Commission for Women, 383 Hall of Administration, 500 W. Temple St., Los Angeles, CA 90012, or call 213/974-1455 to request a report.) A second source which documents SRA is the video, "Ritualistic Abuse: A Professional Overview" (Cavalcade Productions, 7360 Potter Valley Road, Ukiah, CA 95482). Another source is the video, "America's Best Kept Secret" (*Passport* (magazine), 1432 W. Puente Ave., West Covina, CA 91790-1223).

289

2. A pilot study carried out in the Pasadena area estimated that 10 percent of all clients being seen by all therapists in that region had experienced SRA. That is absolutely stunning! A survey of therapists in all of Southern California is being conducted to see if 10 percent applies on a wider basis as well.

3. Please read *A Redemptive Response to Satanism* (in press) by E. James Wilder (Downers Grove, IL: Inter-Varsity Press).

4. Mike Warnke, *The Satan Seller* (New Jersey: Bridge Publishing, 1972), p. 184.

5. The *Cincinnati Enquirer* (March 14, 1987), p. E-5.

6. "America's Best Kept Secret" video, *Passport* (see note #1, this chapter).

7. E. James Wilder's book (in press with Inter-Varsity Press) about helping people keep out of Satanism will blaze a helpful trail.

8. Michelle Smith and Lawrence Pazder, *Michelle Remembers* (New York: Simon & Schuster, Inc., 1980), p. 39. Contains an explanation of how SRA memories are recovered in therapy, which is very similar to Fran's account.

9. "America's Best Kept Secret" video, *Passport*, p. 3 (see note #1, this chapter).

10. Ibid.

11. Judith Spencer, *Suffer the Child* (New York: Simon & Schuster, Pocket Books, 1989). A painstakingly thorough account of an SRA survivor, which illustrates perfectly how those rituals are carried out. The survivor and the therapists believe they would be in danger if their true identities were used; therefore, the names of the author, the therapists and the survivor are disguised, which means the story cannot be verified. Nonetheless, this book seems destined to be a classic, as it brings a lot of light to bear on the process of MPD therapy and on the deadly affects of SRA.

12. Susan J. Kelley, "Ritualistic Abuse of Children," *Cultic Studies Journal*, 5:228. "Reliable estimates of the extent of this problem are not yet available. The majority of professionals are unaware of this form of maltreatment and fail to recognize indicators of ritualistic abuse in histories of victims of child sexual abuse. Also, since children are usually too terrified to disclose the ritualistic abuse, most cases go undetected and unreported. Even when cases are reported, child protective agencies do not categorize them according to whether or not there was ritualistic involvement."

13. Sally Hill, M.S.W., and Jean Goodwin, M.D., M.P.H., "Satanism: Similarities Between Patient Accounts and Pre-Inquisition Historical Sources," *Dissociation* (March 1989), p. 39.

14. *Passport*, p. 4.

Chapter 4   Diagnosing Multiple Personality

1. The International Society for the Study of Multiple Personality & Dissociation (ISSMP&D) publishes a newsletter which reviews new books and articles, a good source for a person who wants to keep up with current issues in treatment of MPD. The ISSMP&D journal, *Dissociation*, presents research-based articles.

2. Judith Spencer, *Suffer the Child* (New York: Simon & Schuster, Inc., 1989).

3. Kristen Kemp, Alan D. Gilbertson and Moshe Torem, "The Differential Diagnosis of Multiple Personality Disorder From Borderline Personality Disorder," *Dissociation* (December 1988).

4. *The Diagnostic and Statistical Manual (Third Edition—Revised)* (1987) does not state that amnesia must be present in order to obtain MPD diagnosis. The two factors listed in that manual which indicate MPD are (1) the presence of two or more distinct personalities or personality states, which (2) recurrently take full control of the person's behavior (p. 272). I believe it is important to distinguish between amnesic and non-amnesic MPD, because amnesia produces different problems in the person's life, so the treatment is different.

5. Colin A. Ross, *Multiple Personality Disorder: Diagnosis, Clinical Features, and Treatment"* (New York: John Wiley & Sons, 1989), pp. 147-57.

Chapter 5   Treatment for Dissociation I
Preparation and Beginning

1. *Moody Monthly* (March 1989), p. 24.

2. Ibid, p. 18.

3. Ibid, p. 23.

4. In *People of the Lie: The Hope for Healing Human Evil* (New York: Simon & Schuster, Inc., 1983), Scott Peck lists the following as characteristics of evil people: (1) consistent destructive scapegoating behavior, which may often be quite subtle; (2) excessive, albeit usually covert, intolerance to criticism; (3) pronounced concern with a public image, and denial of hateful feelings or vengeful motives; and (4) intellectual deviousness, with the likelihood of a mild schizophrenic-like disturbance of thinking at times of stress (p. 129).

5. Ibid, p. 130.

6. James Chu's article, "Ten Traps for Therapists in the Treatment of Trauma Survivors," is a fine overview of this topic.

Chapter 6   Treatment for Dissociation II
Guidelines to Unity

1. This sounds remarkably similar to what Mike Warnke described in his autobiographical book, *The Satan Seller* (New Jersey: Bridge Publishing, 1972). He was a satanic high priest, and his job was to swell the ranks of his local coven in any way he could. He used the same methods as Shadow.

2. Katherine H. Steele, "A Model for Abreaction with MPD and other Dissociative Disorders," *Dissociation* (September 1989).

3. David Speigel, "Treating Multiple Personality Disorder as Post-Traumatic Stress Disorder." Presentation at the Third Annual Conference on Multiple Personality and Dissociation, Orange County, California, 1990.

4. A chapter in Bennett G. Braun's *Treatment for Multiple Personality Disorder* (Washington, D.C.: American Psychiatric Press, Inc., 1986) explains more about drug responsivity for multiples.

5. The books by Spencer, LaCalle, Smith and Pazder, Sizemore, and Allison can provide lots of good information from a first-hand perspective.

6. For therapists who are new with imagery, training and supervision are vital. Coaching and role playing can help sharpen the skills of those on an MPD team.

7. Judith Spencer, *Suffer the Child* (New York: Simon & Schuster, Pocket Books, 1989).

8. Ralph Allison's *Minds in Many Pieces* (New York: Rawson, Wade, Inc., 1980) has a good discussion about the role of the Inner Self-Helper.

9. *The Diagnostic and Statistical Manual (Third Edition—Revised)* (1987).

10. Colin A. Ross, *Multiple Personality: Diagnosis, Clinical Features and Treatment* (New York: John Wiley & Sons, 1989), pp. 147-57.

Chapter 7   God's Perspective

1. This account comes from the Old Testament book of Judges, chapters 6 to 8.

2. "Mind control is the cornerstone of ritual abuse, the key element in the subjugation and silencing of its victims. Victims of ritual abuse are subjected to a rigorously applied system of mind control designed to rob them of their sense of free will and to impose upon them the will of the cult and its leaders. Most often, these ritually abusive cults are motivated by a satanic belief system. The mind control is achieved through an elaborate system of brainwashing, programming, indoctrination, hypnosis, and the use of various mind-altering drugs. The purpose of the mind control is to compel ritual abuse victims to keep the secret of their abuse, to conform to the beliefs and behaviors of the cult, and to become functioning members who serve the cult by carrying out the directives of its leaders without being detected within society at large" (*Report of the Ritual Abuse Task Force*, Los Angeles County Commission for Women, September 15, 1989).

3. David Chilton's *Paradise Restored* (Fort Worth, TX: Dominion Press, 1985) presents the biblical underpinnings of this world view.

4. Charles H. Kraft's book, Christianity With Power (Ann Arbor, MI: Servant Publications, 1989) empowers believing readers and proclaims the power of God for helping.

5. Dallas Willard's *In Search of Guidance* (Ventura, CA: Gospel Light Publications, Regal Books, 1983) has been a great help to me. In pulling biblical and experiential material together, Dr. Willard has built a strong case that God is still eager to give guidance.

Chapter 8   Spiritual Warfare in MPD Therapy

1. Ralph Allison, *Minds in Many Pieces* (New York: Rawson, Wade, Inc., 1980).

2. Ibid, p. 82.

3. Judith Spencer, *Suffer the Child* (New York: Simon & Schuster, Pocket Books, 1989).

Chapter 9   Exorcism

1. Tom White recently authored *The Believer's Guide to Spiritual Warfare* (Ann Arbor, MI: Servant Publications, 1990). I expect this will become a useful and widely read book.

2. Ed Murphy recently contributed a chapter to *Wrestling Against Dark Angels* (C. Peter Wagner, ed.) which will probably become an important spiritual warfare text (Ventura, CA: Regal Books, 1990).

3. M. Scott Peck, *People of the Lie: The Hope for Healing Human Evil* (New York: Simon & Schuster, Inc., 1983).

4. C. Peter Wagner states that when the apostle Paul listed the gift of discernment, it included exorcism because exorcism always followed discernment. Therefore, Wagner believes the gift of exorcism is connected to the gift of

discernment. It is following his teaching that I use discernment-exorcism as a hyphenated word *(Your Spiritual Gifts,* Ventura, CA: Regal Books, 1979), n.p.

5. John White, M.D., "Overcoming Evil With Good." A seminar presented at the 1990 conference of the Christian Association for Psychological Studies—West, Vancouver, British Columbia.

6. *Christian Counseling and Occultism* (Grand Rapids, MI: Kregel Publications, 1972), by Kurt Koch, lists many ways that these temptations can develop.

Chapter 10   Restoration That Endures

1. *Healing of Memories* (Wheaton, IL: Scripture Press Publications, Inc., Victor Books, 1985) by David Seamands provides a fuller discussion of this topic.

2. *The Different Drum: Community Making and Peace* (New York: Simon & Schuster, Inc., Touchstone Books, 1988), by M. Scott Peck, is a good place to delve into understanding the profound effect that life in community holds for individuals.

3. E. James Wilder's book (in press with Inter-Varsity Press) is dedicated to preventing potential victims from becoming cult members and to helping unwilling cult members escape.

4. The Los Angeles County Commission for Women set up a Ritual Abuse Task Force comprised of therapists, SRA survivors and concerned citizens. The Task Force has produced a report which compiles what is known by the members, and is *must* reading for therapists and survivors and for their friends. For those who question the occurrence of SRA, that report is required reading. (Write to Los Angeles County Commission for Women, 383 Hall of Administration, 500 W. Temple St., Los Angeles, CA 90012, or call 213/974-1455 to request a copy of the report.)

BIBLIOGRAPHY

Alexander, Brooks. *The Occult*. Downers Grove, IL: Inter-Varsity Press, 1983.

Allison, Ralph. *Minds in Many Pieces*. New York, NY: Rawson, Wade, Inc., 1980.

Altemeyer, Bob, Ph.D. *The Authoritarian Personality*. The Harvard Mental Health Letter, 7:3 (September 1990), pp. 4-6.

"America's Best Kept Secret." Special Report. *Passport Magazine*, Fall 1986.

"America's Best Kept Secret: A Look at Modern Day Satanism" (video). Passport Enterprises, 1988.

Anderson, Neil T. *The Bondage Breaker*. Eugene, OR: Harvest House Publishers, 1990.

Anderson, Neil T. *Victory Over the Darkness*. Ventura, CA: Regal Books, 1990.

Ankerberg, John, and Weldon, John. *The Secret Teachings of the Masonic Lodge*. Chicago, IL: Moody Press, 1989.

Braswell, Jr. George W. *Understanding Sectarian Groups in America*. Nashville, TN: Broadman Press, 1986.

Brown, Dee. "Adult Survivors of Satanic Ritualistic Abuse." Audio tape recorded at the conference of "The Consortium of California Child Abuse Councils," February 1987.

Carr, Joseph. *The Lucifer Connection*. Lafayette: LA: Huntington House, Inc. 1987.

"A Choice to Share Death: Final Act of Couples' Mystical Beliefs Confirmed 6 Years Later." *The Los Angeles Times*, April 1, 1989.

Cruz, Nicky. *Devil on the Run*. Melbourne, FL: Dove Christian Books, 1989.

DeMar, Gary. *Surviving College Successfully*. Brentwood, TN: Wolgemuth & Hyatt, Publishers, Inc., 1988.

Enroth, Ronald. *The Lure of the Cults & New Religions*. Downers Grove, IL: Inter-Varsity Press, 1987.

Enroth, Ronald. *What Is a Cult?* Downers Grove: IL: Inter-Varsity Press, 1982.

Enroth, Ronald, and Gordon, Melton J. *Why Cults Succeed Where the Church Fails.* Elgin, IL: Brethren Press, 1985.

Franklin, J. "Diagnosis of Covert and Subtle Forms of Multiple Personality Disorder Through Dissociative Signs." *Dissociation* 1:2 (June 1988).

Frederickson, Bruce G. *How to Respond to Satanism.* St. Louis, MO: Concordia Publishing House, 1988.

Gay, Volney P. *Understanding the Occult.* Minneapolis, MN: Fortress Press, 1989.

Groothuis, Douglas R. *Confronting the New Age.* Downers Grove, IL: Inter-Varsity Press, 1988.

Groothuis, Douglas R. *The New Age Movement.* Downers Grove, IL: Inter-Varsity Press, 1986.

Groothuis, Douglas R. *Unmasking the New Age.* Downers Grove, IL: Inter-Varsity Press, 1986.

Harris, Marvin. *Cows, Pigs, Wars and Witches.* New York, NY: Vintage Books, 1974.

Hieronimus, Robert, Ph.D. *America's Secret Destiny.* Rochester, VT: Destiny Books, 1989.

Hill, Sally, and Goodwin, Jean. "Satanism: Similarities Between Patient Accounts and Pre-Inquisition Historical Sources." *Dissociation.* March, 1989.

Hollingsworth, Jan. *Unspeakable Acts.* New York, NY: Congdon & Weed, 1986.

Hubner, John, and Gruson, Lindsey. *Monkey on a Stick.* Orlando, FL: Harcourt Brace Jovanovich, Inc., 1988.

Hunt, Dave. *The Cult Explosion.* Eugene, Or: Harvest House Publishers, 1978.

Johnston, Jerry. *The Edge of Evil.* Dallas, TX: Word Publishing, 1989.

Jordan, James B. *Through New Eyes.* Brentwood, TN: Wolgemuth & Hyatt, Publishers, Inc., 1988.

Kahaner, Larry. *Cults That Kill.* New York, NY: Warner Books, 1988.

Kelley, Susan J. "Ritualistic Abuse of Children." *Cultic Studies Journal,* 5:228.

Kemp, Kristen; Gilbertson, Allan D.; and Torem, Moshe. "The Differential Diagnosis of Multiple Personality Disorder From Borderline Personality Disorder." *Dissociation,* December 1988.

Kluft, Richard P., ed. *Childhood Antecedents of Multiple Personality.* Washington, D.C.: American Psychiatric Press, 1985.

Koch, Kurt. *Christian Counseling and Occultism*. Grand Rapids, MI: Kregel Publications, 1972.

Korem, Dan. *Powers Testing the Psychic & Supernatural*. Downers Grove, IL: Inter-Varsity Press, 1988.

LaCalle, Trula M. *Voices*. New York: Dodd, Mead & Company, 1987.

Larson, Bob. *Satanism The Seduction of America's Youth*. Nashville, TN: Thomas Nelson Publishers, 1989.

LaVey, Anton Szandor. *The Satanic Bible*. New York, NY: Avon Books, 1969.

Marrs, Texe. *Dark Secrets of the New Age*. Westchester, IL: Crossway Books, 1987.

Martin, Walter. *The Kingdom of the Cults*. Minneapolis, MN: Bethany House Publishers, 1985.

Medve, Pamela. "Former satanist decries occult." *Star News*, May 29, 1990, p. A-3, A-4, bottom of page.

Michaelsen, Johanna. *Like Lambs to the Slaughter*. Eugene, OR: Harvest House Publishers, 1989.

Michaelsen, Johanna. *Your Kids and the Occult*. Eugene, OR: Harvest House Publishers, 1989.

Morgan, Robin. *The Demon Lover*. New York, NY: W.W. Norton & Company, Inc., 1989.

"Multiple Personality Disorder: An Overview." (video). Atlanta, GA: Ridgeview Institute, 1987.

North, Gary. *Unholy Spirits*. Ft. Worth, TX: Dominion Press, 1986.

Oke, Isaiah. *Blood Secrets*. Buffalo, NY: Prometheus Books, 1989.

Park, Irene Arrington. *The Witch That Switched*. Spring Hill, FL: 1980.

Parker, Russ. *The Occult, Deliverance from Evil*. Downers Grove, IL: Inter-Varsity Press, 1989.

Peck, Scott M. *The Different Drum*. New York: Simon and Schuster, 1987.

Peck, Scott M. *Omni* interview, October 1988.

Peck, Scott M. *People of the Lie*. New York: Simon and Schuster, 1983.

Phillips, Phil and Robie, Joan Hake. *Halloween and Satanism*. Lancaster, PA: Starburst Publishers, 1987.

Pratney, Winkie. *Devil Take the Youngest*. Shreveport, LA: Huntington House, Inc., 1985.

Pulling, Pat. *The Devil's Web*. Lafayette, LA: Huntington House, Inc., 1989.

Raschke, Carl A. *Painted Black*. San Francisco, CA: Harper & Row Publishers, 1990.

Reisser, Paul C., M.D.; Reisser, Teri K.; and Weldon, John. *New Age Medicine*. Downers Grove, IL: Inter-Varsity Press, 1987.

Rentzel, Lori. *Emotional Dependency*. Downers Grove, IL: Inter-Varsity Press, 1990.

Research Update: Occult Crime: Law Enforcement Primer 1:6. Sacramento, CA: Office of Criminal Justice Planning, Winter 1989-1990.

"Ritual Abuse: Definitions, Glossary, the Use of Mind Control." *Report of the Ritual Abuse Task Force*, Los Angeles County Commission for Women, September 15, 1989. 383 Hall of Administration, 500 W. Temple St., Los Angeles CA 90012.

"Ritualistic Abuse: A Professional Overview." (video). Ukiah, Ca: Cavalcade Productions, 1987.

Rodney-Wilson, Kathleen. "Healing Survivors of Satanic Sexual Abuse." *The Journal of Christian Healing* 12:1, Spring 1990, pp. 9-12.

Ross, Colin A. *Multiple Personality Disorder: Diagnosis, Clinical Features, and Treatment*. New York: John Wiley & Sons, 1989.

Sanders, Ed. *The Family*. New York, NY: Signet, 1990.

"Satanism Haunts Tales of Child Sex Abuse." *Chicago Tribune*, July 29, 1985.

"Satanists' Trail: Dead Pets to a Human Sacrifice." *The Los Angeles Times*, October 19 and 20, 1988.

Schwarz, Ted, and Empey, Duane. *Is Your Family Safe? Satanism*. Grand Rapids, MI: Zondervan Books, 1988.

Seamonds, David. *Healing of Memories*. Wheaton, IL: Victor Books, 1985.

Shaw, Jim, and McKenney, Tom. *The Deadly Deception*. Lafayette, LA: Huntington House, Inc., 1988.

Shuster, Marguerite. *Power, Pathology, Paradox*. Grand Rapids, MI: Academie Books, 1987.

Sire, James W. *Shirley Maclaine & The New Age Movement*. Downers Grove, IL: Inter-Varsity Press, 1988.

Sizemore, Chris C. *A Mind of My Own*. New York: William Morrow, 1989.

Smith, Michelle, and Pazder, Lawrence, M.D. *Michelle Remembers*. New York, NY: Pocket Books, 1980.

"Special Report of Satanism: Evil in the Land." *Moody Monthly*, March 1989.

Spencer, Judith. *Suffer the Child.* New York: Simon & Schuster, Pocket Books, 1989.

Spiegel, David. "Treating Multiple Personality Disorder as Post-Traumatic Stress Disorder." Presentation at the Third Annual Conference on Multiple Personality & Dissociation. Orange County, California, 1990.

Steele, Katherine H. "A Model for Abreaction with MPD and Other Dissociative Disorders." *Dissociation.* September, 1989.

Terry, Maury. *The Ultimate Evil.* Garden City, NY: A Dolphin Book, 1987.

Vanvonderen, Jeff. *Tired of Trying to Measure Up.* Minneapolis, MN: Bethany House Publishers, 1989.

Wagner, C. Peter. *Your Spiritual Gifts.* Ventura, CA: Regal Books, 1979.

Wagner, C. Peter, and Pennoyer, F. Douglas, editors. *Wrestling With Dark Angels.* Ventura, CA: Regal Books, 1990.

Warnke, Mike. *The Satan Seller.* New Jersey: Bridge Publishing, 1972.

Webb, James. *The Occult Establishment.* LaSalle, IL: Open Court, 1976.

Webb, James. *The Occult Underground.* LaSalle, IL: Open Court, 1974.

Wedeck, Harry E. *A Treasury of Witchcraft.* Secausus, New Jersey: Citadel Press, 1961.

Wedge, Thomas W. *The Satan Hunter.* Canton, OH: Daring Books, 1980.

Weldon, John, and Bjornstad, James. *Playing With Fire.* Chicago, IL: Moody Press, 1984.

White, Thomas R. *A Believer's Guide to Spiritual Warfare.* Ann Arbor, MI: Vine Books, 1990.

Willard, Dallas. *In Search of Guidance.* Ventura, CA: Regal Books, 1984.